THE
HISTORY OF
ECUADOR

ADVISORY BOARD

THE HISTORY OF ECUADOR

GEORGE LAUDERBAUGH

The Greenwood Histories of the Modern Nations
Frank W. Thackeray and John E. Findling, Series Editors

 GREENWOOD

AN IMPRINT OF ABC-CLIO, LLC
Santa Barbara, California • Denver, Colorado • Oxford, England

Copyright 2012 by George Lauderbaugh

Library of Congress Cataloging-in-Publication Data

Lauderbaugh, George.
　The history of Ecuador / George Lauderbaugh.
　　　p. cm. — (The Greenwood histories of the modern nations)
　　Includes bibliographical references and index.
　　ISBN 978-0-313-36250-7 (hardcopy : alk. paper) — ISBN 978-0-313-36251-4 (ebook)
1. Ecuador—History. I. Title.
　F3731.L39　2012
　986.6—dc23　　　2011044409

ISBN: 978-0-313-36250-7
EISBN: 978-0-313-36251-4

16　15　14　13　12　　1　2　3　4　5

This book is also available on the World Wide Web as an eBook.
Visit www.abc-clio.com for details.

Greenwood
An Imprint of ABC-CLIO, LLC

ABC-CLIO, LLC
130 Cremona Drive, P.O. Box 1911
Santa Barbara, California 93116-1911

This book is printed on acid-free paper ∞

Manufactured in the United States of America

Contents

Series Foreword   vii

Preface   xi

Timeline of Historical Events   xv

1   Ecuador Today   1

2   Ecuador's Indigenous and Colonial Past   19

3   Independence and the Early Republic, 1795–1859   35

4   Conservative Modernization, 1860–95   53

5   The Liberal Revolution   83

6   Revolution, Reform, Chaos, and War, 1925–48   95

7   Ecuador, 1948–72: Bananas, Democracy,
Populism, and Juntas   115

8   The Oil Boom, Military Reformers, and a
     Second Democratic Parenthesis, 1972–96   131

9   Populism, Political Instability, and the
     Citizen's Revolution   145

Notable People in the History of Ecuador   167

Selected Bibliography   177

Index   183

Series Foreword

The Greenwood Histories of the Modern Nations series is intended to provide students and interested laypeople with up-to-date, concise, and analytical histories of many of the nations of the contemporary world. Not since the 1960s has there been a systematic attempt to publish a series of national histories, and as series editors, we believe that this series will prove to be a valuable contribution to our understanding of other countries in our increasingly interdependent world.

Some 40 years ago, at the end of the 1960s, the Cold War was an accepted reality of global politics. The process of decolonization was still in progress, the idea of a unified Europe with a single currency was unheard of, the United States was mired in a war in Vietnam, and the economic boom in Asia was still years in the future. Richard Nixon was president of the United States, Mao Tse-tung (not yet Mao Zedong) ruled China, Leonid Brezhnev guided the Soviet Union, and Harold Wilson was prime minister of the United Kingdom. Authoritarian dictators still controlled most of Latin America, the Middle East was reeling in the wake of the Six-Day War, and Shah Mohammad Reza Pahlavi was at the height of his power in Iran.

Since then, the Cold War has ended, the Soviet Union has vanished, leaving 15 independent republics in its wake, the advent of the computer age has radically transformed global communications, the rising demand for oil makes the Middle East still a dangerous flashpoint, and the rise of new economic powers like the People's Republic of China and India threatens to bring about a new world order. All of these developments have had a dramatic impact on the recent history of every nation of the world.

For this series, which was launched in 1998, we first selected nations whose political, economic, and sociocultural affairs marked them as among the most important of our time. For each nation, we found an author who was recognized as a specialist in the history of that nation. These authors worked cooperatively with us and with Greenwood Press to produce volumes that reflected current research on their nations and that are interesting and informative to their readers. In the first decade of the series, more than 40 volumes were published, and as of 2008, some are moving into second editions.

The success of the series has encouraged us to broaden our scope to include additional nations whose histories have had significant effects on their regions, if not on the entire world. In addition, geopolitical changes have elevated other nations into positions of greater importance in world affairs and, so, we have chosen to include them in this series as well. The importance of a series such as this cannot be underestimated. As a superpower whose influence is felt all over the world, the United States can claim a "special" relationship with almost every other nation. Yet many Americans know very little about the histories of nations with which the United States relates. How did they get to be the way they are? What kind of political systems have evolved there? What kind of influence do they have on their own regions? What are the dominant political, religious, and cultural forces that move their leaders? These and many other questions are answered in the volumes of this series.

The authors who contribute to this series write comprehensive histories of their nations, dating back, in some instances, to prehistoric times. Each of them, however, has devoted a significant portion of their book to events of the past 40 years because the modern era has contributed the most to contemporary issues that have an impact on U.S. policy. Authors make every effort to be as up-to-date as possible so that readers can benefit from discussion and analysis of recent events.

In addition to the historical narrative, each volume contains an introductory chapter giving an overview of that country's geography, political institutions, economic structure, and cultural attributes. This is meant to give readers a snapshot of the nation as it exists in the contemporary world. Each history also includes supplementary information following the narrative, which may include a timeline that represents a succinct chronology of the nation's historical evolution, biographical sketches of the nation's most important historical figures, and a glossary of important terms or concepts that are usually expressed in a foreign language. Finally, each author prepares a comprehensive bibliography for readers who wish to pursue the subject further.

Readers of these volumes will find them fascinating and well written. More importantly, they will come away with a better understanding of the contemporary world and the nations that comprise it. As series advisors, we hope that this series will contribute to a heightened sense of global understanding as we move through the early years of the twenty-first century.

Frank W. Thackeray and John E. Findling
Indiana University Southeast

Preface

Although I had no idea at the time, this project began in 1962 when my parents, Dale and Virginia Lauderbaugh, encouraged me to become an exchange student in Quito, Ecuador. Little did I know that their support for this adventure would change my life. In Ecuador I was welcomed by two wonderful people, Dr. Alejandro Paz Maldonado and his wife, Fina Durini de Paz, who introduced me to the fascinating world of Ecuador and the culture of Latin America. Ecuador has had a grip on me ever since, and the Paz family has nurtured and supported my interest for the past 49 years.

When I first learned that I would be spending the summer of 1962 in Ecuador, I immediately consulted the *Encyclopedia Britannica* and found a fairly extensive article on my host nation, but it provided little information on Ecuador's political history. Alejandro Paz loved history and introduced me to some of the central characters of Ecuador's past. When I left Ecuador, Fina and Alejandro presented me with Arturo Eichler's *Ecuador: Snow Peaks and Jungle*. The book's classic black-and-white photographs of Ecuador's peoples, historic sites, scenery, and flora and fauna fascinated me and served as a reminder of my extraordinary experience that summer. When I returned home I went to the Carnegie Library in Pittsburgh to find books on Ecuador and discovered *Ecuador: Country of Contrasts* by Lilo Linke. I devoured the thin volume's contents but also found it incomplete, as it did not provide a narrative of Ecuador's political history.

Map of Ecuador. (Cartography by Bookcomp, Inc.)

In 1967 I entered the United States Air Force and began a 25-year career. Other than hosting an Ecuadorian Air Force officer on my first assignment and letters from my exchange family, I had little contact with Ecuador until 1982, when I was assigned to Howard Air Force Base in Panama. Howard served as the hub of military flights to South America and I was soon on my way to Quito, where I reunited with the Paz family after a 20-year absence. The seed that had been planted in 1962 began to germinate as I rediscovered Ecuador and my interest in its history. I began to collect books and articles at libraries in Panama and Ecuador. I was fortunate that my next assignment was to the Air University at Maxwell Air Force Base in Montgomery, Alabama. The Air University Library has an extensive periodical collection and a friendly staff of librarians who went out of their way to locate information on Ecuador for me. Another advantage was a master of arts in military history offered through the University of Alabama. I was encouraged to enroll in this program by the late Dr. Arron Segal, Air War College Visiting Professor of Latin American History, as several of the courses were on Latin American history. My first professor in the program was Dr. Lawrence Clayton, one of the premier historians of Latin America's colonial period and an expert on the Andean nations. Larry encouraged me to visit the University of Alabama and to consider entering a PhD program when I retired from the Air Force. He also thought that my interest in the diplomatic relationship between the United States and Ecuador would be a fertile topic for a dissertation. At Maxwell I also had the opportunity to again host Ecuadorian Air Force officers and they provided additional leads and support for my study of the military ties with the United States.

In 1993, with the strong and enthusiastic support of my family, I began my studies in pursuit of a PhD in history at Alabama. My horizons rapidly expanded as I discovered outstanding sources on Ecuadorian history in both English and Spanish. However, I found the works in English, while excellent, tended to focus on social issues, culture, or economics while political studies tended to cover short periods or a particular movement. When Greenwood Press offered me the opportunity to write *The History of Ecuador* I saw an opportunity to provide a text that would cover some major themes of Ecuador's political past and introduce the central characters of that history. Perhaps a better title would be *The Political History of Ecuador*. It is my hope that this introduction will serve as a guide to scholars seeking to write a comprehensive and detailed account of a particular period or figure of Ecuadorian political history. In keeping with the goal of the Greenwood Histories of the Modern Nations series, I have also included introductory information on Ecuador's cultural, economic, and social history.

Two outstanding teachers, Mr. Alex Kramer in history and Mr. Rudolph (Rudy) Spik in English, prepared me for college and supported my scholarship application for my 1962 exchange. Their influence is still prevalent and very much appreciated. I am particularly indebted to Dr. Jorge Paz and his brother, Ingeniero Carlos Manuel Paz, who over the years continued the hospitality of their parents, opening their homes to me and my family and even taking us to Otavalo on Christmas Day. The example set by the Paz family has been replicated time and time again by many other Ecuadorians.

Dr. Enrique Ayala Mora of the Universidad Andina Simón Bolívar sponsored me as an associate of this fine university during a 1996 research trip. Guillermo Bustos of the university and his wife, Rosemarie Terán Najas, have assisted in my research. Mr. John Sanbrailo, former director of USAID in Ecuador and the current director of the Pan American Development Foundation, guided me in my research both in the United States and in Ecuador. The late Dr. Edward Moseley, former director of the University of Alabama's Capstone International Program, provided a grant for my 1996 trip to Ecuador. Dr. Ronn Pineo, Towson State University, shared much of his research on Ecuador with me and has been a constant source of encouragement. Mr. Bert Romero graciously hosted me during a research visit to Washington. Throughout the years, I have been supported by friends in the Ecuadorian Air Force and I owe a deep debt of gratitude to Brigadier Generals (retired) Rodrigo Bohórquez, Angel Cordova, Colonel (retired) Jorge Cabezas, and Colonel William Orellana for hosting me on so many occasions.

Dr. Daniel Masterson, of the United States Naval Academy, recommended me to Greenwood Press for this project and has provided guidance over the years for this and other endeavors. I extend my sincere appreciation to Kaitlin Ciarmiello at Greenwood Press for editing this work for final publication

Jacksonville State University has supported my work by granting course reductions and funding presentations at conferences. Of special note are my department heads, Dr. Hardy Jackson and Dr. Gordon Harvey, and my colleagues.

Dr. Helen Delpar, retired professor of history at the University of Alabama, carefully read and corrected the numerous typographical errors on the initial draft and also offered substantive suggestions that greatly enhanced the final product. A similar service was provided by Dr. Peter Henderson, professor of history, at Winona State University.

I thank my daughter, Kim, and son, Ken, who endured numerous trips to Ecuador and a four-year assignment in Panama so that their dad could rediscover his life's ambition. I gratefully dedicate this book to my wife, Sue, for her unwavering support at every turn, her careful editing, and her encouragement when I faced despair that I would never finish.

Timeline of Historical Events

1525   Death of Inca emperor Huayna-Cápac. His son Atahualpa inherits the northern territories that comprise much of present-day Ecuador, while his half brother Huáscar inherits the southern portion of the empire and succeeds to the throne in Cuzco.

1526   Bartolomé Ruiz arrives on the Ecuadorian coast in the vicinity of Esmeraldas. Later Francisco Pizarro and Diego de Almagro join him to explore Bahía de San Mateo.

1531   Francisco Pizarro explores the Gulf of Guayaquil and makes contact with local inhabitants on the isle of Puna.

1532   Atahualpa battles the Cañari to consolidate his hold on the northern portion of the empire and engages Huáscar in a civil war. Francisco Pizarro initiates conquest of Peru and captures Atahualpa.

1533   Rumiñahui, uncle of Atahualpa, declares himself governor and organizes resistance in Ecuador to the conquest. Sebastián de Benalcázar commences campaign to capture Quito. After the battle of Tiocajas, Rumiñahui burns Quito.

1534	Benalcázar takes Quito, imprisons Rumiñahui, founds the City of San Francisco de Quito, and builds the Belén Church.
1535	Rumiñahui executed; Galápagos Island explored by Tomás de Berlanga; City of Guayaquil founded.
1536	Quito Cabildo designates Gonzalo Díaz de Pineda the first *alcalde* (mayor).
1539	Gonzalo Pizarro named governor of Quito.
1541	Gonzalo Pizarro and Francisco de Orellana lead expedition into the Oriente.
1542	Orellana reaches the Marañón river and later discovers the eastern portion of the Amazon River. Orellana navigates the length of the Amazon and returns to Spain.
1557	City of Cuenca is founded.
1563	The Audiencia of Quito is established.
1592–93	Tax revolt in Quito, the Revolución de Alcabalas. Viceroy of Peru dispatches troops to quell the revolt.
1618	Birth of Mariana de Jesús Paredes y Flores.
1624	Completion of the Quito to Bahía de Caráquez trail.
1625	Inquisition established in Quito.
1633	Franciscan missionaries establish outposts on the Napo River.
1670	Henry Morgan, the pirate, sends an expedition to the Galápagos.
1671	Defenses at Guayaquil are organized to counter pirate raids.
1687	English and French pirates sack and burn Guayaquil.
1688	University of Quito chartered.
1708	Troops sent to the Jesuit mission at the confluence of the Río Negro and the Marañón to counter Portuguese incursions.
1709	Guayaquil raided by the English pirates William Dampier and Woodes Rogers.
1717	The Audiencia of Quito is made part of the Viceroyalty of New Granada.

1720	The Audiencia of Quito is reincorporated into the Viceroyalty of Peru
1731	Guayaquil fire.
1732	Portuguese attack indigenous groups in the Province of Sucumbíos near the Napo and Aguarico rivers.
1736	The Paris Academy of Science expedition headed by Charles de la Condamine arrives in Quito to make astronomical studies and to mark the equator.
1739	Audiencia of Quito is reincorporated into the Viceroyalty of New Granada
1741	Road built by Pedro de Maldonado links Quito and Esmeraldas.
1764	Great Fire in Guayaquil.
1766	Rebellion of the Barríos breaks out in Quito and is suppressed by 600 troops commanded by Governor Zelaya, who is subsequently named president of the *audiencia.*
1767	Jesuit Order expelled from the Audiencia of Quito.
1768	Strong eruption of Cotopaxi, the highest active volcano in the world.
1777	Under the treaty of San Ildefonso between Spain and Portugal, lands in the Amazon region of the Audiencia of Quito are transferred to Portugal.
1785	Publication of *Reflexiones sobre la viruela* (Reflections on the Epidemic) by Eugenio de Santa Cruz y Espejo.
1787	Espejo exiled to Bogotá.
1789	The Patriotic Society under the direction of Espejo founds the Escuela de la Concordia.
1791	The Patriotic Society of Friends of the Country (Sociedad Patriótica de Amigos del País) is founded.
1792	The first edition of *Primicias de la cultura de Quito,* Espejo's newspaper, is published.
1795	Death of Espejo.
1797	Earthquake destroys Ríobamba.

1808   Supreme Junta formed to recognize Ferdinand VII as the legitimate king of Spain by the patriots El Marqués de Selva Alegre Juan Pío Montúfar, Juan de Dios Morales, Manual Rodríguez de Quiroga, Juan Salinas, Miguel Ríofrío, and Nicolás de la Peña.

1809   Quito Revolt and establishment of a *cabildo abierto* (open council), August 10. The leading members of the *cabildo,* including the Marqués de Selva, are later arrested and imprisoned.

1810   Popular uprising leads to the arrival of royal troops from Peru, who snuff out the revolt and murder many of the leaders of the independence movement.

1812   Quito Constitution is declared. Royal troops defeat a patriot army commanded by Carlos Montúfar and reestablish Spanish control of the *audiencia.*

1814   Ferdinand VII restored to the Spanish throne.

1818   Antonio Ante attempts to depose the Spanish government; he is captured and imprisoned in Ceuta, a Spanish fortification in West Africa.

1820   A group of young revolutionaries take control of Guayaquil, expel Spanish officials, and install José Joaquín Olmedo as the new civil authority.

1821   At the direction of Símon Bolívar, General Antonio José de Sucre arrives in Guayaquil and secures the port for the New Granada government.

1822   Sucre defeats Spanish forces in the Battle of Pichincha overlooking Quito. The independence of Ecuador is secured. Símon Bolívar and José de San Martín meet in Guayaquil. The Supreme Junta is dissolved and civil authority is vested in Bolívar, while Sucre is appointed intendant of the Department of Ecuador.

1824   Gran Colombia establishes the Department of the South with three provinces: Ecuador, Azuay, and Guayaquil.

1828   Conflict with Peru results in the blockade of Guayaquil and other ports.

1829   Guayaquil surrenders to Peruvian forces. Cuenca occupied by Peru. Sucre defeats Peruvian army at Tarqui on February 27. Bolívar takes personal command of Colombian forces with the object of expelling Peruvian forces from Guayaquil. The Treaty of Guayaquil reestablishes the border between Gran Colombia and Peru.

1830   An assembly of prominent citizens meets in Quito and signs an act of independence from Gran Colombia, naming the new state Ecuador, and installs Juan José Flores as provisional president. The departments of Guayaquil and Cuenca follow and join the new state. A constitutional convention meets at Ríobamba, ratifies the first constitution, and names Flores president of the republic and José Joaquín de Olmedo vice president.

1832   Ecuador takes possession of the Galápagos Islands.

1833   War of the Chihuahuas. Quiteño Libre movement begins opposition to Flores regime. Vicente Rocafuerte leads Guayaquil in revolt against Flores and blockades the city.

1834   Flores and Rocafuerte reach an accord to alternate terms as president.

1835   Rocafuerte becomes president of Ecuador, the first native-born Ecuadorian and first civilian to hold that office. Ecuador's share of the debt from Gran Colombia's War of Independence is set at 21.5 percent.

1836   Equator monuments, originally erected by the French Geodetic Commission, are restored at Caraburo and Oyambaro.

1838   Military school founded in Quito.

1839   General Flores begins second term as president. Treaty of Peace, Friendship, Commerce, and Navigation signed with the United States

1840   Spain recognizes Ecuador as an independent country. First theater is constructed in Guayaquil. First steamship is built in Guayaquil shipyards.

1843   "Charter of Slavery" is ratified by a Constitutional Assembly, giving General Flores eight additional years in power. Vicente Rocafuerte goes into exile in Peru.

1844   Gabriel García Moreno forms Sociedad Filotécnica, a secret group in opposition to Flores. Rocafuerte writes a series of manifestos against the Flores regime.

1845   March 6 Revolution, supported by Rocafuerte, Olmedo, and Generals Antonio Elizade and José María Urbina, topples the

Flores government and results in the Treaty of Virginia. Under the agreement, Flores leaves Ecuador for Spain; he promises not to return for two years but retains property and family privileges. Vicente Ramon Roca becomes president.

1846   García Moreno founds *El vengador* newspaper.

1848   Street lights installed in Guayaquil.

1849   Pope Pius IX elevates the Bishopric of Quito to an Archbishopric. Nicolás Joaquín de Arteta y Calisto is named the first archbishop.

1850   Beatification of Mariana de Jesús.

1851   President Diego Naboa overthrown and exiled. Slavery abolished by interim president José María Urbina.

1852   Sixth constitution adopted provides for popular election of the president. Jesuits expelled.

1854   National Library is founded.

1856   Francisco Robles is elected president. Indian tribute abolished.

1858   Ecuador breaks relations with Peru and a brief war follows.

1859–60   Civil war erupts, Roble's regime falls, and a provisional government is established.

1861   Gabriel García Moreno becomes constitutional president.

1862   Brief war with Gran Colombia, in which García Moreno is taken prisoner. Peace Treaty with Gran Colombia. Ecuador signs concordat with the Vatican and Jesuits return to Ecuador.

1863   War with Gran Colombia; Treaty of Pinsaquí ends war.

1864   Insurrection against García Moreno led by General Tomás Maldonado fails. Maldonado is executed. Eloy Alfaro and others also rebel against the government. García Moreno orders construction of the National Astronomical Observatory to commence.

1865   García Moreno defeats forces of General Urvina in Battle of Jambelí, and 45 rebels are executed. Ecuador issues first postage stamps. Jerónimo Carrión is elected president.

1866   Ecuador declares war on Spain. Ecclesiastical privileges are restored including church tribunals free of state regulation. Juan Montalvo publishes *El cosmopolita* newspaper.

1868 An earthquake devastates the cities of Otavalo, Ibarra, and Atuntaqui, killing 20,000 people. García Moreno is tasked to rebuild the province. The Bank of Ecuador is founded in Guayaquil.

1869 García Moreno declares himself supreme leader of the republic. Ecuador adopts its eighth constitution, known as the Black Charter, and García Moreno is elected president for the second time. Moreno suspends payment on the foreign debt. The Military Academy, Polytechnic School, and School of Law and Theology are established. Construction started on model prison.

1871 Telegraph lines installed along national highways, mandatory primary education introduced, National Observatory opened.

1873 National road from Quito to Sibambe is completed. Ecuador dedicates itself to the Sacred Heart of Jesus. Juan Montalvo publishes *La dictadura perpetua* (The Perpetual Dictatorship).

1875 García Moreno is elected to a new term but is assassinated on August 6. Francisco Javier León serves as interim president. Later, Antonio Borrero is elected president.

1876 Revolution of September 8, led by General Ignacio Veintemilla with the support of Eloy Alfaro, Juan Montalvo, and other Ecuadorian Liberals, topples the Borrero government by December 24. Veintemilla rules as supreme chief.

1877 José Ignacio Checa y Barba, the Archbishop of Quito, is murdered for his opposition to Veintemilla, and the conservatives revolt.

1878 The Ambato Convention declares Veintemilla president and writes Ecuador's ninth constitution.

1879 Construction starts on the National Theater or Theater Sucre in Quito.

1882 Veintemilla declares "The Transformation" and assumes dictatorial powers. Veintemilla's opponents, known as the Restorers, launch the War of the Restoration.

1883 The "Restoration Army" takes Quito, establishes the pentavirate as a provisional government, and Veintemilla goes into exile. A Constituent Assembly makes José María Plácido Caamaño interim president, and he is later elected under a new constitution. The Central University in Quito reopens.

1884   Construction begins on the National Basilica.

1884–1895   Ecuador enjoys eight years of political stability under Presidents
              José María Plácido Caamaño and Antonio Flores Jijón. The Na-
              tional Library is established. These years see improvements in
              public education, the railroad extended, the national census
              completed, and the expansion of roads and port facilities.

1893   Ecuador participates in the World's Colombian Exposition in
              Chicago.

1895   Liberal revolution led by Eloy Alfaro commences.

1896   Fire destroys much of Guayaquil.

1897   Contract is signed with Archer Harman for the construction of
              the Guayaquil and Quito Railway.

1898   Ecuador adopts the gold standard as the basis of its money.

1900   Civil Registry established to record births, deaths, and other
              vital statistics.

1901   Leonidas Plaza Gutiérrez assumes the presidency.

1902   Civil marriage and divorce law established.

1906   Eloy Alfaro succeeds in a coup against the government of
              Lizardo García and assumes power as supreme chief. He con-
              tinues Liberal reforms, including separation of church and state.

1908   Guayaquil and Quito Railway is completed.

1909   The centennial of the Sovereign Junta of Quito is celebrated with
              an International Exposition and the dedication of the Heroes
              Monument in the Plaza Grande in Quito.

1910   War with Peru. Ecuador rejects proposal by the King of Spain
              regarding possible border settlement. Spain discontinues me-
              diation efforts.

1911   Eloy Alfaro refuses to relinquish power, is deposed, and is sent
              into exile in Panama. Emilio Estrada assumes the presidency but
              dies on December 22.

1912   Civil war breaks out as Eloy Alfaro returns. Alfaro is de-
              feated, taken prisoner, and murdered by a mob on January 28.

	Subsequently, Leonidas Plaza Gutiérrez is again elected president.
1914	The cacao boom ends as World War I results in import restrictions to Europe.
1915	Expansion of rail system begins with construction of lines to Esmeraldas and Cuenca.
1916	Debtor's prison is abolished and the eight-hour workday is established.
1918	The Rockefeller Commission begins sanitation campaign to rid Guayaquil of yellow fever and other diseases.
1920	The first trans-Andean flight is completed by Elia Liuts in the plane *Telégrafo I,* and radio communication is established between Quito and Guayaquil.
1922	A general strike by workers and the poor of Guayaquil results in hundreds of deaths.
1925	A revolt by junior officers initiates the July Revolution, and a military junta is established to introduce reforms.
1926	The Kemmerer Mission arrives in Ecuador to restructure government finances and the banking and monetary systems.
1927	The Central Bank of Ecuador and other government financial institutions are established based on the recommendations of the Kemmerer Mission.
1928	A new constitution promulgates social reforms and gives women the right to vote.
1932	Congress nullifies the election of Neptalí Bonifaz. The War of the Four Days follows.
1933	José María Velasco Ibarra is elected president for the first time.
1934	Jorge Icaza publishes his famous novel, *Huasipungo* (The Villagers).
1935	Velasco Ibarra declares himself dictator and is later deposed.
1937	Ecuador reestablishes relations with the Vatican
1941	Ecuador and Peru fight a brief war over disputed territory. Peruvian troops occupy El Oro Province.

1942   Ecuador signs Río Protocol ceding most of the disputed territory to Peru; Argentina, Brazil, Chile, and the United States agree to be guarantors of the agreement. The United States builds air bases and naval facilities at Salinas and on North Baltra Island in the Galapagos.

1944   Government of President Carlos Arroyo del Río is overthrown. Velasco Ibarra assumes the presidency for the second time.

1945   Ecuador joins the newly created United Nations.

1946   The United States transfers military facilities to Ecuador.

1948   Galo Plaza Lasso is elected president; Ecuador enters extraordinary period of political stability (1948–60).

1949   An earthquake destroys Ambato and other areas of the central highlands.

1950   Banana boom accelerates as exports exceed $100 million.

1951   Ecuador signs military assistance agreement with the United States.

1952   Velasco Ibarra is elected president, assumes the office for the third time, and completes his only full term (1952–56).

1957   Railroad from Ibarra to San Lorenzo is completed.

1960   Velasco Ibarra is elected president and renounces the Río Protocol.

1961   Velasco Ibarra is overthrown by a military coup. Carlos Julio Arosemena assumes the presidency.

1963   Arosemena is deposed; a military junta rules.

1966   The military junta is ousted. First Clemente Yerovi Indaburu and then Otto Arosemena Gómez are named interim presidents.

1968   Velasco Ibarra returns to the presidency for the fifth and final time after winning his fourth election.

1969   Ecuador joins the Andean Group.

1970   Velasco Ibarra declares himself dictator and refuses to recognize parliamentary election results.

1971   The state-owned oil company CEPE is formed.

1972   Velasco Ibarra is overthrown by a *golpe de estado;* a military junta headed by General Guillermo Rodríquez Lara governs.

1973   The military government announces a five-year development plan.

1975   Rodríquez Lara is removed in a bloodless coup. A triumvirate of army, navy, and air force commanders assumes power and governs.

1978   A new constitution that permits illiterates to vote is approved by a plebiscite.

1979   Velasco Ibarra dies, Jaime Roldós Aguilera is elected president, and Ecuador returns to civilian rule.

1981   Ecuador and Peru clash over border in Cordillera del Condor region, President Roldós dies in a plane clash, and Vice President Osvaldo Hurtado assumes the presidency.

1984   León Febres Cordero is elected president, marking the first peaceful transfer of power under the new constitution.

1985   Pope John Paul II visits Ecuador.

1987   A massive earthquake breaks oil pipeline and causes other damage in four provinces.

1988   Rodrigo Borja Cevallos of the Democratic Left Party is inaugurated as president.

1990   Indigenous uprising starts movement for greater participation in national politics.

1991   President Borja presents plan for peaceful resolution of the territorial dispute with Peru at the United Nations.

1992   President of Peru visits Ecuador.

1995   Military encounter with Peru in the Cordillera del Condor region. Ecuador downs seven Peruvian aircraft and defeats Peruvian incursion.

1996   Jefferson Pérez wins Ecuador's first-ever Olympic gold medal by winning the 20-kilometer race walk at the Atlanta games.

1997   President Abdalá Bucaram Ortiz is forced out of office by Congress for mental incapacity, ending a period of political stability.

1998   Ecuador and Peru sign a peace accord that settles the long-standing territorial dispute.

2000   Ecuador adopts the U.S. dollar as its national currency, replacing the sucre. President Jamil Mahuad Witt is ousted by a military coup inspired by protests organized by Confederación de Nacionalidades Indígenas del Ecuador (CONAIE), the largest indigenous organization.

2001   For the first time in history, Ecuador's national soccer team qualifies for the World Cup.

2005   President Lucio Gutiérrez is removed from office by a constitutional coup.

2006   The national soccer team again qualifies for the World Cup, advances to the second round, and is eliminated by England 1–0. Team receives hero's welcome upon return.

2007   Rafael Correa Delgado becomes president of Ecuador

2008   Ecuador adopts its 20th constitution.

2009   Ecuador does not renew lease of a section of the Manta air base to the United States, and the U.S. Air Force detachment departs.

2010   Barracks rebellion by national police fails. President Correa remains in office.

2011   Ecuador expels the U.S. ambassador for a disparaging report on a Correa appointee that was revealed by the website WikiLeaks. The United States responds by expelling the Ecuadorian ambassador.

1

Ecuador Today

Ecuador, one of the smallest nations of South America, located on the west coast between Colombia on the north and Peru on the south and east, makes up in diversity what it lacks in size. Straddling the equator, from which it derives its name, Ecuador encompasses only 109,000 square miles—approximately the size of Colorado or one-half the size of France. Ecuador has been described by one author as a "country of contrasts."[1] This is indeed an apt description of Ecuador's geography and peoples. It also partially explains the nation's traditional lack of political cohesion, which has plagued its quest for stability and development.

ECUADOR'S GEOGRAPHICAL FEATURES

Seldom does one find such varied geographical features in so compact an area as in Ecuador. Geographers have divided the republic into three continental regions—the Costa, Sierra, and Oriente—and one insular region—the Galápagos Islands. Each region displays a wide variety of characteristics. On the Costa, for example, one encounters semiarid conditions in the vicinity of the Pacific port of Manta; yet less than 100 miles to the northeast, the port of Esmeraldas is situated near a lush tropical rain forest.

The highlands are divided into a multitude of different environments and climates by two great chains of the Andes—the Cordillera Occidental and the Cordillera Oriental. Along the famed Avenue of the Volcanoes, the traveler is awestruck by the towering peaks of Cayambe, Cotopaxi, Antisana, and the highest of all, Chimborazo, at 20,561 feet. Yet, near this great spine of snow-covered peaks one can view tropical rain forest and fertile valleys as well as the barren expanse of the high plain or altiplano.

The gateway to the Oriente region is on the eastern slope of the Cordillera Oriental. Until recently the Oriente was lightly settled and developed. However, the 1970s witnessed dramatic changes to this region, which has become the center of Ecuador's petroleum industry.

The Galápagos Islands, located 620 miles off Ecuador's coast, have been incorporated as a province of Ecuador. Because they are sparsely inhabited and development is limited due to their unique plants and wildlife, they do not currently play a significant role in national political life. However, the islands are playing an increasingly important role in Ecuador's expanding tourism industry.

Ecuador's varied, exotic, and rugged geographical features have contributed to the separation of its peoples. Until recently land transportation has been difficult, and many Ecuadorians seldom ventured beyond the immediate milieu of their villages or hamlets. In addition, central governments have experienced difficulty in exerting control or even maintaining a presence in many of the remote corners of the country. This has made it difficult to establish a sense of national, rather than local, identity among large segments of the population. Finally, the Andes have bifurcated the political and economic life of the nation into two competing zones, the Costa and the Sierra. Politics in Ecuador has been largely a tale of two cities: (1) Guayaquil, the bustling, tropical, Pacific port and (2) Quito, the once sedate colonial highland capital.

The Costa

The coastal region extends from San Lorenzo in the north to Tumbéz in the south and ranges in width from 12 to 112 miles. The northern coastal area in the province of Esmeraldas is characterized by mangrove swamps, a humid climate, and tropical rain forest vegetation. Heavy rainfall in this area results in frequent flooding and villages are often accessible only by boat. On the other hand, Manabí Province, to the immediate south, experiences short winters, long, dry summers, and little rainfall. These conditions are caused by the warm El Niño current as well as the cold Humboldt current. In recent years the El Niño effect has brought torrential rain, which has had a devastating effect on the normally arid area. Manabí is endowed with long stretches of beach that have largely escaped the curse of beachfront development.

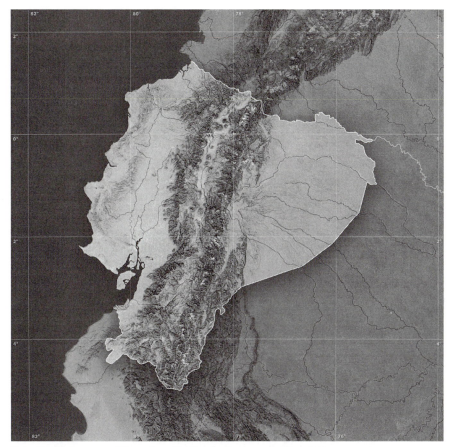

Topographic map of Ecuador. (© iStockphoto.com/Frank Ramspott)

Guayas Province enjoys a variety of climatic and vegetation zones. The Santa Elena peninsula, the westernmost point on the South American continent, is a resort area that includes the city of Salinas. Dry temperate weather prevails most of the year, making Salinas a vacation destination for many Ecuadorians. The Guayas and Daule rivers create a large alluvial plain and eventually drain into the Gulf of Guayaquil. Surrounding the port city of Guayaquil are the fertile lowlands with their abundant supply of water, which are ideal for growing bananas, rice, sugar cane, and cacao. In addition, the Guayas is navigable to oceangoing vessels, making Guayaquil one of the world's busiest seaports. The climate in this part of Ecuador is tropical with a significant amount of annual rainfall.

El Oro is the southernmost of the four coastal provinces. The climate is tropical wet/dry and the vegetation is very similar to that of Esmeraldas, with

numerous mangrove forests. The largest city in El Oro is Machala, with an estimated population of 400,000.

The Sierra

The northern sierra region starts near the Colombian border at the city of
Tulcán in Carchi Province and extends to the south of Quito. Tulcán is famous
for the sculptured hedges of its cemetery garden, which are in the forms of
animals, geometric designs, and houses. South of Tulcán in the province of
Imbabura is the warm and fertile Chota Valley, which produces sugarcane,
flowers, and fruit. The largest city in this part of Ecuador is Ibarra, the provincial capital (population of 108,000), situated at a comparatively low altitude of
7,000 feet. Known as the "White City" for its whitewashed colonial buildings,
Ibarra enjoys a temperate climate of eternal spring. South of Ibarra are three
towns that are a magnet for tourists. San Antonio de Ibarra is the home of
wood carving artisans, Cotacachi is the center of master leather workers and
Otavalo is the hub of the thriving weaving industry that produces quality
textiles that are world renowned.

Quito, with a population of 1.5 million, described by several travel writers
as the crown jewel of the Andes, is the political and cultural center of the nation.

The town of Otavalo in the northern highlands is famous for exquisite woven
products. (Courtesy of Sue Lauderbaugh)

Once considered a sleepy backwater, Quito changed dramatically during the oil boom of the 1970s. Its colonial center, however, still retains its historic charm and has been declared a patrimony to mankind by the United Nations. Magnificent churches and convents built in the colonial period have been expertly restored and contain priceless works of art. The Plaza Grande is the symbolic center of the Ecuadorian nation with a statue in the center honoring the heroes of independence from Spain. The Carondelet, the executive mansion and office for Ecuador's president, is on one side of the Plaza Grande. Other buildings on the plaza include the National Cathedral, Quito's municipal office, and the archbishop's offices and quarters. The modern section of Quito spreads to the north, where a multitude of high-rise buildings house banks, commercial enterprises, shopping centers, hotels, apartments, and government agencies. Quito is also a city of museums, theaters, and universities that contribute significantly to Ecuador's intellectual vibrancy.

The 19th-century German naturalist Alexander Humboldt aptly labeled the route south of Quito the "Avenue of the Volcanoes." The eastern and western cordilleras running north to south form the sides of a large valley. The valley is segmented by lesser mountains that run east to west, creating a series of intermountain basins that range in altitude from 7,000 to 9,000 feet. The rich volcanic soil and favorable climate are advantageous to agriculture and much of Ecuador's food is produced in this region. The scenery is breathtaking as the volcanoes, Antisana (18,717 feet / 5,704 meters), Illiniza (17,277 feet / 5,263 meters), Cotopaxi (19,347 feet / 5,897 meters), Tungurahua (16,457 feet / 5,016 meters), and Chimborazo (20,703 feet / 6,310 meters), are snow-covered year round. Tungurahua has erupted in recent years, spewing ash and fire and causing evacuation of nearby towns. The two largest cities in the central highlands are Ambato and Riobamba. Ambato (population 154,000) produces textiles, fruits, flowers, distilled spirits, and leather goods. Riobamba (population 125,000) is a commercial center for the indigenous population of Cotopaxi Province.

Cuenca is the fourth-largest city in Ecuador (population 304,000) and is the hub of the southern sierra. The city is a major crafts center for the production of ceramics, jewelry, weavings, and paja toquillas, better known as Panama hats. Other industries include textiles, furniture, and automobile tires. Ingapirca, Ecuador's largest Inca ruins, are north of Cuenca near the town of Cañar. Cuenca is also an important cultural center with numerous museums, colonial buildings, and one of the largest cathedrals in South America.

Loja Province, the most remote of the southern sierra provinces, is a rich agricultural region producing cattle, sheep, grains, and flowers. Loja City (population 130,000) serves as the provincial capital, is home to two universities, and has maintained its colonial architectural identity through careful urban planning.

Mount Cotopaxi is the highest active volcano in the world. (© Xura | Dreamstime.com)

The Oriente

A visit to Ecuador's eastern region confirms that this is indeed a "country of contrasts." The Papallacta Pass at 13,400 feet (4,100 meters) is one of the gateways to the Oriente. The journey takes one through the frigid, dreary, snowy, and sepia-toned environment of the high Andes. Once the summit is reached and the sudden steep descent begins, the scenery becomes otherworldly. A vast expanse of verdant rain forest seems to stretch endlessly and the Andean chill soon gives way to tropical heat and humidity. Myriad rivers begin their serpentine paths to feed the mighty Amazon and eventually empty into the Atlantic Ocean 2,000 miles away. This area is a naturalist's dream come true as it is home to more than 500 species of birds and a vast variety of jungle mammals, including pumas, tapirs, monkeys, and the spectacled bear, the only bear in all of South America. The plant life of the Oriente is so varied that it has defied complete classification by botanists and new discoveries are still being made. The Oriente is also home to various indigenous groups discussed later in this chapter.

Until the 1960s only the fringes of the Oriente were known to the rest of Ecuador and the world. The discovery of oil in the early 1960s led to an inevitable influx of settlers from other parts of the country, especially the southern highlands. Nueva Loja, better known as Lago Agrio (Sour Lake), became the center of Ecuador's oil boom, which blossomed in the 1970s. The Trans Andean Pipeline soon connected Lago Agrio with the Pacific port of Esmeraldas. The pipeline and roads built to support its construction and maintenance served as conduits for colonization. Lagro Agrio and the surrounding area grew so fast that the Ecuadorian government created the province of Sucumbíos. In addition to oil, the Oriente is a center of the growing eco-tourism industry. Popular destinations include the Cofan village of Sabelo, the river Conoaco, the town of Coca, Garzacocha Lake, Sachaurcu, Capiguarocha Lagoon, Limoncocha National Park, Pañacoca, and Puerto Misahuallí.[2]

The Galápagos

Ecuador took official possession of the Galápagos Archipelago in 1832, a remarkable acquisition as the islands had long been used by some of the great European powers. The islands were first discovered in 1535 by Tomás de Berlanga, the bishop of Panama, when his ship was blown off course. He named them Las Encantadas (The Enchanted) in response to their mist-shrouded, otherworldly appearance and their unusual wildlife, typified by giant tortoises and iguanas. In 1835 the English naturalist Charles Darwin visited the islands and chronicled their flora and fauna. Darwin's experiences in the Galápagos contributed significantly to his ideas about evolution and natural selection, and his account of the islands later brought them international acclaim.

There are 19 volcanic islands and numerous islets lying astride the equator, 600 miles west of mainland Ecuador. The islands encompass a land area of 3,075 square miles spread over 36,000 square miles of ocean. The population in 2009 was estimated to be 19,000. The islands have English, Spanish, and Ecuadorian names. In 1892 Ecuador officially designated the group the "Archipiélago de Colón" to commemorate the 400th anniversary of the European discovery of the Western Hemisphere. The largest island is Isabela, approximately 82 miles long, covering an area of 1,700 square miles. Isabela is typical of the islands in its lava composition. The five other larger islands are Santa Cruz, Fernandina, San Cristóbal, San Salvador, and Santa María.

The unique native animals and plants remain the main attraction of the islands. The Galápagos tortoise is thought to be the longest-lived animal on earth. There are only nine mammals, two bats, and seven rodents indigenous to the islands. There are no amphibians, few reptiles, and only 80 species of birds. Nevertheless, animal life is of extreme scientific importance because it developed during centuries of isolation from humans in an austere environment that has led to unique adaptive changes.

The Galápagos pose both opportunities and problems for the Ecuadorian government. Much of the area has been designated as national parks and wildlife refuges. Approximately 160,000 tourists visit the Galápagos each year, generating revenue for the country. However, as the influx of visitors increases, so does the threat of extinction to many of the endangered species native to the islands.

THE PEOPLE

Demographers experienced difficulty in accurately determining Ecuador's population before 1950, when the first official census was completed. It also proved difficult to define race and ethnicity and to establish meaningful percentages of each in the general population. Usually, Ecuadorians considered people to be white if they were light skinned, of European ancestry, and could read and write.[3] Many people who presented the same physical features were classified as mestizo if they were poor and illiterate. Likewise, a person of pure Indian blood was classified as a mestizo if he spoke Spanish and wore European-style clothing. Another problem was the ethnic bias of various observers who published population estimates. For example, in 1865 the Ecuadorian geographer Manuel Villavicencio, desiring to boost his nation's international prestige, overestimated the population at 1,108,420 persons and divided Ecuador's population into whites (54.3 percent), Indians (41.7 percent), mestizos (3.3 percent), and blacks (0.7 percent).[4] Foreign observers may also have had a racial bias and emphasized the nonwhite population. George Earl Church, sent to compile a special report on Ecuador in 1881 for the U.S. Senate, concluded that Ecuador's population was 1,000,000. Church estimated the racial classifications as 10 percent white, 60 percent Indian, and 30 percent mixed.[5] Perhaps the most meaningful estimate of Ecuador's 19th-century population was provided by Theodore Wolf in his acclaimed book about Ecuador's geology and geography. Wolf estimated Ecuador's population to be 1,272,000 in 1892, of whom 50 percent were Indians and the remainder were mestizos, mulattos, and zambos. He calculated that the white population was less than 1 percent in the countryside and small towns. However, Wolf observed that the white population comprised one-eighth of the urban population in Guayaquil, Quito, and Cuenca, the third-largest city.[6] Furthermore, only a very small portion of the population participated in the political life of the country. In general the group that held political power in Ecuador was white and of Spanish descent. Evidence to support this is twofold. First, Ecuador's constitution restricted the right to vote based on gender, literacy, property ownership, and income—and all but the first of these were decided advantages of the whites of Spanish ancestry. In the election of 1875, considered one of the most open in Ecuador's history, only 45,000 people out of an estimated population of 800,000 voted.

Ecuador's population in 2011 is estimated to be 14.5 million. The generally accepted ethnic breakdown of the population is mestizo 65 percent, Amerindian 25 percent, white and others 7 percent, and black 3 percent.[7] This statistical breakdown, however, is an oversimplification and does not always reflect the genetic makeup of the population. For example, a person who is genetically an Indian can be considered a *cholo,* the Ecuadorian term for mestizo, if he or she speaks Spanish, dresses in a Western costume, and generally adopts the social customs of the majority. An additional complication is that younger generations of Ecuadorians, whose ancestors often described their background as *criollos, gente buena* (the good people) or white, today self-identify as mestizo.

While some Ecuadorian whites might consider themselves mestizo, it does not mean that this racial classification has disappeared. Generally, Ecuadorian "whites" speak Spanish, emphasize their European ancestry, and dress like Europeans or North Americans. There is still an emphasis on the importance on being light skinned and exhibiting other Caucasian traits. This is mostly evident in popular magazines such as *Vistazo,* which often features pictorials and advertisements that are not of typical Ecuadorians. Throughout much of Ecuador's turbulent history there has been tension between the masses and the white oligarchy that held political and economic power.

The term *Indian* or *indio* is likewise misleading as it implies a homogeneous group, which is far from the reality of Ecuador. In fact, Ecuador's "Indians," especially politically active ones, do not like that term, and prefer "indigenous peoples" as an alternative. There is also great diversity among Ecuador's indigenous peoples. The largest group are the Quichua, who mostly inhabit the sierra regions and comprise nearly 90 percent of the indigenous population. The term *Quichua* or *Quechua* must also be used with caution and is useful mostly in identifying linguistic commonalties. The indigenous peoples of the highlands are very diverse, wear different costumes, and can be fiercely loyal to their local communities and unique customs. Some of the highland Quichua include the Caranqui, Otavaleños, Cayambi, Quitu, Panzaleo, Chibuelo, Salasacan, Tugua, Waranka, Puruhá, Cañari, and Saraguro. These groups may be further subdivided by the village they live in and each may speak in a distinctive dialect of the Quichua tongue.

Ecuador's Oriente region is home to the second-largest indigenous population of about 100,000. The Oriente Quichuas, who have ties to the highland Quichua, are the largest group, numbering about 40,000. They migrated into the Amazon region before the arrival of the Spanish and are further divided into the Canelos and Quijos. Long considered the "civilized Indians" of the Ecuadorian Amazon, the Oriente Quichua are noted for their decorative pottery made by the primitive hand-coiling method rather than using a potter's wheel.

The Shuar are the next largest of the Oriente's indigenous peoples, perhaps the most notorious for their ancient tradition of shrinking the heads of their enemies, a practice that has long been banned by the government. Despite the ban, and all indications that the Shuar no longer engage in this grisly activity, it remains a matter of fascination for scholars and tourists alike with faux

shrunken heads available for purchase in souvenir shops throughout the republic. The Shuar, once called Jívaros by outsiders, were the subject of Victor
Wolfgang Von Hagen's 1937 travel account, *Off with Their Heads,* a book that
long fueled North America's imagination that Ecuador was an exotic destination. It is estimated that the Shuar population, located in Pastaza, Morona
Santiago, and Zamora Chinchipe provinces in the south central Oriente, now
exceeds 40,000. They are one of the indigenous groups whose lifestyle has
changed dramatically in the last 40 years and they are very active in national
politics.

The Huaorani occupy the central provinces of Orellana and Pastaza. For
many years the group, which has a unique language, were called Aucas, the
Quichua word for savages. For centuries the Huaorani engaged in near-
perpetual warfare with their Oriente neighbors as they fiercely defended their
once isolated domain. The Huaorani were master hunters whose blowguns
shot poison darts to kill a variety of game, including howler monkeys, once
part of their diet. Males traditionally were clad only in a cotton loincloth while
women wore simple skirts. The Huaorani seldom had contact with the outside
world until Protestant missionaries flew into their territory in 1955. In 1967 oil
was discovered on Huaorani lands and this resulted in sudden changes in
lifestyle.

The Oriente is also home to smaller but no less interesting native groups including the Achuar of Orellana and Pastaza, the Cofán of western Sucumbíos
Province, the Siona and Secoya who inhabit the eastern section, and the smallest band, the Záparos of central Pastaza, who barely escaped the introduction
of infectious diseases such as measles, smallpox, and flu. Unfortunately, some
Oriente groups did not survive contact with the rest of the world including
the Arda, Bolana, Bracamoro Chirino, and Tete. These are the known groups;
other bands may have disappeared over the ages and there is the remote possibility that other groups remain to be found.

Ecuador's coastal region has the least number of indigenous people as this
region was sparsely populated in the pre-Colombian period. The northwestern province of Esmeraldas is home to the Awá, Chachis or Cayapa, and the
Epera. The Tsachilas are a small but well-known group that reside in the in-
land city of Santo Domingo in the tropical zone of Pichincha Province. The
Tsachilas, commonly known as the Colorados, wear bright red achiote paste
in their hair to repel insects, and paint their bodies with stripes. These practices have largely been discontinued except for the benefit of tourists. The
Colorados have long been a favorite of tourists due to the proximity of Santo
Domingo to both Quito and Guayaquil. Other coastal indigenous groups include the Mantas of Manabí and the Huancavilcas of Guayas.

The number of black Ecuadorians has been the subject of much debate, with
figures ranging from as many as 800,000 to as few as 56,000. Current estimates

range from 3 percent to 5 percent of the total population, or 435,000 to 725,000. Afro-Ecuadorians largely live on the coast where they work on banana plantations, shrimp farms, and other agricultural enterprises. Esmeraldas Province has the highest concentration of blacks and some towns, including San Lorenzo, are predominately black. The Chota Valley in Imbabura is also heavily populated by Afro-Ecuadorians. African slaves were brought into Ecuador by the Spanish to work the colonial sugar plantations in the Chota Valley that were established by Jesuits. Some groups in Esmeraldas claim to be the descendants of slaves who were shipwrecked on a voyage from Panama. These former slaves established free communities on the coast and were long known as the Cimerrones. Blacks were marginalized throughout much of Ecuador's history and subject to discrimination. In the past decade blacks have been more assertive in seeking political rights, equality, and social justice.

The town of San Lorenzo on Ecuador's northwest coast is the home of this Afro-Ecuadorian. (Courtesy of the author)

THE HUMAN CONDITION IN ECUADOR

Ecuador remains a poor country; however, not as poor as it once was. For example, 38.3 percent of the people live below the poverty line, an alarmingly high number, but a vast improvement over statistics from the end of World War II when the poverty rate was nearly 70 percent. Another achievement has been a dramatic increase in the literacy rate, which has reached 91 percent as compared to a meager 44 percent in 1954. Life expectancy has improved to 76.81 years for males and 79.84 years for females, figures close to those of Western Europe or the United States. Despite this progress, Ecuador is one of the least developed nations in Latin America, as indicated by a Human Development Index of 0.772 (as compared to the Latin American average of 0.82), ranking it 89th out of 177 countries evaluated by the United Nations. Other UN rankings of note include: 110th in per capita gross domestic product, 101st in people without access to potable water and 74th in underweight children. Many Ecuadorians have become frustrated with the lack of social progress and economic opportunity and have migrated to the United States or Europe.

POLITICAL CHANGES

The idea that a white elite ruled Ecuador persisted well into the 20th century. However, mestizos became politically active in the aftermath of the Liberal revolution of 1895, which brought General Eloy Alfaro Delgado, a mestizo, to power. The mestizo majority has dominated the political life of the country in the past 50 years, dispelling the notion that political power is exclusively in the hands of a white oligarchy. An interesting development is the emerging political assertiveness of Ecuador's indigenous populations over the past 20 years. Throughout Ecuador's national history, with a few exceptions, indigenous peoples did not participate in politics and generally accepted the social order imposed by the whites and mestizos. In addition, many of the Oriente indigenous groups lived in remote areas and had little interaction with the rest of the nation. Four factors explain the emergence of Indian activism. First, the discovery of oil in the Oriente in 1967 on lands occupied by indigenous peoples, most notably the Huaorani, signaled the end of isolation and soon threatened their way of life. Second, the Ecuadorian constitution of 1978 granted the right to vote to illiterates and the largest segment of the population in that category were the indigenous. Third, nongovernmental organizations (NGOs) supported the rights of indigenous groups. Fourth, the mistaken idea that the Indians were by nature passive and not capable of or interested in participating in national politics came to an end.

In the 1970s many regional groups were formed to present the grievances of specific groups. In 1985 indigenous leaders organized the Confederation of Indigenous Nationalities of Ecuador (CONAIE), which became the largest group to represent indigenous concerns and demands. In 1990 CONAIE organized the *Levantamiento Indígena* (Indian Uprising) that stunned the government of President Rodrigo Borja, who agreed to negotiate with the group, thus giving it legitimacy. Similar protests were conducted throughout the 1990s and in January 2000 CONAIE demonstrations toppled the government of Jamil Mahuad. Indigenous political participation has not been limited to protest. Pachakutik, or the New Awakening and Revolutionary Change Party, was organized in 1996 to participate in the legitimate political system. Pachakutik has elected members to the national legislature, won local elections, and presented candidates for the presidency. It is fair to state that the indigenous political movement in Ecuador has been one of the most consistent and long lasting in the past two decades of Ecuador's convoluted political scene. The recent political history of Ecuador is detailed in subsequent chapters.

THE ECONOMY

Historically Ecuador's economy has been dominated by one product (monoculture) which has subjected the country to periods of boom followed by dramatic downturns. The first major economic boom was generated by cacao, the key ingredient in the production of confectionery chocolate. From 1885 to 1922 cacao accounted for 65 to 70 percent of the value of all exports. The cacao boom financed modernization projects such as railroads, electrification, port improvements, and other projects that were part of the Liberal Party's agenda (see chapter 5). World War I interfered with Ecuador's export of cacao to Europe, and by the 1920s increased competition and a blight on Ecuadorian plantations ended Ecuador's advantage. Ecuador remains a major exporter of cacao today but it now is much less important to the economy.

Ecuador's second economic boom (1947–60) centered on bananas. Until 1934 Ecuador's banana production was minimal and comprised less than 1 percent of total exports. In 1933 the United Fruit Company (UFCO) purchased the vast Tenguel cacao plantation to experiment with banana production in Ecuador as a potential backup to its Central American plantations. Following World War II, UFCO's foresight proved fortuitous as the Sigatoka Leaf Spot and Panama disease, as well as natural disasters, limited output from its Central American operations. There was also a sharp increase in demand, especially in the reviving European market, and Ecuadorian production soared. By 1950 Ecuador was the world's leading banana producer, a status it holds to the present day. However, by 1955 Ecuador faced increased competition from other banana-producing countries and its dominant share of world production started to decline.

The third economic boom started in the 1970s when viable amounts of petroleum became exploitable in Ecuador's heretofore remote Oriente region. A pipeline completed in 1973 linked the rich oil fields near Lago Agrio with the Pacific port of Esmeraldas and began to yield a daily output of 195,000 barrels of crude. Ecuador's economy grew at an annual rate of 11.4 percent over the next several years. The oil boom had a dramatic impact on the country and there were hopeful signs that some of its long-standing problems could be overcome. For example, per capita income rose to $1,180 by 1981, placing Ecuador on equal footing with Peru and Colombia. The oil boom also resulted in infrastructure improvements throughout the country. Unfortunately it also subjected Ecuador to the ups and downs of the world petroleum market, which often had a ripple effect on Ecuador's uneven economic growth. Governments used oil revenues as collateral for development loans, and deficit spending mitigated some of the gains from the initial boom.

Petroleum remains the major product of Ecuador's export-driven economy, accounting for 58 percent of total export earnings in 2007. Other products include bananas ($1.3 billion), shrimp ($613 million), canned fish ($ 671 million), flowers ($469 million), and automobiles ($383 million).

A major economic development was the decision in 2000 to adopt the dollar as the national currency. This controversial measure halted inflation and helped Ecuador out of its economic slump of 1999. From 2000 to 2006 Ecuador achieved one of the strongest economic growth rates in Latin America at 4.6 percent per year. Moreover, per capita income grew from $1,296 to $3,670 by 2008 and the poverty rate dropped from 51 percent to 38 percent by 2006. This growth was spurred by a number of factors including rising oil prices, increased consumer demand, the development of new exports such as flowers, and the growth of remittances ($3 billion a year) from Ecuadorians working abroad. Despite these encouraging trends, Ecuador faced a number of challenges in 2011. Fluctuation in oil prices, a decrease in remittances due to the recession in the United States and Europe, and an ambitious social spending program could threaten the modest prosperity that the country has recently enjoyed.

RELIGION

The vast majority of Ecuadorians (90 to 95 percent) are Roman Catholic, reflecting the historic experience of Latin America with Spain or Portugal. Moreover, it is only recently that other Christian faiths have gained a foothold in Ecuador. Mainline Protestant groups including Methodists, Anglicans, Lutherans, and Baptists came to Ecuador at the end of the 19th century but had little success in winning converts. After World War II, Evangelical and Pentecostal groups arrived and began winning converts. By 1986 there were 250,000 practicing Pentecostals in the country and today there are over 260 congregations. Other North American groups that have had influence in Ecuador include the Church of Jesus Christ of Latter Day Saints (Mormons) and the Seventh Day Adventists. Ecuador is also home to a small number of Jews and Muslims, but their influence is minimal.

The Ecuadorian Catholic Church has 4 archdioceses, 10 dioceses, more than 140 religious orders, and about 1,000 parishes. There are four Catholic universities, two radio stations, and two television stations. As in most of the rest of the world, there is an acute shortage of priests in Ecuador, especially Ecuadorian ones. Nevertheless, the Catholic Church remains one of the best organized institutions in the country, although its political influence is greatly diminished.

The first Spanish building in Quito was the Belén Church (1535), and the fact that it still stands, and is still used, is a testament to the enduring influence of the church in Ecuadorian history. The Belén church is a modest structure, but the various religious orders soon constructed magnificent sanctuaries including San Francisco and the Jesuits' opulent La Compañía. The church also owned haciendas and *obrajes* (workshops), and it administered hospitals, orphanages, almshouses, and schools. As in the rest of Latin America in the colonial period, the church was second only to the crown in wealth and power. The church was also successful in converting most of the indigenous people of Ecuador to the faith, a remarkable achievement considering the multitude of languages, geographical barriers, and the deep-seated beliefs that existed before the arrival of the conquistadors. The Catholic missionaries realized that the Indian's religious beliefs and customs could not easily be swept aside and so decided to take a path of accommodation. The result was a blending of native religion with Catholicism that is uniquely Ecuadorian. This syncretic type of Catholicism can be seen during festivals and holy days, in the architecture of churches and in religious icons displayed throughout the country. Since priests and monks were the most educated men in Ecuador, they had a profound impact on Ecuador's cultural identity, influencing art, music, architecture, literature, and history. In addition, Mariana de Jesús, who was named a saint by Pope John Paul II in 1985, is the first Ecuadorian woman of historically recognized significance.

The Catholic Church's influence was profound throughout most of the 19th century. Gabriel García Moreno, Ecuador's great caudillo president (1861–65, 1869–75) saw the church as the only institution that could unify the country and provide it with the moral underpinning to become a modern civilized nation. García Moreno dedicated Ecuador to the Sacred Heart of Jesus and attempted to establish a theocratic state. Citizenship was available only to

practicing Catholics. The Vatican was granted control of education and ecclesiastical courts were restored. This was clearly the apogee of Catholic influence and power in republican Ecuador.

The Liberal Revolution of 1895, led by General Eloy Alfaro, was a turning
point in Ecuador's religious history. The Liberals sought to separate church
and state and to take over, or at least regulate, functions that the church had
previously performed, including education. Alfaro was the first Ecuadorian
president to invite Protestant missionaries into the country and permit them
to evangelize. These first missionaries gained few converts, but over time they
had an impact, especially in the area of community service and development.

In 1931 Clarence Jones, a pioneer in Christian gospel radio, and Reuben
Larson, a Christian and Missionary Alliance evangelist, established in Quito
the first missionary radio station outside the United States. The station's call
letters are HCJB (Heralding Christ Jesus's Blessings) and its slogan is "The
Voice of the Andes." From its humble beginnings as a 200-watt station, HCJB
grew into an Evangelical radio broadcasting giant with its signals now reaching
80 percent of the earth's surface. The impact of HCJB on Ecuador was immediate and dramatic. It introduced a new technology, encouraged the development of commercial radio, informed Ecuadorians of local, national, and world
events, provided educational and health information and cultural and enter-
tainment programs, and assisted the government with emergency broadcasts
during natural disasters. The mission also provides health and social services
through a variety of programs. In 1960 HCJB introduced television to Ecuador.
While HCJB won relatively few converts to the Protestant faith, it garnered the
respect of the people and the government and has been honored on several
commemorative issues of Ecuadorian postage stamps. Of all the Protestant
organizations in Ecuador, HCJB is the most enduring.

The Summer Institute of Linguistics (SIL) is an evangelical Protestant group
that arrived in Ecuador in 1952 to begin an outreach to the isolated indigenous
groups in the Oriente. One of SIL's goals is to translate the Bible into even the
most obscure languages. It missionaries were among the first to make contact with the Huaorani Indians. Unfortunately, five missionaries were brutally slain by the Huaorani in 1956. Several of the slain missionary's widows,
including Elisabeth Elliot, continued the mission and eventually established
a relationship with them. The role of SIL in assisting oil companies with the
task of convincing the Huarorani to permit drilling on their lands is a matter of
great controversy. The institute denied involvement, but the Ecuadorian government expelled the group in 1981.

The Catholic Church did not sit idly by while Protestant groups gained
converts through the use of technology and by offering social services. In the
1960s, liberation theology, a new view of the role of the church in people's
lives, came to the fore in Latin America. Adherents to liberation theology were

committed not only to meeting the immediate needs of the poor but also to structural changes that they believed would result in long-term social justice. Archbishop Leonidas Proaño (1910–88) took up the mantle of liberation theology. He fought for improved working conditions, health care, land reform, and educational opportunity for Ecuador's indigenous groups. In 1976 Proaño organized an international conference to discuss the programs he had implemented and to share ideas with other archbishops from Latin America. The meeting was sanctioned by the Vatican but was perceived as a threat by Ecuador's military government. The government arrested Proaño and 17 other archbishops on the trumped-up charge that they were plotting to overthrow the government. Proaño was later nominated for the Nobel Peace Prize.

Religion has always been an important part of every Ecuadorian life and remains so today. The vast majority of Ecuadorians remain Roman Catholics. Protestant missionaries have had some limited success in Ecuador and about 5 percent of the population belong to Protestant denominations. Protestant groups, most notably HCJB Radio, have had an impact on Ecuador beyond their scanty numbers. In the 21st century, Ecuador is more religiously diverse than ever and its citizens are free to practice their faiths openly.

Ecuador is certainly one of the most beautiful countries in the world, but it is also one of the most puzzling. While rich in natural resources, too large a portion of its population suffers in poverty. It offers breathtaking vistas and natural wonders, yet it does not attract large numbers of tourists. Ecuador has avoided problems that confront its two neighbors. For example, there has never been any significant insurgency such as Sendero Luminoso in Peru or the Revolutionary Armed Forces of Colombia, FARC. Narcotics trafficking has only recently become a problem and has not yet reached the scale that plagues Colombia and Mexico. Nevertheless, Ecuador has encountered more than its share of political upheavals in the past 15 years. More than one author has described Ecuador as an enigma and at least one used it as the title of his book.[8] Subsequent chapters will attempt to explain the enigma that is Ecuador.

NOTES

1. Lilo Linke, *Ecuador: Country of Contrasts,* 3rd ed. (London: Oxford University Press, 1964).

2. Rob Rachowiecki, "The Oriente," in *Insight Guides Ecuador,* ed. Tony Perrottet (Boston: Houghton Mifflin, 1995), 279–302.

3. Linda A. Rodriguez, *The Search for Public Policy: Regional Politics and Government Finances in Ecuador, 1830–1940* (Berkeley: University of California Press, 1985), 24.

4. Ibid., 25.

5. Ibid.

6. Ibid., 26.

7. *CIA World Fact Book,* https://cia.gov/library/publications/the-world-factbook/geos/ec.html.

8. See David Schodt, *Ecuador: An Andean Enigma* (Boulder: Westview Press), 1987.

2

Ecuador's Indigenous and Colonial Past

Vestiges of Ecuador's indigenous and colonial heritage can be seen through-out the country today; however, there are few pre-Colombian historical sites. For example, the largest Inca ruin, Ingapirca, located in the southern high-lands near Cuenca, is relatively small when compared to sites in Peru such as the world-famous Machu Picchu. What is more evident are the descendants of the early inhabitants, who comprise an estimated 25 percent of the popu-lation. They represent a variety of traditions and linguistic groups and since 1990 have assumed an active role in Ecuadorian politics. On the other hand, Ecuador's Spanish colonial heritage is more profound and long-lasting. For example, colonial churches, monasteries, and public buildings still stand in Quito, Cuenca, and other cities. Moreover, Spanish is the language most spo-ken by present-day Ecuadorians and the Roman Catholic religion the most practiced. In addition, mestizos comprise the largest segment of Ecuador's ethnic makeup and their culture and traditions were strongly influenced by Spain's colonial rule. Imperial Spain's political and economic institutions have also left their mark on Ecuador.

PRE-COLUMBIAN CIVILIZATIONS

Ecuador's pre-Columbian history is only now being fully examined by archeologists and other scholars. The arrival period and origin of the first Ecuadorians remains uncertain. There is archeological evidence that humans arrived in Ecuador around 8000 BCE, but some suspect that it was much earlier. The Valdivia culture located on the Santa Elena Peninsula dates to 3500 BCE and was once considered the earliest site. Other prehistoric sites are found in other coastal provinces and throughout the northern, central, and southern highlands. While Ecuador may have been the site of some of the earliest human habitation in South America, its indigenous populations were widely scattered and diverse. By the time of the Inca invasion in 1473 there were nine major linguistic groups on the coast: the Malaba, Cayapa, Nigua, Compaz, Caraques, Manta, Chono, Hunacavilca, and Puna. The six large language groups of the sierra were the Pasto, Otavalo-Caranqui, Panzaleo, Puruhá, Cañar, and Palta. The Oriente was home to the Cofán, Coronado, Quijo, Macas, Jivaro, Omagua, Tucanoans, Kandoshi, Zaparoans, and Panoans.[1] The variety of these groups in terms of language, culture, and development cannot be overemphasized.

The coastal groups were loosely organized into tribes or small cheifdoms with an agricultural system that produced corn, yuca, sweet potatoes, papayas, and other crops. This diet was supplemented by game and fish. While there was trade and other peaceful interaction between the coastal groups, they were also frequently at war with each other. However, these conflicts did not result in regional consolidation; thus the number of chiefdoms was much larger than the nine linguistic groups previously referred to. The indigenous coastal population is thought to have been between 546,000 and 571,000 in 1532.[2]

The sierra groups had the most sophisticated agricultural and trading systems. The agricultural system included the exploitation of lands in different environments determined by altitude, irrigation, fertilization, terracing, and draining fields. Products that could not be produced were obtained through an elaborate system of trade. Foods obtained through agriculture were supplemented by hunting. Small local communities were dispersed throughout the highlands but were not completely independent as they were tied to a larger group or chiefdom, headed by a *cacique* (chief) by a tribute system. The chiefdoms often had populations in excess of 10,000. The largest pre-Columbian population was concentrated in these highland groups and is believed to have numbered over 800,000.[3]

The various indigenous groups that lived in the Oriente were the most diverse and the least developed of the ancient peoples of Ecuador. They were seminomadic because agricultural production was limited, and relied more

Indigenous children wear costumes similar those of adults.
(Courtesy of Sue Lauderbaugh)

on hunting and gathering than the sierra and coastal indigenous groups. War was frequent as each small band, led by a shaman, protected its territory. The population of Oriente groups is estimated to have been approximately 156,000.[4]

THE INCA CONQUEST

The expansion of the Inca Empire into Ecuador is important because it changed the economic, social, political, and religious life of many of the indigenous groups, especially in the highlands, and, in many ways, paved the way for the subsequent Spanish conquest and colonization. The Inca subjugation of the highland groups proved to be difficult and time-consuming. As a result, the southern sierra was under Inca rule for approximately 60–70 years and the north for only 30–40 years. It appears that the Inca had little influence on coastal populations and none on the groups in the Oriente.

According to the Spanish chronicles, the Inca invasion of Ecuador began around 1463 when the ninth Inca, Pachakutik Inca Yupanqui (1438–71), ordered his son and future Inca, Tupa Inca Yupanqui (1471–93), to lead 200,000 warriors into northern Peru. After taking northern Peru, Tupa Inca Yupanqui proceeded to battle the fierce Cañari at Tomebamba, the present-day city of Cuenca in the southern highlands. A protracted war with the Cañari ensued and delayed Tupa Inca's Yupanqui's campaign into the northern highlands. His successor, Huayna Cápac (1493–circa 1527), is credited with incorporating the northern regions, including the city of Quito, into the empire. These military campaigns were very destructive and thousands were killed. The Incas established military control by building forts, roads, and *tambos* (store houses and rest stops) that supported the army. Once military control was established, political dominance followed through the establishment of administrative centers, the introduction of loyal colonists know as *mitimaes,* and the relocation of rebellious elements to distant southern areas of the empire. The Incas also enticed local chiefs to become part of the new order by offering them gifts and privileges.

The Incas soon imposed their political and economic structures on the conquered areas. Distinct ethnic groups were organized into provinces and subdivided into units known as *hanan* and *hurin* moieties. Each province was theoretically comprised of 40,000 people under a governor appointed by the emperor in Cuzco. The Incas also employed a decimal system that arranged the population into tribute-paying groups of 10, 50, 100, 1,000, and 10,000. A local *kuraka* was in charge of each grouping and given special privileges including tax exemptions. The most striking economic change was that all lands and resources became the property of the Inca state, whereas previously, they had been held privately. The new system was imposed to increase agricultural productivity in order to support the Inca upper class, the army, and religious leaders who were not involved in agriculture. This necessitated an expansion of land usage, which was accomplished by improving irrigation, terracing, and the introduction of new crops such as oca, sweet potatoes, sweet manioc, and peanuts. The Incas also improved the llama herds, increased cotton production, and exploited salt deposits. The Incas imposed *mita,* a labor draft system that required commoners to perform public services on a rotational basis. *Mita* tasks included maintaining roads and bridges, stocking the *tambos,* constructing public buildings, and harvesting public lands. The

Incas also conscripted people for permanent public service. The conscripts or *yanaconas* were often skilled artisans including potters, weavers, gold and silversmiths, and carpenters. The *yanaconas* were exempt from *mita* service. Another group of conscripts were beautiful women known as *aklla* who were forced from their villages to provide services to state officials, including the Inca. Some *aklla* served as concubines for the Inca while others were used as gift wives to the nobility. Other women called *mamakuna* were assigned to the temples. *Mamakuna* who were virgins were sometimes sacrificed to the sun god. Another change was the introduction of Quechua as the official language of the empire and in time it became the most widely spoken language in the highlands of Ecuador.

Another significant outcome of the Inca Conquest was the growth of Quito and its status as the northern capital of the northern quarter of Tawantinsuyu, as the empire was known in Quechua. Huayna Cápac was particularly enamored with Quito and established a royal court there that rivaled Cuzco. It was in Quito that Huayna Cápac fathered Atahualpa, reportedly his favorite son, with one of his many wives. Huayna Cápac preferred Quito to Cuzco and died there in 1526 or 1527. Huayna Cápac's sudden and totally unexpected death, most likely caused by smallpox or measles, resulted in a power struggle between Atahualpa and his half brother Huáscar for control of the empire. Huáscar was the son of Huayna Cápac and his sister and was considered by Inca officials based in Cuzco to be the legitimate heir. After his father's mummified remains were escorted to Cuzco, Atahualpa declared himself king of Quito and independent of Huáscar's realm. Huáscar sent an army into the northern quarter of the realm to end Atahualpa's pretensions. Huáscar's army was soundly defeated in a battle near present-day Ambato. In 1531 Atahualpa ordered his generals to invade northern Peru to capture Huáscar. The culminating battle of the War between the Brothers resulted in a complete victory for Atahualpa's forces and the capture of Huáscar. Ecuadorians celebrate Atahualpa as their first great national hero and he has been designated the "Creator of Quitonian nationality."[5]

THE SPANISH CONQUEST

In 1524 Francisco Pizarro, an illiterate former swineherd from Extremadura, Spain, led an expedition from Panama to explore the west coast of South America in search of the fabled city of El Dorado. Little was found on the first voyage other than rumors of a great empire farther to the south. Pizarro returned in 1526, explored the coast of Ecuador, and encountered a large group of hostile indigenous at Esmeraldas. The expedition also intercepted an Inca trading raft with a cargo of silver, rubies, and fine woven products. Pizarro established an encampment on Gallo Island near Tumaco,

Colombia, and ordered his ships to return to Panama. The governor of Panama, convinced that the expedition was a failure, later sent ships to bring Pizarro and his men back. Realizing that his return would be the end of the mission, Pizarro and 13 others remained on Gallo Island while his partners in Panama petitioned for funds to renew the exploration. A rescue vessel arrived five months later and Pizarro used it to probe farther south. At the mouth of the Tumbez River he made contact with a representative of Huayna Cápac and also found evidence of the riches of the Inca Empire when he viewed gold ornaments being made by temple artisans. Convinced that he had found a civilization that would rival Cortés's Mexico in wealth, Pizarro returned to Panama to organize a conquering force. When the governor of Panama refused to back Pizarro's venture he returned to Spain and presented his plan to King Charles I. Charles I was so impressed with Pizarro and his findings that he appointed him governor and captain general of Peru. After recruiting his four half brothers, Pizarro returned to Panama, and with the support of Diego de Almagro, his main partner, organized an expedition of conquest.[6]

In January 1531 Pizarro set sail with 180 men and 37 horses on three small caravels and landed on the northern coast of Ecuador. He plundered a peaceful village and found gold and emeralds, which he send back to Panama to fund supplies and to lure additional recruits. He also received word that the highland area of the empire was engulfed in civil war. He traversed coastal Ecuador with little resistance. Pizarro was soon joined by Sebastián de Benalcázar and 30 additional soldiers of fortune. Another 100 men commanded by the legendary Hernando de Soto joined Pizarro by the time he reached Puná Island in the Gulf of Guayaquil. From Puná, Pizarro pressed on to Tumbez, which he found in ruins, a result of the raging civil war between Huáscar and Atahualpa. Pizarro then marched across the arid land south of Tumbez and founded the city of Piura, the first Spanish city in Peru.

On September 24, 1532, Pizarro led a column of 105 infantrymen, 62 horsemen, and a friar out of Piura into the highlands of northern Peru in search of Atahualpa, gold, and glory. The Spaniards passed unmolested through the narrow trails cut out of the sides of canyons that wound ever higher until they reached a valley near the Inca city of Cajamarca on November 15, 1532. An advance party, led by de Soto, had made contact with Atahualpa and his legions and had arranged a meeting in Cajamarca the following morning. Pizarro did not wait for the emperor to arrive and entered Cajamarca. Pizarro and his officers concocted an audacious but risky plan to capture Atahualpa when he entered the central plaza in Cajamarca. Atahualpa and his retinue of unarmed thousands finally arrived in Cajamarca in the twilight hours of November 16. Pizarro dutifully sent the Dominican friar Vicente de Valverde to demand that Atahualpa submit to the authority of the king of Spain and to accept Jesus as his lord and savior. When Atahualpa threw the Bible that

Valverde offered him to the ground, the trumpets sounded and the Spaniards attacked with determined fury. The indigenous were caught completely by surprise and retreated in panic toward the walls surrounding one end of the plaza. Unable to escape, thousands of indigenous people were trampled, suffocated, or killed by Spanish steel lances and swords. Atahualpa was captured and held for ransom and control of his realm. During his imprisonment Atahualpa ordered the execution of Huáscar, an act that later led to his own demise. After the ransom was delivered, Pizarro decided that Atahualpa was no longer useful and ordered that he be tried for regicide and conspiracy against Spain. He was found guilty and sentenced to die by burning at the stake. This sentence was commuted when Atahualpa converted to Catholicism; he was strangled rather than suffering death by fire, an ignominious end for the first Ecuadorian.

Pizarro soon marched south from Cajamarca to seize Cuzco, the capital of Tawantinsuyu. He took the city in November 1553. As Pizarro marched south, Benalcázar was ordered to proceed north from Piura with 140 men to conquer the northern quarter of the Inca Empire. In August 1534, at the base of the Chimborazo Volcano, aided by fierce Cañari warriors, he routed but failed to destroy an imperial army commanded by the Inca general Rumiñahui. Rumiñahui retreated to Quito, all the while destroying storehouses, armories, temples, and any building that was of use to the enemy. Following this battle near the city of Ríobamba, Benalcázar was confronted by a rival expedition commanded by Pedro de Alvarado, the governor of Guatemala. Benalcázar and Diego Almargo convinced Alvarado to abandon his venture in exchange for treasure. Most of Alvarado's troops joined Benalcázar's force for the assault on Quito. Rumiñahui stubbornly fought the invaders as they advanced on Quito. The great Inca general ordered Quito burned and then abandoned it. Benalcázar eventually captured Rumiñahui and had him executed. This pyretic Spanish victory explains why there are few remains of Inca buildings in Quito today. On December 6, 1534, Benalcázar founded the city of San Francisco de Quito. The previous year he had founded the city of Guayaquil, but it was soon retaken by Huancavilca warriors. Francisco de Orellana, another conquistador, drove the Huancavilca from Guayaquil and rechartered the city in 1538. Thus the historically intense rivalry between Quito and Guayaquil has deep roots.

Benalcázar build a fine home in Quito, established a municipal government, and oversaw the construction of the Belén Church. He left Quito in 1536 in search of gold and glory in Colombia and became the governor of Popayán. In December 1540, Gonzalo Pizarro, half brother of Francisco, was appointed captain general. He arrived in Quito and began organizing one of the great adventures of the conquest period. The conquistadors were disappointed when they found little treasure in Quito or the surrounding area. It was rumored that Rumiñahui had removed all treasure and stored it in caverns on the slopes of the eastern cordillera. Gonzalo Pizarro was determined to locate the lost treasure and to exploit the natural resources of the Oriente, especially cinnamon. He set out from Quito in February 1541 with Francisco de Orellana, his second in command, 210 Spanish soldiers of fortune, and 4,000 indigenous porters. The arduous journey over the cordillera and the descent into the rain forest took its toll. By the time the adventures reached the Coca River, over half the party had died or deserted. The remainder were malnourished, half-naked, and totally exhausted. Pizarro decided to send Orellana, 57 Spaniards, and 200 indigenous downriver in search of food in a ship that had been hastily built on the Coca. Orellana proceeded but found no food source. The current of the Coca was swift and it was impossible to return upstream. The Coca flows into the Napo, a main tributary of the mighty Amazon. Incredibly, Orellana traversed the length of the Amazon to the Atlantic Ocean and eventually returned to Spain. He named the river after encountering a group of fierce female warriors during his journey. Orellana's discovery and exploration was the beginning of Ecuador's claim that it is an Amazonian nation entitled to access to the great river.

When Orellana failed to return, Pizarro assumed the party was lost. He led a few survivors back to Quito in August 1542 and found Peru in an ongoing civil war. The problems started with disagreements between Francisco Pizarro and Diego de Almargo over the distribution of treasure and the division of conquered territory. Almargo was defeated, found guilty of treason, and executed. However, his followers continued the struggle and Francisco Pizarro was assassinated on June 26, 1541. The chaos created by the feuding conquistadors, reports of abuse of the native populations, and the fear that independent fiefdoms would emerge caused the Spanish crown to pronounce the New Laws of 1542. The New Laws had little immediate impact but they clearly signaled the intent of Spain to establish administrative control and strip the conquistadors of power. In 1544 the Viceroyalty of Peru was established and Blasco Núñez de Vela arrived in Lima as the first viceroy, the king's direct representative in his new kingdom of Peru.

Núñez de Vela attempted to impose his rule on the colony but met fierce opposition to his arbitrary actions and pronouncements. He was soon arrested by the *oidores* (judges) of the Audiencia (court and advisory unit) of Lima. In 1546 the viceroy was shipped off to Panama but convinced the ship captain to free him at Tumbes. There he rallied support to retake the viceroyalty, marched north to Colombia, and united with Sebastian de Benalcázar. The rebels, led by Gonzalo Pizarro, defeated the royalist army and killed Núñez de Vela at the battle of Añaquito north of Quito on January 18, 1546. However, Gonzalo Pizarro's triumph was short-lived as he was defeated by a royalist army in 1548, convicted of treason, and hanged. The death of the younger Pizarro ended the tumultuous times of the conquistadors and brought orderly colonial rule to Ecuador.

THE SPANISH COLONIAL PERIOD

In theory Spain's colonies in the Western Hemisphere were the personal possessions of the king and his authority was absolute in Ecuador. The crown established the Council of the Indies in 1524 to carry out all colonial administration in the king's name. The council was located in Madrid and established all the laws and regulations governing the political, economic, social, educational, and religious aspects of colonial life. Commerce was governed by the Board of Trade, with headquarters in Seville. The Board of Trade established a closed trading system that permitted trade solely between each colony and Spain. Intercolonial trade was limited, and commerce with other nations prohibited. The principal colonial administrative units were the viceroyalty, the *audiencia* (court, legislative, advisory unit), and the *cabildo* (municipal council). Rural areas populated by large numbers of indigenous had different administrative units variously known as *reducciónes* or *repúblicas de indios.*

Ecuador was governed directly by the Viceroyalty of Peru from 1544 to 1563 with no intermediate administrative unit other than the local *cabildos.* In 1563 the Audiencia of Quito was established and had authority over a territory that was much larger than present-day Ecuador. The *audiencia,* also known as the Kingdom of Quito, extended northward into present-day Colombia and included the city of Cali. The southern boundary encompassed portions of northwestern Peru, while the ill-defined eastern border ran far into the Amazon River basin. In reality much of the territory of the *audiencia* was unexplored and its exact boundaries never clearly delineated. Nevertheless, the Audiencia of Quito later provided Ecuadorian nationalists with the geographical vision of what their nation should include. In addition, the lack of clear colonial boundaries resulted in extended territorial disputes and conflicts with Colombia and Peru.

Spanish colonial control in Ecuador was centered in the sierra, where the indigenous population was completely subjugated. Spanish Quito was constructed on top of the second Inca capital and became the largest city in the colonial period. Other Spanish cities and towns were soon founded in the intermountain basins of the Ecuadorian Andes. The larger ones, from north to south, include Ibarra, Ambato, Ríobamba, Cuenca, and Loja. While the sierra was the most populated area of colonial Ecuador, it was also isolated from the rest of the world by its geography and the failure of the Spanish to fully integrate the coast and lowlands into a cohesive political and economic entity.

With the exception of Guayaquil, much of the coast and the lowland areas remained unconquered. The indigenous populations north of Manta were displaced, not by Spaniards, but by shipwrecked Africans slaves who were to be transported to Peru. The blacks killed or drove off the native males and took the women as wives or concubines. The offspring of these unions were called *zambos* or *cimarrónes* and succeeding generations created a semiautonomous area with its own unique culture. Today the descendants of this unique group are the largest segment of the population in the city of San Lorenzo and other northwestern coastal towns. The Oriente, for the most part, remained unexplored.

Quito was the center of Spanish religious, cultural, social, and political life in colonial Ecuador. El Belén Church was the first Spanish building constructed in the new city and mass was celebrated to commemorate Quito's new beginning. The original El Belén was lost to history but a later church replaced it in 1612 and is situated on the site of the first mass. Spain's religious mission in Ecuador is exemplified by the magnificent churches, monasteries, and convents built during the colonial era, most of which still stand and are in daily use, making Quito a living museum. Friar Jadoco Ricke began construction of the Monastery of San Francisco in 1534. The massive structure, constructed in Renaissance Greco-Roman neoclassicism, took nearly 70 years to complete, and houses some of the great works of art, including sculpture by the famous indigenous artisan, Caspircara. Other Catholic orders arrived and also built architectural wonders including Santo Domingo (1580), San Agustín

Friar Jadoco Ricke began construction on the San Francisco Church and Monastery in 1534. (© Ammit | Dreamstime.com)

(1606), and La Merced (1701). The Jesuits began La Compañia de Jesús in 1605 and created one of the finest examples of Rococo style in the world. It is the most visited church in Ecuador today. In addition to these, dozens of convents and smaller churches were built throughout Quito and the surrounding area. In addition to providing spiritual services, the Catholic Church organized hospitals, schools, universities, orphanages, and almshouses. It trained artisans, engaged in many enterprises, and provided funding for both private and public projects. From Quito missionaries from the regulated orders set out into the hinterlands to convert the natives with unrelenting zeal, while the secular clergy tended to the needs of the Spanish population. By 1736 Quito boasted a grand central plaza with the palace of the *presidencia* (presidency of the *audiencia*) on one side, and a cathedral, bishop's palace, and city hall on the others.

The social structure of colonial Ecuador mirrored Spain's other New World possessions. *Peninsulares,* Spaniards born in Spain, held the most important government and ecclesiastical positions and were considered the societal elite. In Ecuador, peninsular Spaniards were called *chapetónes.* Criollos, the progeny of Spanish parents, but born in Ecuador, were next in the social pecking order. Criollos were often large land owners, heads of important commercial

A statue honoring Ecuador's Independence Heroes is in Quito's Plaza Grande. (© iStockPhoto.com/Loic Bernard)

enterprises, militia officers, and lesser government and church officials. Mestizos, the offspring of a Spaniard and an indigenous person, comprised the largest Hispanized group in colonial times. This diverse group held a wide range of occupations and their social and economic status varied greatly. Indigenous people were supposedly the next rung on the social ladder, but in reality were the most marginalized group. However, indigenous peoples who became Hispanic by adopting Spanish names, language, and costume could be elevated to mestizo status. While Africans officially had the lowest societal status, they often fared better than the indigenous. For example, household slaves were often in charge of indigenous servants known as *yanaconas*. As presented previously, Africans living in coastal areas enjoyed a certain autonomy by living in relative isolation. There were many other racial classifications in the Spanish colonial social system, such as *cholo, mulatto,* and *zambo,* to list only a few. In addition, family relationships were often tangled and complex, resulting in great racial diversity. Social lines were not always easily defined and it is evident that some from the lower racial classes were able to obtain *criollo* status in the second half of the 18th century.

While the formation of cities was an important aspect of the colonial era, the Ecuadorian economic engine was agriculture. Because Ecuador did not have the mineral wealth that Peru yielded, the emphasis was on increasing the agricultural output of the indigenous-populated rural areas. *Encomienda* and *mita* were the systems adopted to meet that end. Under *encomienda* Spaniards were placed in charge of large numbers of indigenous people and their lands. The *encomendero* (overseer) was charged with converting the indigenous to the Catholic faith, providing ongoing religious services, organizing agricultural production, defending of the area, and collecting tribute. The *encomendero* was not granted title to the land or ownership of the indigenous, but could use their labor for personal gain and to pay operating expenses. In effect, *encomienda* was a form of indigenous slavery that enriched the *encomenderos.* The highland *encomiendas* were the breadbasket of colonial Ecuador, providing wheat, beef, potatoes, and other crops for local consumption. They also yielded wool and cotton, the raw materials needed for the manufacture and export of textiles.

Francisco Pizarro initially granted 14 *encomiendas* in Ecuador, but they were soon subdivided and others were added.[7] It is estimated that there were nearly 500 *encomiendas* in the colonial period. The Spanish Crown attempted to mitigate the abuses of *encomienda* by limiting inheritance of the grants to two generations. By the end of the 18th century, the *hacienda* system replaced most of the encomiendas. A *hacienda* was a large landed estate that was owned by a peninsular or more likely a criollo Spaniard. Indigenous labor was contracted to work the fields in exchange for a plot of land on which the criollo could raise subsistence crops to support his family. Indigenous labor became bound to the land in a system of land tenancy similar to sharecropping in the United State know in Ecuador as *huasipungo.*

Not all indigenous people lived and worked on *encomiendas.* The Spanish also established *reducciónes,* planned towns where large numbers of the indigenous were concentrated from previously scattered villages and hamlets. The *reducciónes* or *repúblicas de indios* were headed by a *kuraka* (chief) who oversaw the town and acted as a liaison between the indigenous masses and a *corregidor,* the Spanish official who oversaw several towns in a specific area designated as *corregimiento.* Usually each indigenous town was assigned a certain craft and expected to produce products in excess of local needs in *obrajes* (sweatshops). Conditions in the *obrajes* were often abusive, including long hours, family separation, and harsh discipline if production quotas were not met. Typical crafts included weaving, woodcarving, and leather work. Indigenous artisans proved to be very skillful and produced quality products despite the harsh conditions. The legacy of the colonial *obrajes* can be seen throughout Ecuador today in much more benign settings where family-owned cottage industries have replaced the sweatshops. Prominent examples include the exquisite textiles of Otavalo, the fine leather products produced in Cotacachi, and the extraordinary carved wooden figures of San Antonio de Ibarra. In addition to generating products and paying tribute, the inhabitants of the *reducciónes* were required to perform *mita,* one year of public service on a rotational basis to build roads, churches, *obrajes,* and public buildings, or perform a host of other tasks. *Mitayos* were paid for their labor, but the wage was so low that they borrowed from the *corregidors* and *kurakas* and became heavily indebted. Thus *mita* evolved into a system of debt peonage that was augmented and sustained by the *repartimiento de mercancías,* the forced sale of products at high prices. As debts were never paid in full, they were passed on to the next generation, guaranteeing a labor supply for the *obrajes* and other enterprises and creating a class that lived in virtual serfdom.

Guayaquil also developed as an important commercial center. As a port it served as Ecuador's window on the outside world and the outlet for sierra textiles, hardwoods, and other products, as well as cacao from coastal plantations. Goods from Spain, the Philippines, and Peru passed through the bustling port. Guayaquil's main industry was shipbuilding and its shipyards were the largest on the Pacific coast of South America.

In 1736 a team of scientists from the French Academy of Sciences, led by Charles Marie Louis de la Condamine, arrived in Ecuador to determine the exact location of the equator in order to resolve scholarly arguments over Isaac Newton's theory of the size and shape of the earth. This nine-year scientific mission had a dramatic impact as La Condamine, Joseph de Jussieu, botanist, Pierre Bouguer, astronomist, Jean Godin des Odonais, physicist, and Dr. Jean Seniergues introduced enlightenment ideas that questioned tradition and

These Otavaleñas are attired in traditional costumes. (Courtesy of Sue Lauder-baugh)

emphasized natural rights.[8] The works of Voltaire, Jean-Jacques Rousseau, and John Locke eluded Spanish censors and were widely read by criollo intellectuals. The expedition succeeded in charting a portion of the equator with amazing accuracy and built pyramid monuments to mark the location. The French academicians were accompanied by two Spanish officers, Jorge Juan y Santacilla and Antonio de Ulloa, who later authored the four-volume *A Voyage to South America*, a work that provides one of the most accurate descriptions of Ecuador in the colonial period. An example of the conflicted attitude of the colonial population toward the expedition was the murder of Dr. Seniergues by an angry mob while he attended a bullfight in Cuenca.[9] The La Condamine expedition also resulted in worldwide attention of a previously obscure area of the Spanish Empire and later was a factor in the selection of Ecuador as the nation's name. Ecuador takes pride in its historic role of promoting scientific discovery and has built Mitad del Mundo (Middle of the World), a museum and park north of Quito at the site of the French team's first pyramids. The country also prides itself for supporting space exploration in the 1960s when NASA, the U.S. space agency, built a tracking station near Mount Cotopaxi.

A thorough study of Ecuador's indigenous and colonial history is essential for understanding the nation's current identity and problems. The ambivalent attitude of the place of the indigenous in Ecuador's history is one example. Ecuadorian nationalists point out that the country was never fully integrated into the vast Inca Empire and maintained a distinct identity. Atahualpa is exalted as the first Ecuadorian. The resistance of Rumiñahui and others to the Spanish Conquest is a source of pride. On the other hand, the indigenous populations have often been viewed as an impediment to development and until recently have not had a voice in the political life of the country. In the aftermath of the Spanish Conquest, Ecuador became more Hispanic than indigenous and the largest segment of today's population identifies with those traditions. From Spain, Ecuador inherited the Roman Catholic religion, the Spanish language, the idea of the city, legal and governmental concepts, social structure, and many other economic and cultural institutions. Geographical Ecuador was an outcome of the creation of the Audiencia of Quito. Seeds of nationalism were inadvertently planted by the mother country when the La Condamine expedition was allowed into the colony. The very name of the country is but one outcome of its rich colonial past.

NOTES

1. Linda Newson, *Life and Death in Early Colonial Ecuador* (Norman: University of Oklahoma Press, 1995), 25–116.

2. Ibid., 61–78.

3. Ibid., 26–59.

4. Ibid., 79–115.

5. Pío Jaramillo, *La nación Quiteña* (Quito: n.p., 1947), 147.

6. Loren McIntyre, *Incredible Incas* (Washington, DC: National Geographic Society, 1975), 120–38.

7. Nicanor Jácome, "Economía y sociedad en el siglo XVI," in *Nueva historia del Ecuador*, vol. 3, ed. Enrique Ayala Mora (Quito: Corporación Nacional, 1995), 145.

8. For a detailed account of the expedition refer to Robert Whitaker, *The Mapmaker's Wife* (New York: Basic Books, 2004).

9. Victor Wolfgang von Hagen, *Ecuador and the Galapagos Islands* (Norman: University of Oklahoma Press, 1949), 32–35.

3

Independence and the Early Republic, 1795–1859

In many ways Ecuador's revolt against Spanish rule was typical of the rest of Latin America, caused by ideals of the Enlightenment, the examples of the American and French revolutions, the Bourbon reforms, economic factors, and the conflict between criollo and peninsular Spaniards. On the other hand, the Ecuadorian experience was unique. For example, the first manifesto declaring independence in 1809 did not proclaim lofty ideals of liberty but rather faulted the president of the Audiencia of Quito for his poor leadership. Another distinct feature is the cast of characters who inspired or led the fledgling nation to independence from Spain followed by independence from Gran Colombia. These men and women became the first heroes and heroines of the new republic and in many cases initiated traditions that impact Ecuador today. The idea of Ecuador as a nation was born during this period, although the extent of its national territory would not be completely defined until 1998.

ESPEJO: PRECURSOR OF ECUADORIAN INDEPENDENCE

The Bourbon monarchy, inspired by the technical advances of the Enlightenment, initiated programs that became known as the Bourbon reforms, designed to improve the efficiency of its colonial administration and to increase the economic output of its colonies. For Ecuador, the creation of the Viceroyalty of New Granada in 1717, which included much of present-day Ecuador, Colombia, Venezuela, and Panama, proved a most important administrative reform. The viceroyalty was dissolved in 1723 but reestablished in 1739. The vice regal capital was Bogotá. The separation of the Audiencia of Quito from the Viceroyalty of Peru would later allow Ecuadorian patriots to define their vision of national territory to encompass the borders of the former colonial *audiencia*, as well as dictate Ecuador's inclusion in the republic of Gran Colombia from 1822 to 1830. While not evident at first, the redrawing of colonial administrative units stirred a nascent nationalism.

The reformers planted another nationalist seed when new lucrative and powerful colonial administrative positions were staffed mostly by peninsular Spaniards rather than criollos, the local Spanish colonists who had been born in the New World. This schism of the mostly white upper class of colonial society into competing camps proved to be critical to the emergence of independence sentiment and ultimate action. In addition, as many of the enterprises of the colonies were criollo-owned, the reformers encouraged the formation of organizations to improve economic output known as Amigos del País (Friends of the Country). The initial idea was to use these groups to discuss new techniques in farming, mining, or manufacturing. However, these groups were soon also discussing political philosophy, issues, and events stemming from the Enlightenment, including the works of Rousseau, Montesquieu, Locke, and Paine as well as the examples of the American and French revolutions.

In Quito, Francisco Eugenio de Santa Cruz y Espejo, a physician, intellectual, and journalist, served as the leader (secretary) of the Sociedad Patriótica de los Amigos del País (Patriotic Society of Friends of the Country). Under the Spanish caste system of racial classification, Espejo was a *zambo*, as his father was black and his mother indigenous. However, Espejo's keen intellect enabled him to overcome discrimination and prejudice to become a member of the criollo elite. Espejo also was the editor of the society's newspaper, *Primicias de la cultura de Quito* (First Fruits of Quito's Culture). Between 1792 and 1795, Espejo used the paper and other forums to advocate for complete independence from Spain and the establishment of a republic. He also proposed radical social change, including nationalization of the clergy, confiscation of property held by religious orders, and the expulsion of peninsular Spaniards. Espejo's manifestos caught the attention of Spanish officials, who had him arrested and imprisoned. Espejo died while incarcerated but not before he won over to the patriot cause some notable criollos, including Juan Pío Montúfar y Larrea, the second Marquis of Selva Alegre, who would later lead the first revolt against Spanish rule. Espejo's audacious writings and speeches made him the intellectual father of Ecuadorian independence and the nation's first political martyr.

THE SOVEREIGN JUNTA OF QUITO: SOUTH AMERICA'S FIRST CRY FOR INDEPENDENCE

The outside event that touched off the conflagration of the war for Spanish America's independence was Napoleon's invasion of Spain in 1808. The Spanish king Charles IV soon abdicated and this was supposed to pave the way for his son Ferdinand VII to assume the throne. Spain's political chaos and a nasty guerilla war resulted in the emperor placing his brother, Joseph Bonaparte, on the Spanish throne. The removal of Ferdinand VII coupled with Joseph's reforms, including the abolishment of feudalism, restrictions on church authority, and the integration of Spain into Napoleon's Continental System, caused a reaction in Ecuador. On December 25, under the leadership of Selva Alegre, a junta was formed to support Ferdinand VII, provide for the defense of the fatherland, and to preserve the Catholic faith. Vice regal authorities soon stifled this initial conspiracy.

The group went underground and after meeting in the house of Manuela Cañizares, a prominent resident of Quito, declared the Sovereign Junta of Quito as the legitimate government to replace the *audiencia*. The date was August 10, 1809, which is Ecuador's official independence day. Selva Alegre was named president, and the bishop of Quito, José Cuero y Caicedo, became vice president. The Spanish garrison in Quito supported the junta and placed the president of the *audiencia* under house arrest. The Sovereign Junta gained legitimacy when a *cabildo abierto* (open council) composed of prominent citizens approved the junta's acts. The junta proclaimed its objectives as preservation of the true religion, defense of the fatherland, and defense of the legitimate monarchy of Ferdinand VII. The junta also condemned Manuel de Urriez, the Conde Ruiz, the president of the *audiencia,* for being absolutely inept and decrepit. The junta ruled Quito for three months but was unable to convince Cuenca and Guayaquil to join the cause. A power struggle broke down the unity of the junta and the revolt had little appeal to the masses. The viceroys of both Peru and New Granada condemned the revolt and sent troops to put it down. Selva Alegre fled on October 5 and royal troops gained control on October 28 as the Conde Ruiz returned to his position. More than 100 patriots were arrested and tried for treason. Forty-six were condemned to death and the rest were to be exiled. On August 2, 1810, a mob attempted to enter the prison and free the patriots before their sentences were carried out, but Spanish soldiers panicked and fired on the prisoners in their cells, massacring more than 70 men.

Five weeks after the massacre, Lieutenant Colonel Carlos Montúfar, a son of Selva Alegre, and a special commissioner representing the Junta Central of Spain, arrived in Quito to restore order and to calm the populace. Carlos Montúfar, with the support of a criollo committee, established the Superior Junta of Government with the Conde Ruiz as president and Selva Alegre as vice president. Given Selva Alegre's previous condemnation of the count, the junta's meetings were not without considerable acrimony. Nevertheless the junta held power from September 1810 until December 1812.

On October 11, 1811, Quito again revolted and declared independence. Selva Alegre left the junta and in January he became president of the Free State of Quito. The viceroy of Peru dispatched another royalist army commanded by General Toribio Montes, who crushed the uprising and forced Selva Alegre into exile. Montes then governed until 1817. It appeared the royalists had won and Ecuador remained firmly in the empire's grip until 1820.

From 1808 until 1820 the center of the Ecuadorian revolt was in Quito and surrounding areas. In 1820 the locus of rebellion shifted to Guayaquil. The port city, led by José de Villamil and León Febres Cordero, revolted successfully on October 9. Several of Febres Cordero's descendants would become president of Ecuador and others still aspire to that office. A provisional government was established and presided over by the poet José Joaquín Olmedo. A *cabildo abierto* soon bestowed legitimacy on the new government and an appeal was made to Quito and Cuenca to join. The Guayaquileños organized a patriot army and dispatched it to the central highlands. Cuenca declared independence on November 3, 1820. However, on November 22 the royal army prevailed at the battle of Huachi near the city of Ambato and the patriots retreated to the coastal region.

In February 1821 Simón Bolívar, the liberator of Venezuela and Colombia, dispatched reinforcements and military supplies to the Guayaquil patriots. Bolívar wanted to drive the Spanish from the Audiencia of Quito and to incorporate it into his newly created Republic of Gran Colombia. At the time the Guayaquil rebels were considering three options: join Gran Colombia, join Peru, or create a small independent republic. Bolívar's actions ultimately proved decisive in Guayaquil becoming part of Gran Colombia. In addition to providing troops and supplies, Bolívar dispatched his most trusted general, Antonio José de Sucre, to Guayaquil to rally the patriot forces and to secure the *audiencia* before General José de San Martín arrived with a Peruvian patriot army. Sucre arrived in May, raised an army, and led it into the sierra with the objective of taking Quito. After initial victories, Sucre's force was defeated at the second battle of Huachi on November 22. Sucre signed an armistice and withdrew to Guayaquil.

In early January 1822 Sucre renewed operations to drive the Spanish from the Ecuadorian highlands by first marching south and taking the town of

Machala in the coastal lowlands. He then led his 1,700 men to the southeast to Saraguro where he linked up with the Peruvian Division that had been sent by San Martín. With his army now numbering nearly 3,000, Sucre turned to the north toward Cuenca. Spanish forces abandoned the city and Sucre liberated it on February 21. The patriot army marched along the spine of the western cordillera, freeing Riobamba on April 12 and Latacunga on May 2. The patriot army was reinforced by the famous Colombian Alto Magdalena Battalion and the Albion Battalion, a mercenary group of Scots and Irish, for the final assault on Quito. The Spanish commander, General Melchor Aymerich, had blocked the direct approaches to the Valley of Quito and Sucre wisely chose not to attack them head on. Instead he conceived a daring flanking maneuver and led his men along the slopes of the Cotopaxi volcano, into the Chillos valley and behind the Spanish position. On the night of May 23–24, the patriot army ascended the Pichincha Volcano overlooking Quito but was spotted by Royalist forces. Aymerich decided to attack before the Patriots had established an impregnable position on the high ground. The battle began at 9:30 in the morning and was fought at an altitude of 11,500 feet. After three hours of intense fighting on difficult terrain, the royalist forces, demoralized by the slaughter of their elite unit by the Albion Battalion, retreated to Quito. On May 25 Sucre and his victorious army entered Quito in triumph. The general had earned his place in Ecuadorian history as a great liberator and is today a national hero despite his Venezuelan birth. His remains occupy a place of honor in the national cathedral in his adopted city. He was also honored for many decades when Ecuador's national currency was named the sucre. The Battle of Pichincha produced another national hero in Lieutenant Albdon Calderón, a teenager who was seriously wounded but selflessly refused to leave his position. He died the following day and his memory is honored by the Albdon Calderón Star, one of the highest of Ecuador's military decorations.

On June 16 General Simón Bolívar made his triumphal entry into Quito amid the adulation of the population, who lined the narrow streets or perched on balconies to cheer and catch a glimpse of the liberator. Later at a victory ball, Bolívar, a widower, was introduced to Manuela Sáenz de Thorne, the half sister of one his military aides and one of the most beautiful women in all of Quito. Sáenz was from one of Quito's wealthiest families, but her illegitimate birth had hindered her claim to her maternal inheritance. She was married to an English merchant, many years her senior, whose business interests were in Peru. She had only recently returned to Quito to pursue her inheritance claim when her chance encounter with Bolívar occurred. Bolívar and Sáenz were attracted to each other and a romantic relationship soon followed. In time "Manuelita" would become Bolívar's trusted aide and the archivist of his most important papers. Of greater importance were her heroic actions on September 25, 1828, when she thwarted an assassination attempt directed at

Bolívar and earned the sobriquet *Libertadora del Libertador* (Liberator of the Liberator). After Bolívar's death in 1830, Sáenz's political influence waned to the extent that she was exiled from Ecuador in 1835. She lived the remainder of her life in Paita, Peru.[1]

THE GUAYAQUIL MEETING

Ecuador was free of Spanish rule but its political future remained uncertain. Would the former Audiencia of Quito be part of Gran Colombia or Peru? What would be the status of Guayaquil? The issue was partly settled when Bolívar marched into Guayaquil on July 11, 1822, and soon abolished Olmedo's government. San Martín arrived on July 26 to discuss the status of Guayaquil and to formulate plans to deliver the final blow to Spanish forces in Peru. The question of Guayaquil's political future was moot as Colombian forces were in firm control. Bolívar annexed the city into Gran Colombia. Mystery shrouds the other issues that the two great men discussed as there is scanty documentation of their deliberations.[2] After the meeting San Martín returned to Lima and abruptly resigned his military command and position as Protector of Peru. He left his native Argentina for Paris, where he lived until his death in 1850.

THE GRAN COLOMBIAN EXPERIENCE, 1822–30

For eight tumultuous years Ecuador remained part of Bolívar's Gran Colombia, a nation that included most of present-day Venezuela, Colombia, Ecuador, and Panama. Ecuador was designated the District of the South and was further divided into three departments: Quito, Guayaquil, and Cuenca. While Ecuador's membership in Gran Colombia was brief, it had long-lasting consequences. Regional differences emerged among the northern and central highlands represented by Quito, the coast, which was heavily influenced by Guayaquil, and the southern sierra where Cuenca dominated. Cuenca often served as the deciding vote in political impasses between Quito and Guayaquil. Another consequence was the dominance of Venezuelan and Colombian military men who served as the intendants (governors) of the three departments and held 12 of the 15 general officer positions. Moreover, for much of the period the head of the Department of the South was General Juan José Flores, a Venezuelan who would ultimately lead Ecuador out of its union with Gran Colombia. Another result was a territorial dispute with Peru that persisted for nearly 170 years. Finally, Ecuador was burdened with an exorbitant debt that was supposedly its share of the cost of the Wars of Independence. The small nation has never been able to overcome this shaky financial start.

During the Wars of Independence, Juan José Flores was a young officer who showed promise in a number of battles.[3] In 1826 Bolívar promoted Flores to the rank of general and appointed him governor of the "Department of Ecuador." While the appointment of Flores was due, in no small part, to his extreme loyalty to Bolívar, the young Venezuelan had also demonstrated intelligence, political acumen, and the ability to maintain order. The general was also vain, ambitious, and opportunistic. He had taken control of Quito on his own in late 1824 and his later official appointment was also a matter of a fait accompli. Flores soon established friendships with certain factions of Quito's elite. In 1825 he solidified his status by marrying Mercedes Jijón y Vivanco, a member of a prominent aristocratic family. While it was clear that Flores considered Quito his home and Ecuador his country, he was considered an outsider and a usurper by his political opponents, a stigma that Flores battled for the rest of his life.

Nevertheless, Flores made significant contributions to the future of Ecuador and at times demonstrated personal courage and extraordinary leadership skills. He successfully guided Ecuador through the disintegration of Bolívar's bold vision of a confederation of Andean states that included Gran Colombia, Peru, and Bolivia. In April 1827 the Third Division of the Peruvian patriot army invaded the departments of Azuay and Guayas in an attempt to detach them from Gran Colombia. Flores blunted the initial assault and then raised an army of 5,000 to defend Ecuador from subsequent incursions. After raising the army, Flores cheerfully accepted Bolívar's orders placing Marshall Sucre in command, and accepted a subordinate position. Flores achieved military glory on February 28, 1829, during the crucial battle of Tarqui when he exhibited extraordinary valor and helped deal the Peruvians a stinging defeat. After the battle, Sucre awarded Flores the Medal of Tarqui and promoted him to the rank of division general.

Flores's heroics at Tarqui mitigated, but did not completely eliminate, the animosity that some native citizens of Ecuador held against him. While the battle of Tarqui temporarily stifled Peru's attempts to incorporate Ecuador into its territory, it did not forestall the breakup of Gran Colombia. Opposition to Bolívar's dictatorship was widespread and included factions in Venezuela, Colombia, and Ecuador. Flores, however, remained committed to keeping Ecuador in the nation and refused to abandon his mentor, Bolívar, until events dictated otherwise.

Venezuela broke from Gran Colombia on January 13, 1829, when General José Páez, a former lieutenant of Bolívar, declared its independence. Páez's declaration inspired rebellions in other parts of the republic, including the Department of Ecuador. Flores pleaded with Bolívar to officially visit Quito to bolster support against secession, but to no avail. The beleaguered liberator was facing fierce opposition in Bogotá and was in declining health from the ravages of tuberculosis. By May 1830 it was apparent that the District of the South was seriously contemplating separation. The leading citizens of Quito formed a *cabildo abierto* (open council) and invited Flores to play a pivotal part in the independence movement. Flores accepted and on May 13 he was named Supreme Civilian and Military Magistrate. A few days later Guayaquil joined the newly formed state. Despite his acceptance of this key post, Flores had hopes of a reconciliation with a Gran Colombia headed by Bolívar. These aspirations were dashed on June 4, when Marshal Antonio José de Sucre was ambushed and murdered while traveling from Bogotá to Quito at Berruecos, a remote village in southern Colombia. Sucre was on a reconciliation mission and his tragic death ended the last possibility of Ecuador remaining part of Gran Colombia.

THE FIRST FLORES PRESIDENCY 1830–34

On September 22, 1830, attired in his army dress uniform and festooned with his numerous military decorations, 30-year-old Juan José Flores swore "by God and the Holy Scriptures to uphold the Constitution," and assumed the presidency of the newly created República del Ecuador.[4] The constitution that Flores swore to uphold provided for a federal form of government that granted equal representation to Ecuador's three departments with a 30-member unicameral Congress. On paper it provided for separation of powers between the executive, legislative, and judicial branches, although this proscription has rarely been followed. Popular participation was limited to literate male property owners and thus excluded most of the adult population. Not surprisingly, the constitution, written largely by Flores's supporters, gave considerable power to the president, including the appointment of government officials, judges, and high church officers. The Roman Catholic Church was declared the official state religion to the exclusion of all others. Moreover, the state was responsible for collecting the church tithe. Flores and his vice president, José Joaquín Olmedo, were granted a four-year term of office. Ecuador's first constitution, while including some concepts from the U.S. Constitution such as the separation of powers, was a very conservative document. And, unlike the U.S. Constitution and American presidents, Flores and many future Ecuadorian presidents followed it only when convenient. Perhaps the most significant aspect of the 1830 constitution was selecting the name Ecuador for the meridian line through the new nation rather than the more traditional Quito, although even that decision was a controversial matter for opponents of the charter.

Flores first wanted to determine the national territory of the republic. On December 20 he decreed that the former Department of Cauca, once part of Gran Colombia and in dispute with New Granada, was part of Ecuador.

Flores's bold decision resulted in a confrontation with New Granada and established a precedent for Ecuadorian foreign and defense policy over the next 168 years. Ecuador contended that its national territory should be based on the boundaries of the colonial Audiencia of Quito. Under this assumption Ecuador included the lowlands of the Amazon and Marañón rivers to the east and south and the Department of Cauca to the north. Unfortunately Ecuador's neighbors, Colombia, Peru, and Brazil, disputed this demand and saw an opportunity to expand at Ecuador's expense. The immediate impact of Flores's claim to Cauca was an attempt by New Granada's General Rafael Urdaneta to topple his government. Urdaneta's plot failed, but New Granada's determination to retain Cauca was backed by superior military force. In December 1832 Flores reluctantly conceded that Cauca was part of New Granada. He signed the Treaty of Pasto, relinquishing Ecuador's claim and accepting the Carchi River as the border between the two countries.

Flores's failure to obtain the Cauca region was partially offset by his decision to annex the Galápagos Islands in 1832. This decision, almost unnoticed at the time, brought into Ecuador's national domain one of the most exotic and scientifically important archipelagos on the earth. The islands also were of strategic importance, especially during World War II, when the United States would build an air base on Baltra Island. Today the Galápagos are an international nature preserve and a favorite tourist destination.

On the domestic front, Flores soon learned that Ecuador is a very difficult country to govern. Opposition to Flores centered in El Quiteño Libre, an organization formed in 1833 to promote liberal republicanism. Among the society's founders were Colonel Francis "Francisco" Hall, an English mercenary and hero of the Battle of Pichincha, and Vicente Rocafuerte, a liberal politician and intellectual from Guayaquil. Hall, Rocafuerte, and Pedro Moncayo, the editor of the society's newspaper, also called *El Quiteño libre,* campaigned for freedom of the press, religious freedom, and a curb on the power of the Catholic Church, and open transparent government. Ironically, given Hall's background, the society railed against the foreign military men who had taken up residence in Ecuador and their political influence. Of course, this was a direct attack on Flores and he did not take it lightly. When the society published a pamphlet, *Las facultades extraordinarias,* that was highly critical of Flores and his policies, the president requested and on September 14, 1833, obtained extraordinary powers from the Ecuadorian Congress to suppress the opposition. Soon Pedro Moncayo was exiled. In Guayaquil, Vicente Rocafuerte led a revolt. A more alarming incident was the assassination of Colonel Hall and three other members of the society on October 10, 1833.

Rocafuerte's opposition expanded into the "War of the Chihuahuas," so called because of Rocafuerte's ownership of a large hacienda in the Mexican state of Chihuahua. The "war" coincided with Rocafuerte's campaign to become president of Ecuador, making violence part of the process that is all too frequent in Ecuadorian politics. Flores outwitted Rocafuerte and took him into custody when he returned from Peru with military supplies for the revolt. Flores decided to end the violence that was consuming the country. He pardoned Rocafuerte and agreed to alternate the presidency with his rival with the stipulation that he, Flores, would retain command of the army.

In his first term as president of Ecuador, Flores achieved what only a few of his successors would: he completed his constitutional term. He had added the Galápagos Islands to Ecuador's territory and settled the dispute with New Granada over the northern boundary. He was unable to resolve Ecuador's chaotic financial system and his attempts to provide education and social services to Ecuador's impoverished masses never materialized.

Several trends emerged during the first Flores presidency that have plagued Ecuadorian politics ever since. First was the willingness of Flores to use repression in an attempt to silence a critical press. Second, the opposition to Flores was not a loyal opposition and resorted to intrigue and armed uprisings in an attempt to seize power. Third, all too soon the elite leadership bifurcated into two broad factions: liberals and conservatives. Fourth was the realization that the army played a significant role in internal politics. Finally, personalities played a decisive role in Ecuadorian politics, now centered on Flores and his rival Rocafuerte rather than the ideologies that each advocated. While the personal aspect of Ecuadorian politics would often become rancorous, Flores demonstrated that it need not plunge the nation into a long civil war when he reached a compromise with Rocafuerte.

VICENTE ROCAFUERTE: ECUADOR'S FIRST NATIVE-BORN PRESIDENT, 1835–39

In many ways Vicente Rocafuerte y Rodríguez de Bejarano was Ecuador's first citizen of the world. Born into a prominent Guayaquil family in 1783, Rocafuerte had the advantage of a first-class European education and years of international travel. He was an intellectual who devoured books on the political ideas of the Enlightenment. In addition to his native Spanish he spoke five other languages fluently. A sojourn in the United States (1821–23) convinced Rocafuerte that his native land should attempt to emulate its political institutions and inspired him to write *Necessary Ideals for Every Independent American Nation which Wishes to Be Free.* In this manifesto he proposed constitutional law, representative government, public education, economic growth, agricultural modernization, and trade as paths to development that all the new republics of Latin America should pursue. He also translated and appended the Declaration of Independence, the Articles of Confederation, and the U.S. Constitution to his book. Rocafuerte gained diplomatic experience when he joined

Mexico's mission to gain recognition from Great Britain, serving in London from 1824 to 1829. He resided in Mexico from 1829 to 1832 and then returned to Ecuador, where he immediately became involved with opponents of Flores.

While governing as supreme chief of Guayaquil, Rocafuerte summoned a constitutional convention, thus establishing another trend in Ecuadorian politics: new leaders writing new constitutions to suit their vision for governance. Ecuador's second constitution eliminated any thought of rejoining Gran Colombia, made native birth a qualification to be president, created a bicameral legislature, allowed for local elections, and expanded suffrage. It also provided for a system of provincial representation in the House of Deputies while retaining equal representation in the Senate for the three regions. Despite Rocafuerte's objections, the Roman Catholic Church remained the official religion to the exclusion of all others.

The constitutional convention elected Rocafuerte president on August 8, 1835, ending a year of political chaos in which competing *caudillos* ruled the sierra and coastal regions. With his legitimacy established, Rocafuerte set about initiating reforms. He formed the National Guard as a counterbalance to the armies of local warlords. He founded military and naval academies in an attempt to professionalize the armed forces. Rocafuerte introduced public education for girls when he invited Isaac Wheelwright, an American educator, to set up a school based on the Lancaster method of instruction. He expropriated the Dominican Colegio de San Fernando and implemented a secular curriculum. Several laws were passed that lessened the influence of the Catholic Church and curbed its abuses. For example, the number of religious holidays sanctioned by the state was reduced and entry into religious orders was prohibited to anyone under the age of 25. Rocafuerte oversaw the preservation of colonial-era art and the restoration of the famous equator monuments that had been erected by a French scientific expedition in 1740. He liberalized Ecuador's judicial system by introducing the jury system in criminal proceedings and appointed a commission to codify national law. Rocafuerte's energetic and reform-minded administration ended peacefully on January 31, 1839, with the expiration of his constitutional term. It was the first time that there was a peaceful transfer of power from one president to the next, which would be a rare occurrence throughout Ecuador's history.

THE SECOND FLOREANO, 1839–45

Surprisingly, Juan José Flores chose to continue some of Rocafuerte's programs, including completion of the port of San Lorenzo on the northwestern coast. However, foreign affairs consumed most of Flores's attention. He renewed efforts to acquire Pasto, which resulted in a disastrous war with New Granada. Disputes over Ecuador's southern border led to a break in diplomatic relations with Peru and set the stage for Ecuador's most vexing international problem, which would not be resolved until 1998. On the other hand, Flores negotiated a treaty with Spain that recognized Ecuador's independence.

Flores became embroiled in a dispute with Congress and dissolved the body in 1841. The tension and conflict between the executive and legislative branches has permeated Ecuadorian politics ever since. When the Congress reconvened in late 1842 to select Flores's successor, it failed to do so and thus provided an opening for the general to remain in power. Flores chose to maintain a facade of legitimacy and ordered a new constitutional convention. His handpicked delegates drafted a document that was labeled "The Charter of Slavery" by the opposition because it provided for an eight-year presidential term and permitted reelection. The Charter of Slavery also curbed the powers of Congress by having it convened only at four-year intervals. A special commission or council of state comprised of five senators was authorized to approve presidential decrees when congress was not in session. Clearly, Flores was attempting to perpetuate himself in power and had reneged on his agreement with Rocafuerte to alternate the presidency every four years. Nevertheless, on April 1, 1843, the convention dutifully elected Flores to his third term with only two dissenting votes.

Flores's political maneuvering caused a strong reaction from Vicente Rocafuerte. From Peru, where he had been exiled, the former president published *A la nación*, 13 essays highly critical of Flores and his sycophants who had continued him in power. In Quito, the two academic groups, the *Filantrópico-Literaria* and the *Filotécnica*, published anti-Flores polemics. One of the opposition group's members was Gabriel García Moreno, who advocated the extreme measure of tyrannicide and plotted the president's assassination. García Moreno's story demonstrated the convoluted nature of Ecuadorian politics as he was destined to become Ecuador's Conservative dictator and in this position made Juan José Flores commander of the army! In a twist of fate, García Moreno was the first president of Ecuador to be assassinated and his assailants justified their act as tyrannicide.

Flores also angered high officials of the Catholic Church when he insisted that they swear an oath to state control of ecclesiastical patronage, which was contrary to the Vatican's tradition. Government toleration of non-Catholic worship was another reason the Roman Church began to oppose the president. The imposition of a head tax on all Ecuadorian males aged 22–25 spurred violent protests throughout the country.

In February 1845, Vicente Ramón Roca, a Guayaquil businessman, organized a revolutionary movement to topple the Flores regime. Key participants included Rocafuerte, Olmedo, and Generals José María Urbina and Antonio Elizalde. On March 6, 1845, the revolution began in earnest in Guayaquil and soon spread to the rest of the country. Flores won several battles but soon realized that he could not defeat the rebels. A provisional triumvirate consisting of Roca, Olmedo, and Diego Noboa y Arteta negotiated a peace agreement, the Treaty of Virginia, with Flores in June 1845. Under this agreement Flores agreed to resign the presidency and leave Ecuador for two years. He also resigned as commander of the army but was allowed to retain his rank. His family was granted immunity from harassment and prosecution. In addition, Flores was promised a 20,000-peso yearly salary and would be allowed to return to Ecuador after his two-year exile. Flores left Ecuador for Europe on June 25 and his adversaries soon called a new convention to write yet another constitution and to select a new president.

The Treaty of Virginia brought a very temporary period of tranquility to the troubled Andean republic because the revolutionary government reneged on its obligations to Flores, who spent the next 13 years plotting his return to Ecuador by organizing filibustering expeditions in Europe, the United States, and Peru.[5] All attempts proved fruitless, but Flores was not mollified until García Moreno invited him to return in 1859 and placed him in command of the army.

The next 14 years of Ecuadorian history saw periods of stability interrupted by periods of political chaos, culminating in the Terrible Year of 1859, when civil war swept the country. In addition to Flores's intrigues, there were numerous conflicts between Liberals and Conservatives. As always there was tension between the church and state over a host of issues, with the question of control of church appointments causing the most controversy. Moreover, internecine feuds within these broad political coalitions caused even more chaos. Personal allegiance, or *personalismo,* to a particular *caudillo* became more important than ideology. Ironically, Ecuador's fourth constitution intended to mitigate these trends by declaring the sovereignty of the people and extending the right to vote to all male adult citizens.[6] The convention elected Vicente Ramón Roca, a Conservative, to the presidency. The convention also nullified the Treaty of Virginia and mandated that Flores's holdings in Ecuador be confiscated.

Roca presided over four years of relative calm, attributable in no small part to his steady leadership and honesty. He thwarted all attempts by the Flores faction to restore the exiled general to power. Esmeraldas, formerly a territory on the northwest coast, was granted provincial status, a concession by Roca to coastal Liberal interests. Roca's most significant achievement was that he completed his constitutional term, providing his country with a much-needed period of stability. However, a flaw in the 1845 constitution, the requirement that Congress elect the next president by a two-thirds majority, ended this brief respite. When Congress could not agree between the two leading candidates, General Antonio Elizade and Diego Noboa Arteta, Manuel Ascásubi, the sitting vice president, assumed the presidency despite the fact that there was no constitutional basis for this. In his defense Ascásubi did what many Ecuadorian politicians had done and would continue to do: ignore the constitution whenever it was convenient. Despite his dubious claim to the presidency, Ascásubi governed effectively for a year.

The effective and honest government of Ascásubi did not deter Elizade and Noboa from plotting to overthrow the government and to move the capital from Quito to Guayaquil. They found a powerful ally in General José Urbina, who assumed control of Guayaquil Province in February 1850. Civil strife became widespread when Diego Noboa was declared Supreme Chief of the Republic on March 2, 1850, while at the same time Ascásubi stubbornly claimed to be the legitimate president. The issue was resolved when Ascásubi agreed to step aside on June 10. Noboa governed as supreme chief until the predictable constitutional convention convened on December 7 and made him interim president. For the fifth time in only 20 years Ecuador drafted a new constitution. Of course the new charter contained the usual flowery verbiage about republican government, checks and balances, and separation of powers. It did correct the flaw of presidential election by Congress by now requiring only a simple majority instead of the two-thirds vote required by the fourth constitution. As in the past, the sitting interim president, in this instance Noboa, was elected to a four-year "constitutional term."

Noboa lacked the political instincts required to remain in power in Ecuador. Although he was from the Liberal coastal elite, he allowed the Jesuit Order to return to Ecuador, a decision that angered his core supporters on the coast. He also purged the military officer corps by ordering 163 officers removed from the active rolls. Noboa foolishly exiled General Elizade, who had been a fellow conspirator in the coup against Ascásubi. The hapless president appeared to also support the return of Flores. These decisions angered General Urbina, who ordered Noboa arrested and then sent him into exile to Costa Rica in September 1851. Urbina ruled as supreme chief on the coast until he defeated government forces and entered Quito later in the month. Ecuador's sixth constitution was soon promulgated; Urbina was "elected" president and assumed his constitutional term on September 6, 1852.

Urbina ruled with an iron fist and used his own praetorian guard, black soldiers from the Taura Battalion, as his enforcers. The Tauras were infamous for intimidating voters at elections and forcing contributions to the national treasury. Urbina's opponents were often confronted by the Tauras and escorted out of the country. While the dictator promoted primary education, he undermined the university system through his "liberty of studies" program that allowed students to bypass the classroom and study on their own. Under this program the faculty merely administered exams when students felt they were ready.

Urbina's popularity rested both on his ability to keep General Flores out of the country and on his anticlerical policies. He expelled the Jesuits and allowed the Freemasons to open lodges. He expropriated some church property, took control of ecclesiastical patronage ,and regulated seminaries and monasteries. These actions, however, appealed only to the Liberal faction in Ecuador. Conservatives, on the other hand, were outraged and protested vigorously. The Conservatives found a champion in Gabriel García Moreno, who denigrated Urbina in his famous "Ode to Fabius," branding the dictator as a "perjurer, a barbarian, a brigand, swindler, liar and calumniator."[7] Urbina ruled for four years despite García Moreno's polemics and completed his constitutional term. He then campaigned for his friend and colleague General Francisco Robles to succeed him. Robles had no trouble winning the 1856 presidential election; after all, he had Urbina's Tauras to insure that a majority voted the right way. Robles and Urbina were so closely linked that their Conservative opponents derisively referred to them as "the Twins." At least Robles's accession to the presidency negated the need for a new constitution.

General Robles attempted to implement Liberal programs in education and Indian relations. Congress abolished the head tax on Indians, a form of tribute that had existed since the arrival of the Spanish conquistadors. The curriculum of schools in Latacunga and Loja was improved through the introduction of math and science. These modest gains were more than offset by Robles's battle with the Conservatives, which intensified in 1857. Dr. Gabriel García Moreno, the rector of the Central University, mayor of Quito, and a senator from Pichincha Province, was the most spirited of Robles's detractors. García Moreno used his weekly newspaper, *La unión nacional,* to attack Robles and Urbina, as well as other Liberals and Freemasons.

Neighboring Peru challenged Robles over the disputed boundary. Ecuador attempted to trade land in the Oriente to British creditors in exchange for a reduction in its external debt. Peru objected on the grounds that the area was Peruvian territory. Peru also restated its claim to the entire Oriente as well as parts of Pichincha Province and areas near Guayaquil. The dispute resulted in a break in diplomatic relations between the two countries and soon led to hostilities. In 1858 Peru declared a blockade of the Ecuadorian coast. In January 1859 Peruvian troops took the Island of Puna in the Gulf of Guayaquil and advanced to the mainland south of the city.

The Peruvian invasion should have unified the country, but it had the opposite effect, and Ecuador experienced 12 months of civil strife that became known as "the Terrible Year." Robles and Urbina tried to maintain control, but one critical decision resulted in chaotic upheaval. Congress had granted authority for the capital to temporarily be moved from Quito to Riobamba as a defensive measure. This was accomplished in late 1858, but the Twin Generals next decided to move the capital to Guayaquil, the center of their political support. This was obviously a political rather than a strategic decision and it inspired a rebellion in Quito. The city fathers of Quito declared the Robles government illegitimate because the constitution had been violated by the relocation of the capital to Guayaquil without congressional authorization. A triumvirate, consisting of Gabriel García Moreno, Jerónimo Carrión, and Pacífico Chiriboga, was installed as a provisional government. In the southern highlands Cuenca and Loja declared their autonomy. Robles retained control of Guayaquil and the nearby provinces of Manabí and Esmeraldas.

General Urbina had a short-lived success against the triumvirate army by taking Quito. When Robles attempted to raise money by forced contributions and confiscation of private property, his support began to dwindle. His army was defeated in a battle in Imbabura Province north of Quito. A popular uprising in Quito soon followed and the historic capital was returned to the triumvirate government on September 4, 1859. Two days later a revolt in Guayaquil resulted in General Guillermo Franco declaring himself supreme chief of both the city and the surrounding province. Realizing that he no longer had support, Robles resigned and fled to Peru. He was soon followed by General Urbina. The Twins would not return to Ecuador until 1876.

Meanwhile General Franco consolidated his hold on the three coastal provinces and hoped to eventually control all of Ecuador. He found support from Peru's president, General Ramón Castilla. Franco and Castilla signed a treaty in which Peru would obtain all of the Oriente in exchange for recognizing the Franco regime as the legitimate government of Ecuador. The agreement backfired on Franco, and Manabí Province soon defected from his confederation. While Franco was plotting with Peru, García Moreno was making proposals to the French minister, Emile Trinité, to make Ecuador a protectorate of France. Unlike Franco's schemes, Gracía Moreno's entreaties were not known until 1861.

The triumvirate recalled the former president, Juan José Flores, from exile and placed him in command of their army. Flores had little trouble in taking Guayaquil. Franco sought safe passage out of the country on a Peruvian warship. The triumvirate now ruled all of Ecuador and set about the task of establishing a permanent government.

On January 10, 1861, yet another national assembly set about the task of writing a new constitution and selecting a new president. At first García Moreno was named interim president but soon he was elected to a four-year term. García Moreno assumed the presidential sash on April 2, 1861, and a new era of Ecuadorian history began.

During this formulative period, 1795–1859, a national identity emerged that would contribute to Ecuador's birth and growth as an independent nation-state. For example, Espejo presented the idea of nationhood through his essays in Ecuador's first newspaper. The Sovereign Junta of Quito took the first bold political step toward independence in all of Spanish America and forever made August 10 Ecuador's independence day. The massacre of 70 patriots on August 2, 1810 resulted in martyrs who are immortalized on national monuments and in history textbooks.

Ecuador's brief confederation within Gran Colombia was also important in determining the nation's future. Perhaps the most important aspect was the incorporation of Guayaquil into the District of the South, ending the notion that the port city was potentially part of Peru. The Gran Colombian experience gave Ecuador a geographical shape. Even the name Ecuador is derived from this period, when the southern district of Gran Colombia was sometimes referred to as the District of Ecuador.

The 1830 split with Gran Colombia solidified Ecuador's nascent nationalism. The first constitution designated the name Ecuador and established Quito as the capital. This was not without some controversy as Ecuador is the only nation in the world named for an imaginary line. Some Ecuadorian scholars have commented that it may also be an imaginary country. Despite this criticism the nation has taken great pride in its name and has used it to promote tourism. The Mitad del Mundo (Middle of the World) park and science center, just north of Quito, is but one example of this geographical identity.

Juan José Flores became Ecuador's first president amid a storm of controversy because he was a foreigner. The fact that Flores's foreign origin caused concern is but another example that an Ecuadorian national identity had taken hold by 1830. Of course this accusation was somewhat unfounded because Flores was born in Venezuela, which was not a country until 1829. In other words, Flores was a citizen of Gran Colombia just as his "Ecuadorian" opponents were. In addition he had a long history in the District of the South and had married a local woman.

A number of trends became apparent in the first three decades of independent nationhood. For instance, the disagreements between Liberals and Conservatives came to the fore. These ideological differences resulted in bitter, and at times violent, encounters that have plagued Ecuadorian politics more or less continually ever since. Another trend was *caudillismo* or the rule by strongmen who are unwilling to relinquish power according to constitutions. Most, but not all, of the early *caudillos* were military men. Militarism or *militarismo* became another aspect of Ecuadorian politics as generals used the army as a base of political support. Even the civilian presidents, Rocafuerte and Roca, realized that courting the military was necessary if they were to complete their terms of office. Personal power or *personalismo* is perhaps the most significant and long-lasting trend. For example, supporters of Flores became *Floristas* rather than identifying with the president's political ideology. Some men who started out as Liberals later became Conservatives, but their ultimate loyalty usually rested with the particular leader they followed.

Constitution writing was also a hallmark of this period, as six constitutions were ratified, an average of a new constitution every five years. At first glance, these six Ecuadorian constitutions appeared to be models of classic liberalism that guaranteed individual rights and provided for separation of powers and a system of checks and balances. The reality was quite different. With the exception of the first one, the main purpose of Ecuadorian constitutions was to provide a shroud of legitimacy on governments that had assumed power through force. Moreover, presidents and their political opponents tended to ignore the lofty principles of the fundamental law of the land. Therefore, one would gain little understanding of the early Ecuadorian political system by only studying its myriad constitutions.

The trends of *caudillismo, personalismo,* and *militarismo* would continue and, indeed, be expanded upon by succeeding presidents. This certainly was the case of Ecuador's next great *caudillo,* Gabriel García Moreno, who would lead the small Andean republic into an extended period of stability and modernization.

NOTES

1. For an excellent scholarly biography of Manuela Sáenz, consult Pamela S. Murray, *For Glory and Bolívar: The Remarkable Life of Manuela Sáenz* (Austin: University of Texas Press, 2008).

2. For more information on the meeting refer to Gerhard Masur, "The Conference of Guayaquil," *Hispanic American Historical Review* 31, no. 2 (1951): 189–229.

3. Information pertaining to Flores in this section is from Mark J. Van Aken, *King of the Night: Juan José Flores and Ecuador, 1824–1864* (Berkeley: University of California Press, 1974).

4. Ibid., 50.

5. For an account of Flores's military expeditions organized in the United States refer to Charles H. Brown, *Agents of Manifest Destiny: The Lives and Times of the Filibusters* (Chapel Hill: The University of North Carolina Press, 1974).

6. Frank Macdonald Spindler, *Nineteenth Century Ecuador* (Fairfax: George Mason University Press, 1987), 41.

7. Ibid., 48.

4

Conservative Modernization, 1860–95

ECUADOR IN 1860

In 1860 García Moreno took charge of an Ecuador that was suffering from political and social disorder. The nation was nearly bankrupt and what little infrastructure existed was crumbling. With virtually no highway system, the two principal cities of Quito and Guayaquil, although merely 150 miles apart on a direct line, were connected by a tortuous, sinuous, and often impassable mule trail that meandered over 300 miles across the high desert over precipitous ravines and through stifling tropical rain forest. Guayaquil, Ecuador's window on the outside world, fancied itself the "Pearl of the Pacific." In reality it was the pearl only of pestilence. Yellow fever, malaria, and other maladies made Guayaquil one of the deadliest places on earth.

The rarefied air of the highlands made the climate of Quito more tolerable, but this was deceiving. Despite the splendor of her 18th-century cathedrals, churches, and monasteries, the majority of Ecuadorians in the highlands, like the citizens of the coast, lived in abject poverty. The education system, despite the impetus furnished by Ecuador's second president, Vicente Rocafuerte, provided for only the privileged few. Only some 200 primary schools existed in the country when Gabriel García Moreno assumed the presidency.

GABRIEL GARCÍA MORENO, ECUADOR'S SECOND GREAT *CAUDILLO*

Out of the chaos and rancor of 1859, "the Terrible Year," Gabriel García Moreno emerged as Ecuador's next great *caudillo*. He was born in Guayaquil on December 24, 1821, to a socially prominent family but one of modest means. García Moreno's father was a peninsular Spaniard and former minor official in the Spanish government. He emigrated to Guayaquil and attempted to make a living as a merchant. García Moreno's mother was Mercedes Moreno, the daughter of Don Ignacio Moreno, a member of the Guayaquil *cabildo* (town council) and the Order of Carlos III. It was a typically large colonial Spanish family, Gabriel being the fifth son among eight siblings. While Don Ignacio's titles provided the family with social standing, García Gómez's lack of business acumen kept the family in perpetual financial difficulty.[1]

Nevertheless, García Moreno received an excellent education despite his family's economic situation. Father José Primo Betancourt, a Mercederian friar from Quito, provided his primary education. Betancourt taught Gabriel the essentials that he would need to continue his education and indoctrinated him in the conservative teachings and values of the Roman Catholic faith. Perhaps Betancourt's Quito roots contributed to the decision to send the 14-year-old García Moreno to the capital and entrance into the Colegio Nacional de la Universidad to prepare for a university education. A combination of Betancourt's influence, his secondary schooling, and later university experiences resulted in García Moreno's long-standing affection for Quito and the surrounding sierra. His strict Catholic upbringing caused him to consider the priesthood and he took minor orders in 1838. He soon decided that this was not his calling and he subsequently enrolled in the Central University in 1840. In 1844 he graduated with a doctorate of law.

While at the Central University, García Moreno joined two literary societies, Sociedad Filantrópico Literaria and Sociedad Filotécnica, both hotbeds of radical protest against President Juan José Flores. García Moreno stood out as a vehement opponent of the regime and even advocated tyrannicide as an appropriate means to end the Flores dictatorship. The irony of this stance only became apparent 32 years later when García Moreno was assassinated by men who viewed him as a tyrant. Radical politics also inspired García Moreno to try his hand at journalism.

In time García Moreno became the editor and main contributor to four antigovernment publications. These journals usually did not last long and were frequently shut down by the government. His first paper, *El zurriago* (The Whip), was a propaganda sheet that castigated the Roca government (1845–49). *El vengador* (The Avenger) denounced General Flores and his filibustering schemes to return to power. *El diablo* (The Devil) also criticized the

Roca regime but its polemics did not inhibit Roca from appointing, or García Moreno from accepting, a government post in Guayas Province. *La nación* (The Nation), founded by García Moreno in 1853, proved to be the most radical of all. García Moreno and others were briefly jailed and then exiled by the thin-skinned government of José María Urbina. In addition to papers and journals, García Moreno wrote and distributed pamphlets that attacked the various presidents of the republic. One particular issue that galled García Moreno was the allowance of Freemasonry in Ecuador at the same time the Jesuits were expelled. His 1851 pamphlet, *Defensa de los Jesuitas* (Defense of Jesuits), implored the government of Diego Naboa to continue its pro-Jesuit policy even though it offended the Masonic Order. In 1853 he wrote *A Fabio* (To Fabio), a satirical poem that portrayed Urbina as a tyrant.

In addition to his education and radical activism, international travel also shaped García Moreno's beliefs. García Moreno traveled to England, France, and the German States between December 1850 and July 1851. On his way back to Ecuador he spent time in Panama, where he met with some Jesuits who had been expelled from Colombia and who later inspired him to write his famous pamphlet.[2] In 1853 García Moreno was banished to Peru and in April 1855 he left for France. Once in France, García Moreno immersed himself in scientific studies at the University of Paris. For 10 months he studied physics, chemistry, algebra, and calculus. These advanced studies convinced him that they should someday be incorporated into university curriculums in Ecuador. He also attended the Paris World Fair. He was impressed by the national exhibits from the advanced countries and he lamented that Ecuador was not represented by a display. In addition he studied Abbé René Francois Rohrbacher's 29-volume, 27,000-page *Universal History of the Catholic Church,* which greatly influenced him. Rohrbacher's volumes informed García Moreno about the doctrine of ultramontanism. "Ultramontanism essentially asserted the doctrine of papal supremacy in the global struggle emanating from the French Revolution."[3] "Essentially the movement called for the reformation of the Catholic Church by emphasizing the primacy of the pope and the clerical hierarchy. García Moreno also saw in ultramontanism an opportunity to provide national unity based on faith, an alternative to the doctrinaire enlightenment liberalism that had become standard fare in Latin America since independence."[4]

García Moreno returned to Ecuador in November 1856 and shortly thereafter served briefly as the mayor of Quito. There is scant information regarding his record as mayor. He was also appointed rector (equivalent to university president) of his alma mater, the Central University. García Moreno had a most positive impact as rector, establishing new professorships in mathematics and chemistry, improving business practices, funding a chemistry lecture hall, and strengthening academic standards. He even donated his own chemistry equipment, acquired during his French sojourn, to the university. As rector he fought for repeal of the Educational Reform Act, which had lowered standards by allowing students to graduate without the benefit of having ever attended classes. Clearly García Moreno viewed education as essential to Ecuador's modernization and later as president he would work tirelessly to improve the system at all levels. García Moreno was also elected to the Senate in 1857 and soon became the leader of the Conservative Party before and during the 1859 civil war, as described in the preceding chapter.

While his education, travel experience, student activism, journalism, and politics were important factors in his rise to power, family connections also played a pivotal role. His controversial marriage to the spinster Rosa de Ascásubi in 1846 is one example. Rosa was 36 and Gabriel only 24, but she was from a prestigious highland family and the sister of his best friend, Roberto de Ascásubi. García Moreno's political opponents accused him of marrying Rosa solely to enhance his political career and even claimed that he had poisoned her when she died in November 1865. His marriage to Rosa provided him with an entry into Quito's high society, improved financial circumstances, and political connections, as Rosa's other brother, Manuel, was vice president and later president of Ecuador. The letters that survive suggest that, at the very least, the two grew in genuine affection and love over time. Unfortunately Gabriel and Rosa's three children died in infancy. Gabriel and Rosa later adopted five of his brother's children. After Rosa died, Gabriel married Marianita, his adopted daughter and niece. Another important family tie was the marriage of his brother, Pedro Pablo, to Virginia Flores Jijón, the daughter of General Juan José Flores, Ecuador's first president and once the target of García Moreno's rage. This marriage allowed for García Moreno's reconciliation with Flores and his appointment to once again command Ecuador's army.

García Moreno was described by Frederich Hassaurek, the U.S. minister resident to Ecuador 1860–64, as "tall and possessed of a wide forehead and forceful eyes" and having a "violent and arbitrary disposition." On the other hand, the U.S. diplomat observed that "the President is a man of a great deal of public spirit and extraordinary energy. He is anxious to promote the material welfare, and to develop the internal resources of the country, and labors incessantly in pursuit of these objectives. He is honest, a quality which cannot be said to be very general in these countries. He is very ambitious, and is intolerant in religious matters, is vindictive against political opponents, a man who wants to do things the right way."[5]

One thing was certain: Gabriel García Moreno was determined to reform, unify, and modernize Ecuador through an ambitious agenda that included a revival of the Catholic faith as the moral underpinning of society and extensive public works projects.

THE FIRST GARCÍA MORENO
PRESIDENCY, 1860–65

Once again a constituent assembly drafted a new constitution, selected a "constitutional" president, and bestowed legitimacy on the new government. Ecuador's seventh constitution attempted to diminish the political power of Guayaquil by mandating proportional representation in the Congress, a provision that favored the more populous highlands. In addition, a new province, Los Ríos, was formed out of the region surrounding Guayaquil, another indication that highland conservatives dominated the assembly. The constitution expanded the powers of the president, weakened the power of the provinces, and provided for a centralized government instead of the existing federal system. Liberals disapproved of the document but were unable to stop its ratification. Another opponent of the new charter was García Moreno, who thought it too restrictive on the powers of the presidency. Nevertheless, the assembly elected García Moreno president of the republic and he took office on April 2, 1861.

NATIONAL SECURITY ISSUES, 1859–63

García Moreno realized that Ecuador, sandwiched between its two larger and more powerful neighbors, Colombia and Peru, was vulnerable to aggression over territorial disputes. In 1859, as a revolutionary leader, he attempted to secure French support. The *caudillo* solicited French aid in a series of letters to the French chargé, one Emile Trinité, in which he proposed a union between Ecuador and France. The letters soon became public and were published in both the Lima and Panama press. However, before France could grant assistance to García Moreno, he consolidated power.[6] The plan again surfaced when M. Benedotti, a special envoy of Emperor Louis Napoleon, arrived in Guayaquil for the purpose of secretly pursuing the scheme of a union or protectorate. On March 15, 1862, Antonio Flores, Ecuador's minister resident to France, met with Napoleon III and offered him the Galápagos Islands and portions of lands on the Amazon River in exchange for French protection against Peru. Another proposal involved the establishment of a monarchy to be known as *Le Royaume-Uni des Andes.* When Napoleon III refused to consider these offers Flores countered by offering the Galápagos in exchange for military training and assistance, a proposal that the emperor also rejected. Nothing ever came of the French protectorate or the proposed monarchy, but they were indicative of García Moreno's anxiety about the security of his nation.

García Moreno saw both a threat and an opportunity when a bitter civil war broke out in Colombia, pitting the forces of the Liberal Party of General

Tomás Cipriano de Mosquera against those of the Conservatives led by General Julio Arboleda. Perhaps Ecuador could take advantage of the situation and expand into southern Colombia. On June 19, 1862, Arboleda's forces crossed into Ecuador near the town of Tulcán in hot pursuit of their enemies. President García Moreno, although he had no formal military experience, organized an expedition of 5,000 men and proceeded to Tulcán. Unfortunately, García Moreno and his army were quickly routed and García Moreno became Arboleda's prisoner. The hapless Ecuadorian president was coerced into signing a secret treaty promising to provide arms and cash in order to secure his release.

Arboleda was subsequently defeated by his liberal rival Mosquera but this did not lessen Colombia's aggression. In fact, Mosquera proposed the recreation of Gran Colombia and announced plans to annex Ecuador. This threat rallied popular support for García Moreno, who raised a 7,500-man army and placed it under the command of General Juan José Flores, his former adversary and first president of Ecuador. Flores marched to Tulcán and invaded the Colombian province of Cauca. At the battle of Cuaspud on November 26, 1863, Flores and his army met with disaster. The army was destroyed, 2,000 soldiers were taken prisoner, and the remainder, including Flores, dropped their arms and ran back to Ecuador. The battle of Cuaspud was humiliating for both Flores and Ecuador, for the army "had been surprised, outmaneuvered, and routed by an enemy force of no more that twenty-five hundred."[7] Ecuador now stood defenseless and García Moreno planned to move the government to Guayaquil where it could be more easily defended, not by a new Ecuadorian army, but rather by impassable roads in the rainy season and the threat of pestilence for which the port city was infamous.[8] However, this particular Colombian crisis ended almost as suddenly and surprisingly as it had begun. In a strange turn of events, Mosquera held out the olive branch, released the 2,000 Ecuadorian prisoners of war, made no demands for territory or reparations, and set aside the plan for a revived Gran Colombia. García Moreno wisely acceded to these generous terms, and for a while relations with Colombia were normalized.[9]

CHURCH AND STATE RELATIONS

García Moreno sincerely believed that the modernization of Ecuador was linked to a revival of the moral authority of the Roman Catholic Church throughout Ecuadorian society. He also believed that Catholicism could unify the country and garner support for his government. In addition, he viewed the church as the one institution that could counter the influence of the military. Therefore, he embarked on a program to restore the power of the church and to partner with it in a number of projects. García Moreno's most important, yet controversial, ecclesiastical policy was the agreement he reached with the Vatican known as the Papal Concordat, signed on September 26, 1862. The Concordat continued the tradition of the Catholic Church as the official church but it went a step further by prohibiting any "dissident cult or any society condemned by the church."[10] This phrase was clearly aimed at the Freemasons, who had lodges in Ecuador and were associated with the Liberal party. It was the opening salvo in García Moreno's battle to rid the country of the Masonic Order.

The article on education illustrated García Moreno's ultramontanism, as it not only allowed for the establishment of parochial schools, but mandated that all schools, including universities, had to conform to Catholic doctrine. Bishops could select textbooks in theology, ethics, and philosophy and could censor any book they felt was contrary to the Catholic faith or established customs. Other powers included free communications without state interference or review between the papacy and the Ecuadorian church, and the re-establishment of church courts with complete jurisdiction over the clergy in all matters including crimes. The president would continue to appoint archbishops and bishops. Moreover, the state could not suppress any religious order nor prohibit the establishment of additional ones. The right of the church to obtain property was affirmed and the state was required to aid in the promotion of the faith. The Vatican agreed to assist García Moreno in his attempt to cleanse corruption from the monastic orders.

Opposition to the Concordat came from two directions. The Liberals decried the restriction on freedom of the press, interference in trade, and censorship, and called it a disgrace to any republic. In addition, the Ecuadorian clergy were upset as bishops feared a loss in revenue if new dioceses were created, while the lower priests wanted to retain the *recurso de fuerza*, the right to appeal church court decisions to secular authorities. Congress objected that the Concordat had not been presented for ratification. García Moreno, in a rare moment of compromise, agreed to submit revisions to Rome. However, the Holy See refused to consider the revisions and García Moreno decided to stand by the treaty, threatening to resign if Congress did not ratify it. His tactic worked and the Concordat was approved with some slight modifications.

MODERNIZATION AND REFORM EFFORTS

García Moreno had come to power with a vision of modernizing Ecuador through infrastructure improvements and reforming the country by ending, or at least curbing, corruption. On both fronts his first presidency proved to be a disappointment. His greatest public work project was constructing a wagon road to connect Quito with Guayaquil, which the president saw as a way to mitigate Ecuador's regionalism, improve commerce, and allow for rapid troop movement. The wagon road began in 1862 but Ecuador's internal strife, coupled with international crises, delayed significant progress until García Moreno's second term. The president led by example in his attempt to end corruption in the treasury department. His efforts in this area led the U.S. minister resident to comment that "his absolute honesty in handling public funds led him to observe strict economy, to improve methods of accounting, and to curb corruption."[11] García Moreno attempted to establish civilian control of the military and declared, "I want the black coat to command the red coat."[12] He reduced the size of the military and ended some abuses. In education he used religious orders to provide schooling for Ecuador's masses and invited the Sisters of Charity, the Sacred Heart Sisters, and the Brothers of Christian Schools to come to Ecuador to start schools. These achievements, while noteworthy, fell far short of what the president had envisioned. He was undoubtedly frustrated that more could not be accomplished because he had to devote so much of his time and energy to combating a vociferous and determined opposition.

THE OPPOSITION AND REPRESSION

Opposition to the García Moreno's government and policies was widespread but lacked unity because each faction had its own agenda. The most serious and persistent opponents of the regime were former presidents José María Urbina and Francisco Robles. Urbina and Robles, derisively called "the Twins" by García Moreno, were supported by Peruvian president Ramón Castilla, who allowed their rebel expeditions to be organized in neighboring Peru. A military expedition launched from Peru was defeated in 1862, as was a pro-Urbina uprising in Guayaquil the following May. General Flores thwarted another attempt to overthrow the government, inspired by Urbina and Robles, at the coastal town of Machala in 1864. Flores died after the Machala revolt and García Moreno decided to take personal command of the army when he was again confronted by Urbina and General Franco in May 1865. Urbina and Franco, using the river steamer *Washington*, managed to capture the *Guayas*, Ecuador's only warship, and subsequently joined forces with a third rebel ship, the *Bernardino*. Apparently the conspirators thought the presence of their small flotilla would result in a popular uprising in Guayaquil and end García Moreno's government.

García Moreno responded to the crisis by declaring the rebels pirates, seeking the intervention of the United States and other powers, and raising an army to put down the revolt. García Moreno and his small army arrived in Guayaquil on June 10 and found the city tranquil. He seized the *Talca*, a British-owned steamer, and proceeded to outfit her as a gunboat. García Moreno then boldly steamed into the section of the Guayas estuary known as the Ca-nal of Jambelí and surprised Robles and Franco. The *Guayas* was sunk dur-ing the opening salvo from the *Talca* and loyalist troops stormed and captured the *Bernardino*. Robles and Franco fled in the *Washington* and later ran it aground and escaped over land to the sanctuary of Peru.

García Moreno's stunning victory at the naval battle of Jambelí, followed by a rout of other fleeing rebels at Santa Rosa, ended Urbina, Robles, and Franco's attempts to oust him during his first term. In the aftermath of this last dramatic assault on his first government, García Moreno decided to deal harshly with captured enemy combatants. Twenty-seven men were tried by court martial and were executed by firing squad. In addition, García Moreno arrested and charged Santiago Viola, an Argentine national, with conspiracy although little creditable evidence was presented to substantiate Viola's in-volvement in the affair. Viola was executed despite entreaties from the diplo-matic corps and García Moreno's own mother.

PLOTS AND REPRESSION

Viola's execution typified the extreme and violent measures García Moreno used in dealing with his enemies during his first presidency. However, he faced many extreme and violent attempts to overthrow his government. Some early plots misfired and the conspirators escaped with impunity. These in-cidents resulted in García Moreno's conclusion that "Prompt and forceful repression is the sole means of restraining the evildoers, who become em-boldened with tolerance."[13] Laws were passed enacting the death penalty for conspirators. The government banished opponents to the remote Napo River region in cases not egregious enough to warrant the death penalty. In 1864 García Moreno's secret police uncovered a plot to assassinate the president and to replace him with General Manuel Tomás Maldonado. Maldonado eluded capture for several months but was eventually captured. Maldonado expected clemency as he was a prominent member of the elite. García Moreno was not sympathetic and had the general summarily executed by firing squad. This internal strife, combined with military invasions from Colombia, greatly impeded García Moreno's plan to modernize Ecuador through infra-structure projects. Thus, at the end of his constitutional term the wagon road was completed only to Riobamba, a distance of less than 100 miles.

THE CARRIÓN AND ESPINOSA INTERLUDES

García Moreno adhered to the constitution that he detested and left office on September 7, 1865, but not before he handpicked his successor, Jerónimo

Carrión. Carrión was a conservative Catholic with a reputation for hard work and honesty but also for being somewhat lacking in intellect. García Moreno was confident that he had placed a sycophant in the presidency and he fully expected Carrión to continue his ultramontane program. Carrión did continue many of the policies including the Concordat and curbs on Liberal influence. However, he was less repressive than his predecessor and proved reluctant to jail, banish, or execute the opposition. There was also a brief respite in the suppression of civil liberties, especially freedom of the press. For instance, Juan Montalvo's newspaper, *El cosmopolita,* reappeared, and new papers including *La América Latina* and *El Sud Americano* commenced publication. Carrión enacted these enlightened policies after he prudently sent the former president on a diplomatic mission to Chile.

After his diplomatic service in Chile, García Moreno returned and resumed his political career by running for the Senate from Pichincha Province. He was dealt a resounding electoral defeat but was later declared the winner due to a technicality concerning his opponent's eligibility. However, the Senate refused to acknowledge this turn of events and denied him the seat. García Moreno's disenchantment with Carrión grew as Congress considered measures to curb the influence of the church. In addition, the former president did not like Carrión's choices for key cabinet positions, especially Manuel Bustamante, who held the foreign ministry portfolio. Carrión attempted to assuage his predecessor by firing Bustamante and others. He also appointed García Moreno to head the army. Once García Moreno accepted the position he forced out Carrión by orchestrating a bill of censure in the Congress. Carrión, realizing that he did not have the support of the army, resigned on November 6, 1867, and the vice president, Dr. José de Arteta, assumed the presidency. Arteta, a 70-year-old Catholic Conservative, proved unacceptable to Liberals and he was soon forced from office. While Pedro Carbo served as interim president, Congress and García Moreno decided to hold a presidential election to complete Carrión's term. In a rare moment of unanimity both García Moreno and Juan Montalvo agreed that Dr. Javier Espinosa was the ideal candidate for the presidency. Espinosa also represented the voice of moderation, another rarity in Ecuadorian politics. While a member of the Liberal Party, he was also a good Catholic who had vehemently opposed the expulsion of the Jesuits while he served in Urbina's cabinet, a stance that made him acceptable to García Moreno and his Conservative supporters. Liberals, on the other hand, saw Espinosa as a moderate who would promote their agenda. Of course, this agreement between the two warring political factions proved to be short-lived. Espinosa was inaugurated on January 20, 1868.

The most important event of Espinosa's brief presidency occurred on August 16, 1868, when a massive earthquake struck Imbabura Province and destroyed the cities of Ibarra and Otavalo. More than 20,000 people were killed, tens of thousands were left homeless, and property damage was widespread. Espinosa appointed García Moreno as the civil and military chief of the province, tasking the former president with restoring order and beginning the reconstruction process. García Moreno demonstrated extraordinary energy and efficiency in dealing with the crisis. He quickly established order and brought in much-needed supplies to feed and clothe the populace. He arranged for burial of the dead and implemented other sanitary procedures to prevent epidemics. He also built hospitals, transported orphans to Quito, and began restoring bridges and highways. While these Herculean efforts did not silence his Liberal critics, they did win over the common people. In many ways, the Imbabura quake provided García Moreno with the opportunity to become a widely popular, if not a beloved, figure to many Ecuadorians.

President Espinosa's appointment of García Moreno to relieve the suffering of Imbabura masked the tensions that had been steadily building between the two men. García Moreno was not satisfied with Espinosa's moderate middle-of-the-road method of governing and opposed many of his cabinet appointments. He decided to again seek the presidency and easily secured the nomination of the Conservative Party. His opponent was the 70-year-old Francisco Javier Aguirre, a noted Liberal and popular author. Despite his newly won popular acclaim, García Moreno was fearful that Aguirre would defeat him in an open election. On the night of January 16, 1869, García Moreno, with the support of the army, launched a *golpe de estado*, removed Espinosa from office, and declared himself supreme chief of the republic.

THE SECOND GARCIAN DICTATORSHIP, 1869–75

Soon after seizing power, García Moreno purged the government of Liberals and sent many into exile, including Juan Montalvo, Pedro Carbo, and General Ignacio de Veintemilla. Montalvo spent the next seven years in exile, mostly in Colombia writing polemics against dictatorship. While García Moreno enjoyed widespread popular support, his opponents were determined to remove him from the Carondolet Palace, Ecuador's executive mansion. The first serious challenge to his authority occurred on March 19, 1869, when General José de Veintemilla attempted a *golpe de estado* in Guayaquil. However the revolt soon petered out after General Veintemilla was killed. With his opponents either banished or dead and his own popularity at an all-time high, García Moreno discerned that it was an opportune time to impose his vision of a united, modern, and Catholic Ecuador. He would unite the country by forming a strong central government that would end the ubiquitous revolts and threats that had plagued Ecuador since independence. Once law and order had been imposed, he intended to transform the nation through universal public education, infrastructure improvements, European immigration, and technology to modernize Ecuador with the best that science had to offer. Finally, reform would be accomplished via the moral foundation that García Moreno fervently believed only the Catholic faith could provide.[14] However, before his vision could move forward his legitimacy had to be established by a new constitution.

THE CONSTITUTION OF 1869

The constitution of 1869 proved to be one of the most controversial in Ecuador's history until the constitution of 2008. To García Moreno and his supporters, the document was a means to end Ecuador's decades of political strife, racial problems, and the overall decadence of society. His Liberal opponents, on the other hand, viewed it as an attack on civil liberties, the separation of church and state, and the system of checks and balances between the power of the president and Congress. Montalvo and other critics labeled it the "Charter of Slavery to the Vatican" and the "Black Charter."[15]

Written and ratified almost exclusively by delegates handpicked by García Moreno, the constitution was indeed a radical departure from Ecuador's previous ones. The constitution greatly expanded the powers of the president by allowing him to rule by decree when Congress was not in session (which was frequently), extended the presidential term to six years, and allowed reelection to a second term. Moreover, the president was given broad powers of appointment including governors, mayors of provincial capitals, and other local executives, and he also had the authority to remove officials anytime he deemed it necessary. Only Catholic males 21 years of age or older who were literate could vote. Freemasons were banned under the charter, as were all non-Catholic religions. The president was designated commander in chief of the armed forces but was also granted the discretion to increase the size of the military without consulting Congress. As in most previous constitutions, the president also had extraordinary powers to quell rebellions by declaring a state of siege. For example, under the new constitution García Moreno was empowered to order searches and seizures without a warrant, banish citizens without judicial proceedings, impose special taxes on his opponents, ban public meetings, and throttle the voice of the press. In addition, the government could seize arms and establish special military tribunals to try dissidents or any opponents of government policies. In sum, the constitution gave García Moreno dictatorial powers and allowed him to implement his vision of a united country with a modern infrastructure sustained by the moral authority of Roman Catholicism.

GARCÍA MORENO'S ACHIEVEMENTS

Emboldened by his newfound popularity, confident of his own abilities, and relieved of previous constitutional restraints, García Moreno initiated ambitious projects of economic and social development during his second presidency. These included government and financial reforms, extensive public works, commercial marketing, education, and improved public administration.

García Moreno realized that he could not transform Ecuador without the help of an honest and efficient bureaucracy that shared his vision of a modern Catholic state. Congress soon passed a series of laws that revised Ecuador's military, civil, and criminal codes, enabling the president to reward military and civilian officials when they met his standards and to punish them when they failed. As in his first administration, García Moreno led by example and continued to be scrupulous in his personal conduct and tireless in carrying out his duties. García Moreno was determined to make the army a professional and apolitical group and curb its independent ways. He used strict new laws to exact loyalty and discipline from the officer corps. On the other hand, he offered incentives including the purchase of modern weapons, standardization of uniforms, and the creation of an improved military academy to assuage the military establishment. Civilian bureaucrats were also held to high standards that were previously unknown in the country. These included requirements that they prepare annual reports on progress, provide accurate accounting of expenditures, and keep regular office hours. As the government was partnering with the Catholic Church on many projects, García Moreno demanded that ecclesiastical officials conform to the same standards. Through sound central leadership corruption was reduced and public administration was greatly improved.

García Moreno understood that political stability was the key to economic development and this partially explains his authoritarian tendencies as well as his quest to remain in power. He realized that political stability would result in increased revenues and investments and also attract American and European immigrants. A diversified economy and pro-business commercial code were other important factors that could contribute to the nation's development. His strong-arm tactics provided Ecuador a measure of stability, and as a result, investments and revenue increases soon followed his second rise to power. Ecuador now marketed a variety of agricultural products, but these commodities still left the country with an export-driven economy. Congress wrote a new commercial code that helped create a favorable business climate. While these were much-needed improvements, the Conservative government was never able to raise enough capital to fully fund the ambitious development agenda set by the president.

The Bank of Ecuador, established in 1869, was indicative of attempts to improve capital availability. While a private enterprise, the new national bank served both the sierra and the coast. The bank issued standardized currency and coins for the first time in Ecuador's history in an effort to replace foreign coins. The bank also loaned money to the government for public works projects. The government also raised capital through import and export taxes, the tithe, and government monopolies on salt, liquor, gunpowder, and legal paperwork. Tax evasion and smuggling were significant problems that the regime was never able to completely resolve.

García Moreno had grand plans to promote Ecuador's agricultural and manufactured products to the world at international fairs and exhibits, but these never reached fruition. Cacao was the leading export and confectionery chocolate had become popular in Europe and the United States. However, it would be another decade until Ecuador would benefit from a boom in the sale of cacao and emerge as the world's leading producer. Rubber was the second most important export. Cinchona bark, from which quinine is made, was another important export and drew the attention of the international medical community.[16] Another promising herb was *cundurango*, which was thought to be a cure for cancer and nearly every other disease. An attempt was even made to provide *cundurango* bark to the United States to treat former president Ulysses S. Grant's throat cancer. The claims of the effectiveness of *cundurango* appear to have been exaggerated, but even today desperate cancer victims journey to Ecuador in hope of a cure. Other exotic exports included fine straw hats made from *toquilla* plant straw and *tagua* nuts used in the manufacture of buttons. *Toquilla* hats would become famous when demand increased during construction of the Panama Canal (1904–14) and they became known as Panama hats.

The creation of a great Ecuadorian highway system was, perhaps, García Moreno's favorite of his many ambitious public works projects. He saw improved roads as the key to economic development as well as a means to achieve balance between the coast and the highlands. He wanted to tie the country together through a coherent grid that would create a national marketplace and also provide a means for highland products to be marketed abroad. While the Incas had incorporated the sierra portions of Ecuador into their realm, they had neglected building roads to the coast, and only paths existed from colonial times. By widening the paths to accommodate wagons and carts and improving the surface, the road could be used in the rainy season. Another objective was to create new secondary roads that connected to the main artery that linked Quito and Guayaquil. Ecuador's rugged terrain, raging rivers, and climate made the task extremely difficult, but these factors did not deter García Moreno. The centerpiece of the new highway system was the wagon road begun during García Moreno's first administration. By 1869 it had reached Riobamba, a little over halfway to Guayaquil. García Moreno wanted it completed and existing roads improved to accommodate two-way traffic in all weather conditions. In 1872 construction crews reached the coastal lowlands at Sibambe. The lowlands presented different engineering challenges, but García Moreno was justifiably proud of what had been accomplished. By any measure, the obstacles overcome by building 71 bridges as well as numerous drainage aqueducts was a great feat of modern engineering. The three-cart-wide road was paved in cobblestone and the coastal plain could now be reached in all weather conditions in a matter of days instead of weeks. Sibambe, however, was 78 miles from Guayaquil and García Moreno had a unique proposal to complete the final link.

García Moreno believed that a railroad could economically connect the national road to lowland communities and Guayaquil. Therefore, he ordered agents to contact Henry Meiggs, the American railroad entrepreneur who had built large sections of Peru's trans-Andean system. When Meiggs and other railroad men rejected Ecuadorian inquiries, García Moreno took the matter into his own hands, purchased two locomotives and steel tracks in the United States, and stored them at Guayaquil. Workers completed the initial construction between Yaguachi and Milagro, a distance of only seven miles, and the inaugural run was made on May 1, 1874. This was impressive but it was also expensive and the project fell some 72 miles short of reaching the national road at Sibambe. Nevertheless, García Moreno had made significant progress in his dream of connecting the coast and highlands and he had introduced the iron horse to Ecuador.

While the highway and rail systems were the centerpieces of infrastructure improvements García Moreno initiated other projects to improve communication. On January 1, 1865, Ecuador issued its first postage stamp, adopting technology first used by Great Britain in 1840. While stamps may seem quaint or even archaic by the today's standards, they were an important advancement in improving communications and fostering national identity. The concept of a uniform rate paid by the sender was a radical departure from the previous practice of payment or refusal by recipients. Not only did the adoption of standardized postage improve internal communications, but it would later link Ecuador to a global system. García Moreno also brought the telegraph to Ecuador and planned to connect Ecuador to the main international cable that ran from Central America to Chile, but this proved unfeasible during his presidency in the face of problems with Peru. He did obtain funding for an internal line, which was completed in 1875 between Guayaquil and the northern highlands and eventually would reach Quito. This was but another example of Ecuador's rapid adoption of technology in this period.

His interest in technology led to the construction of the Astronomical Observatory in Quito's Alameda Park beginning in 1873. García Moreno contracted with the German Jesuit astronomer, J. B. Menten, to bring the latest telescopes and other state-of-the-art instruments to equip the beautifully designed building. Its location, near the equator line, insured the observatory's acclaim by the international scientific community. El Observatorio Astrónomico has stood the test of time, as it is occasionally used by stargazers today.

Guayaquil, Ecuador's window on the Pacific, benefited from García Moreno's modernization projects. Although he was always suspicious of his hometown's political loyalty, García Moreno realized the importance of the city to trade. Harbor improvements included the addition of modern lighthouses, dredging operations to accommodate larger ships, channel markings for safer navigation, construction of sea walls, and the installation of a floating wharf to facilitate the unloading of ships. The installation of gas streetlights was another accomplishment, but an attempt to improve Guayaquil's potable water supply proved unsuccessful.

Improvements were made in other Ecuadorian cites as well. Some of the streets of Quito were paved, streetlights were installed, and the water supply was improved. Ibarra continued its resurrection from the devastating 1868 earthquake and boasted broad avenues, parks, and, most importantly, a potable water system. Cuenca renovated its city hall and Latacunga paved its streets.

García Moreno viewed universal public education as essential to improving the human condition in Ecuador. Above all else, the dictator believed that education would both further his plans to inculcate the moral standards of a Catholic society and create a modern workforce. Therefore, an 1871 law made education for children between the ages of 6 and 12 mandatory in areas where there were at least 20 children in these age groups. This law, coupled with García Moreno's oversight, resulted in a widespread school construction program largely funded by the central government. García Moreno also ordered that schools be properly equipped with furniture, books, maps, and school supplies. The government increased teacher salaries and mandated a curriculum that included the fundamental subjects of reading, writing, and math as well as proper Spanish, Catholic doctrine, and civics. For the first time in Ecuador's history, indigenous children were afforded the opportunity to attend school in large numbers. However, as part of his theme of national unity, all instruction was in Spanish. Of course, given the enormous task at hand, García Moreno's primary education program did not reach all Ecuadorian school-age children. This was especially true in the coastal agricultural zones and on highland haciendas, where children were often used in the fields as labor. Nevertheless, the advancement of primary education in this period was impressive. The number of students increased from 13,700 in 1867 to 32,000 in 1875. The system was segregated by gender but even this was a step forward as the number of schools for girls increased from 41 in 1867 to 164 by 1875. The Christian Brothers administered best-quality boys' schools while the Sisters of the Sacred Heart directed the finest girls' schools.

Considerable progress was also made in secondary education. García Moreno partnered with the Jesuits to expand the secondary school system for boys. The Jesuits' curriculum emphasized science and Catholic moral values, which fit perfectly with the dictator's views. Secondary education for young women, on the other hand, was largely conducted by the Sisters of the Sacred Heart and emphasized subjects to prepare them to be wives and mothers. Many new schools had to be built or old ones renovated to meet the government's objectives. The Jesuits brought laboratory equipment from Europe so that science could be taught in secondary schools. Because secondary education cost tuition, the government offered scholarships to worthy students. While secondary education lagged behind that of the United States, Europe, and even other Latin American nations, Ecuador made significant progress during the second Garcian presidency. Some graduates even continued their education at the university level.

Higher education was also reformed and improved between 1869 and 1875. First García Moreno closed down the Central University in Quito in order to purge it of its liberal faculty. This was not only a political move but also stemmed from a desire to replace the humanistic curriculum with one focused on science. The Central University School of Medicine reopened and the addition of French surgeons and physicians improved the quality of the faculty. The French medical experts introduced modern methods, instruments, and laboratory apparatus. The Polytechnic Institute, founded and staffed largely by German Jesuits, educated undergraduates in the core sciences and prepared them for medical and other postgraduate schools. (Unfortunately, the school would close shortly after García Moreno's death in 1875.) Other specialty schools and colleges were founded and operated with varying degrees of success. These included a midwifery school, teachers' colleges, a school of fine arts, a music conservatory, and various trade schools.

Since colonial times the Catholic Church provided health and social services. García Moreno continued that tradition but increased government funding and oversight of these important operations. Of course, these programs reinforced his vision of unity and morality based on Catholic beliefs. Improved health care was a priority of the administration, second only to education. The government also tried to improve the care of orphans and to reform the criminal justice system, but funding restrictions relegated these to secondary importance.

The charitable orders worked to clean up Ecuador's crowded and filthy hospitals. García Moreno provided funding to allow the Sisters of Charity to improve the quality of health care. In addition to improving existing facilities, the government built new hospitals in many of the provincial capitals. In some instances the sisters brought the first surgeons and modern medical practices to these cities and towns. The Lazarists, another Catholic order, established the San Lázaro hospice in Quito to provide care for the terminally and mentally ill. A similar institution was established in Guayaquil. Hospital administration was improved through inspection, audits, and training of staff in modern medical practices.[17]

For the most part, Catholic orders took responsibility for the large number of orphans, always a problem in 19th-century Ecuador, but one that became more acute after the 1868 earthquake. For example, the French Sisters of Providence ran the main orphanage in Quito. Because orphan boys could often find work with relatives or in adopted homes, the residents of orphanages were disproportionately female. The Sisters of Providence provided a basic primary education at the home and supplemented the curriculum with vocational training in sewing, ironing, and cooking. García Moreno had a surprisingly progressive plan to deal with Ecuadorian criminals and moral deviants that included both punishment and rehabilitation. One example of this progressive vision was the construction of a model prison, the Panóptico, in the capital that replaced the horrific conditions found in the city jail. The government likewise encouraged the replacement of overcrowded jails in local communities and recommended separate facilities for men and women to prevent immoral behavior. The spiritual well-being of prisoners also received attention, as the government sent chaplains into the prisons to preach and conduct prayer sessions. The government offered inmates training programs in the trades in an attempt to prepare them for a productive life in society after they served their sentences. A special effort was made to deal with the problem of women who engaged in vice such as prostitution. Sisters of the Good Shepherd came from France and established a home for wayward females within the confines of the Dominican convent.

AN ASSESSMENT OF GARCÍA MORENO'S NATION-BUILDING VISION

Gabriel García Moreno secured his place in history as Ecuador's first great nation-builder during his second administration. He initiated 178 public works projects between 1869 and 1875, the most ever attempted at that point in time in the poor Andean republic's history. Moreover, the number of infrastructure projects impressed both Ecuadorian and foreign observers, and several, including the Astronomical Observatory, remain in use today. For the first time an all-weather highway linked Guayaquil and Quito. Education, health care, and social services were much improved. The world was beginning to learn of Ecuador's products and a greater sense of national identity had clearly emerged. On the other hand, Ecuador remained a backward nation and, in many ways, García Moreno was a divisive figure. His insistence on using the Catholic Church as a partner in his nation-building schemes drew the ire of his Liberal opponents. His use of repression, coupled with his desire to retain power, would ultimately result in his tragic and brutal assassination.

THE DEMISE OF THE "PERPETUAL DICTATORSHIP"

García Moreno's use of banishment to remote regions of the Oriente, imprisonment, exile abroad, and, at times, summary executions of his opponents resulted in a determined effort to depose him. Two exiles, Eloy Alfaro, a rebel military man, and Juan Montalvo, a writer, became the sword and the pen of Ecuadorian Liberal resistance to García Moreno. The two collaborated during their exile in Panama. Montalvo agitated for García Moreno's overthrow by writing political propaganda while Alfaro organized armed uprisings. On June 10, 1871, Alfaro, Montalvo, and others launched a revolt in the coastal province of Manabí and proclaimed former president General José María Urbina as supreme chief of the republic. However, the revolt failed and it proved to be the last well-organized military expedition against the García Moreno government.

As the 1875 elections neared, García Moreno announced that he would seek another six-year term. The Liberals realized that the election would not be open, free, or fair. The political situation in Ecuador inspired Montalvo to publish his most famous pamphlet, *La dictadura perpetua* (The Perpetual Dictatorship), in Panama on October 2, 1874. In this polemic, Montalvo listed García Moreno's alleged crimes and failed policies and condemned his ultramontane vision for Ecuador. He also called for action, stating, "It is the duty of every American to point out the traitors of the common fatherland, of every republican to fight despotism and its perpetuation, of every man to rise up against iniquity, and to raise his voice on high to heaven."[18] García Moreno prohibited the publication of the pamphlet in Ecuador and found a staunch ally in the archbishop of Quito, who promised to excommunicate any Ecuadorian who dared to read it. Of course Liberal thinkers brought the pamphlet surreptitiously to Ecuador, where it was widely read. García Moreno made matters worse when he closed down another liberal newspaper, *La nueva era* (The New Era), and exiled the paper's editors, Miguel Valverde and Federico Proaño, to Peru. Not surprisingly, García Moreno easily won the 1875 presidential election. While his electoral success owed more to his efficient and honest administration than to his Machiavellian manipulations, his Liberal opponents did not view it that way and a plot was soon hatched to remove him from power.

In May 1875, three young idealists, Roberto Andrade, Manuel Cornejo, and Abelardo Moncayo, began planning to either kidnap or assassinate García Moreno. In July they were joined by the older Manuel Polanco, who had connections to high-ranking officers in the army. They ultimately decided to assassinate the president as the only way to convince the army to join the plot. Polanco reportedly recruited the fifth major conspirator, retired army captain Faustino Lemos Rayo, who held a personal grudge against García Moreno. On August 6, Andrade, Cornejo, Moncayo, and Rayo attacked the president on the promenade of the presidential palace. The conspirators slashed the president with a machete and shot him several times. García Moreno fell 12 feet to the plaza below, but at that point his wounds were not mortal. Rayo continued to attack the helpless president and delivered the fatal blow. Three of the assassins then fled the scene as spectators took the dying president into the nearby cathedral, where last rites were administered. Rayo was captured at the scene and shot to death within the hour by a soldier while being taken to a military headquarters. Cornejo was later captured, tried, found guilty, and executed. Andrade and Moncayo fled Ecuador and escaped justice. Juan Montalvo took undue credit for García Moreno's demise, reportedly exclaiming, " It is not Rayo's steel; it is my pen that killed him."[19]

Despite a turbulent and bloody political history, García Moreno remains the only incumbent Ecuadorian president to be murdered. His death did not result in the dramatic change in Ecuador's politics that the conspirators had envisioned. One unintended consequence of the assassination was that his admirers and collaborators sought his elevation to the status of martyr to the fatherland and Catholic civilization. Soon, however, factionalism engulfed the Liberals and prevented a comprehensive restructuring of the state.

THE BRIEF PRESIDENCY OF ANTONIO BORRERO

García Moreno's death resulted in a power struggle, as he had named no successor within the Conservative Party. The Liberals saw an opportunity to dismantle the government established under the 1869 constitution and soon backed Antonio Borrero Cortázar for the presidency. Interim presidents Francisco Xavier León (August 6–October 6) and José Xavier Eguiguren (October 6–December 9) governed until elections were held. The Conservatives were hopelessly divided, which insured Borrero's election in what was Ecuador's first open and honest election.

Borrero viewed himself as a peacemaker. He attempted to assuage the Conservatives by pledging to protect the Catholic religion, while also promising the Liberals that he would reform the 1869 constitution, known in liberal circles as the Black Charter. In a futile gesture to the Conservatives he appointed General Julio Saénz, one of his opponents in the recent election, minister of war. Borrero's tactics soon backfired as both Conservatives and Liberals refused to compromise. Barely three months into the Borrero presidency the Conservatives attempted an unsuccessful revolt. Borrero was soon challenged from another unexpected quarter, his own Liberal party. Borrero's modest reforms of the constitution included freedom of the press and an expansion of the franchise, but this was not enough to please his erstwhile Liberal supporters, who demanded a new constitution. Juan Montalvo, Eloy Alfaro, and other young Liberals began organizing protests, urging Borrero to scrap the 1869 constitution and to purge his cabinet of Conservatives. Montalvo's new periodical, *El regenerador,* was relentless in its criticism of Borrero and the Catholic Church. On August 19, José Rafael Arízaga, the minister of the interior, ordered provincial governors and church officials to shut down papers that attacked church dogma or encouraged dissent. On September 8, the Liberals launched a coastal revolt under the tutelage of General Ignacio de Veintemilla. In a convoluted turn of events, Conservatives supported Borrero, who remained in power in the highland region. Veintemilla soon disappointed Montalvo, who eventually realized the general was simply using the Liberal cause to seize personal power. When Montalvo wrote essays attacking Veintemilla, the former was banished to Panama. In December 1876, Veintemilla's and Urbina's armies defeated pro-Borrero forces in key battles. Borrero fled the country and Veintimilla declared himself supreme chief.

THE VEINTEMILLA DICTATORSHIP, 1877–83

Veintemilla realized that he needed to solidify his hold on power by courting the Liberal Party and that a reversal of García Moreno's ecclesiastical policy was a convenient and expeditious way to obtain that objective. Through a series of decrees he secularized education, curbed clerical political participation, made it a crime to promulgate revolution in the name of the church, suspended the Papal Concordat, and reinstated governmental ecclesiastical patronage. The clergy reacted by organizing a mass protest that resulted in a riot. Then, on March 30, 1877, Archbishop José Ignacio Checa y Barba was murdered while celebrating mass on Good Friday. The method used in the murder was particularly despicable as the prelate was poisoned with strychnine mixed in the sacramental wine. The archbishop was a strong critic of

Veintemilla, whom many assumed was behind the murder. Veintemilla's meddling in an investigation that never resulted in an arrest reinforced this opinion. Additional anticlerical policies led to Veintemilla's excommunication and ultimately to a revolt by Conservative forces.

A Conservative army, led by General Manuel Santiago Yépez and supported by Colombian Conservatives, converged on Quito in late October 1877. Veintemilla was able to thwart the attack and apparently bribed Yépez to end his opposition to the regime. Other Conservative leaders were not so fortunate and were sentenced to death by court-martial, later commuted to five years in prison. Despite this rare gesture of humanity, Veintemilla was soon besieged not only by Conservatives but Liberals as well.

Liberal opposition to Veintemilla stemmed from his request for troops from Colombia to assist in the defeat of the Conservative army. Three thousand Colombian troops had been dispatched to Quito but they arrived too late to be of use. Nevertheless, Colombia demanded a payment of 10,000 pesos to defray the cost of the expedition and refused to withdraw the troops until the bill was paid. Montalvo's paper intensified criticism of Veintemilla and condemned his attempt to forge an alliance with Colombian Liberals. Another dispute arose over Ecuador's ninth constitution, which offered concessions to both Liberals and Conservatives but was largely viewed as a ploy to legitimize the Veintemilla government. These factors, coupled with Veintemilla's despotic tactics, kept Ecuador in a state of tension. On the coast Eloy Alfaro continued to plot Veintemilla's overthrow and was thrown into a jail known as the *Infiernillo* (Little Hell). In September 1879 Montalvo left the country and launched a pamphlet campaign against the regime from Panama. Between March 1880 and January 1882 Montalvo published *Las Catilinarias, o la espada de dos filos* (The Catilinarias, or the Two-edged Sword), 12 pamphlets that highlighted Veintemilla's tyranny, crimes, and corruption. As pressure from Liberals intensified, Veintemilla turned to Conservatives for support. In 1882 a new Concordat was ratified with the Holy See. The president then promoted José Ignacio Ordóñez to the archbishopric of Quito, a stunning gesture to the right as it was Ordóñez who had previously excommunicated the president.

Veintemilla's overtures to the Conservatives had little effect as they continued to distrust him and held him accountable for the murder of Archbishop Checa y Barba. The Liberals, on the other hand, were disillusioned with the rampant corruption that pervaded the regime and the harassment of their prominent party leaders by Veintemilla's henchmen. The constitution barred Veintemilla from a second consecutive term in office. At first he planned to control the 1882 election and have a surrogate become president so that he could rule from behind the scenes. When it became apparent that the Liberals would not cooperate, Veintemilla temporarily relinquished power to a sycophant, journeyed to Guayaquil, took command of troops, and prepared to launch an *autogolpe* (self-coup). On March 26 a coalition of military officers, government officials, prominent citizens, and the Municipal Council of Quito proclaimed Veintemilla Supreme Chief of the Republic. The event, known as the Transformation, suspended the 1878 constitution and officially established Veintemilla as dictator, although he certainly had acted as one during his "constitutional" term.

THE WAR OF THE RESTORATION

Veintemilla's establishment of a personal dictatorship accomplished a rare feat: Conservatives and Liberals united. The War of the Restoration aimed at removing Veintemilla from power and reestablishing constitutional government. In April 1882, Eloy Alfaro, the old campaigner, initiated the first uprising in the coastal province of Manabí, during which Veintemilla's soldiers captured Miguel Valverde, Alfaro's right-hand man and minister general of the provisional government. Valverde was subjected to brutal torture, including 300 lashes. This incident only inflamed the determination of the Restorers to rid the country of the dictator. From his exile in Paris, Juan Montalvo used the atrocity in a manifesto, *Azotes por virtudes* (Stripes for Virtues), that implored the citizens of Ecuador to overthrow the tyrant.

After Alfaro's defeat, the Restorers turned their attention to the highlands and organized a three-pronged attack on Quito. In the north, Conservative and Liberal exiles joined forces and marched south from Colombia. A Liberal army was organized in the central highlands and was later joined by one composed of Liberals and Conservatives from the southern sierra region. On January 12, 1883, Quito fell to the Restorers and they soon established a provisional government, dominated by Conservatives but with a smattering of Liberals. This government, however, had control only in the capital and the highlands.

Alfaro renewed his campaign in Esmeraldas and Manabí, achieved success, and named a Liberal provisional government ruled by a triumvirate comprised of Pedro Carbo, General José María Sarasti, and himself. Veintemilla still clung to power in Guayaquil and hoped to defeat Alfaro by forming an alliance with the highland Conservatives. This attempt failed and Guayaquil capitulated to a Restoration army on July 9, 1883, ending the Veintemilla regime. Veintemilla went into exile and did not return to Ecuador until 1907. Once again Ecuador had rid itself of a strongman bent on personal power. The Restorers agreed to convene a constituent assembly to write Ecuador's 10th constitution and to unite the country under one government. José María Plácido Caamaño was designated interim, and later, constitutional president.

Caamaño was a Conservative and the unity that had been achieved between Conservatives and Liberals during the War of the Restoration proved short-lived.

CONSERVATIVE AND PROGRESSIVE GOVERNMENTS, 1884–95

The collapse of the Veintemilla dictatorship ushered in a period of constitutional governments led by three civilian presidents: José María Plácido Caamaño (1884–88), Antonio Flores (1888–92), and Luis Cordero (1892–95). For the most part, an oligarchy that included the hierarchy of the Catholic Church, highland hacienda owners, the officer corps, and other traditional elements of Ecuadorian society supported the three presidents. All failed to mollify the discontent of the Liberals, who waged nearly continual insurgencies with the *montoneros,* the paramilitary arm of the party. Caamaño and Flores would renew García Moreno's vision of modernization by attempting infrastructure improvement projects. Flores tried to end the conflict between Liberals and Conservatives by creating the moderate Republican Party. On the surface Ecuador appeared to have found political stability while elections were held and the constitution followed for an extraordinary 12 years. In the end conservatism and moderation would give way to the Liberal Revolution of 1895.

CAAMAÑO: A RETURN TO GARCÍAN POLICIES

A weak attempt at bipartisanship was made in writing the 1884 constitution by including three Liberals on the nine-member drafting committee. The final document, however, was decidedly conservative. Following a long-standing tradition, the constituent assembly decided to confirm interim president Caamaño in a constitutional four-year term rather than holding elections to decide the presidency. Liberals felt that this maneuver denied General Eloy Alfaro the presidency. The Liberal-Conservative feud that had plagued the republic since its inception returned with a vengeance.

One Ecuadorian historian described Caamaño as "the ghost of García Moreno." The president's neo-Garcían agenda included public works, educational improvements, administrative reforms, and expanding the role of the Catholic Church in national life. He expanded the highway network by constructing roads over the eastern cordillera into the Oriente and repaired the existing national road. The railroad was extended to 45 miles and smaller lines were built to access coastal gold mining regions. Caamaño's greatest public works accomplishment linked Quito with all the provinces, save Esmeraldas, by telegraph. His government expanded public education with the addition of 21,000 students between 1884 and 1888, reopened the Central University, and improved it with the rechartering of the Institute of Sciences. The Astronomical Observatory was repaired and new equipment procured. The Botanical Garden was created and improvements were made to the Polytechnic School and the military and naval schools. Government administration was vastly improved as indicated by the creation of the National Archives, the introduction of scrupulous accounting procedures in the treasury, and reform of the customs service, including the suppression of smuggling. On a more ominous note, Caamaño created a new national police force to cope with internal disorder. The president also courted high-ranking church officials by developing programs that fully supported Catholic doctrine. For example, the law establishing the new national police force prohibited blasphemy, acts of irreverence, and the presentation of plays contrary to religion, morality, and good customs. Construction began on the National Basilica of the Sacred Heart of Jesus, a physical testimony to the fact that church and state were once again operating in harmony.

Of course Caamaño drew the ire of Liberal journalists. Juan Montalvo continued his vitriolic condemnation of the president and the church from his self-imposed exile in Europe. The journalist and prominent attorney Juan Benigno Vela did not enjoy the luxury of exile and suffered the consequences. Vela, who was blind, opposed Caamaño with editorials in his newspaper, *El combate.* A decree was passed prohibiting the practice of law by blind persons, an obvious attempt to persecute Vela. When this failed to silence him, the government threw him in prison. Caamaño survived Alfaro's numerous attempts to oust him by military force and served out his constitutional term.

ANTONIO FLORES JIJÓN: A MIDDLE PATH IN ECUADORIAN POLITICS

Presidential elections were slated for March 1888 and, to his credit, Caamaño did not attempt to remain in power. Instead he proposed the candidacy of Dr. Antonio Flores Jijón, the son of Ecuador's first president and Ecuador's minister to France in 1888. Flores won the election against only token opposition, garnering 29,555 votes to Alfaro's 777 and Montalvo's 56. Flores returned to Ecuador and assumed the presidency but soon realized that his election was clouded by fraud. He submitted his resignation, but Congress unanimously rejected it. Flores was also destined to complete his constitutional term, a rarity in Ecuadorian politics.

Antonio Flores was well qualified by family connections, education, experience, and temperament to be a successful president of Ecuador. Of course, as the son of the first president, he had unique insight into the history of Ecuadorian politics, starting with his birth in the Presidential Palace. Unlike Juan José Flores, his "Ecuadorian-ness" was beyond reproach. Not only had he been born in Quito, but his mother, Mercedes Jijón y Vibanco, was from one of the most prominent families in the republic. As a child Antonio Flores was tutored by Simón Rodriguez, the famous mentor of Símon Bolívar, the great liberator. He completed his secondary education at a prestigious academy in Paris and he earned a doctorate in law at the venerable San Marcos University in Lima. After completing his doctorate, he was appointed to the chair of universal history at San Marcos and gained a reputation as a brilliant scholar. Diplomatic assignments to Washington, Paris, Rome, and London afforded him a broader worldview than most Ecuadorian politicians. On the other hand, Flores had spent only 16 of his 55 years living in his native land and lacked firsthand knowledge of the contemporary political scene.

Flores astutely concluded that Ecuador's political scene was hopelessly bifurcated by the Liberal and Conservatives. Therefore he proposed a *via media* (middle path) and formed the Ecuadorian Republican Party, pledging it to moderation, progressivism, and free enterprise. He also sought to heal the deep-seated animosity of the Liberals and offered both Alfaro and Montalvo diplomatic posts. Both refused, demonstrating a stubborn unwillingness to compromise, but Juan Benigno Vela accepted a cabinet position. Flores also freed 43 political prisoners and offered amnesty to many exiles.

Flores was strongly committed to modernization, and initiated improvements in education and public works, as well as government administration. Educational improvements included the reestablishment of the School of Fine Arts, increased funding for the Central University, founding of the National Library, the establishment of a vocational school in Latacunga, new elementary schools in Alausí and Zumara, and much-needed high schools for girls there and in Otavalo. The Flores administration purchased and distributed Reverend Dr. Federico González Suárez's *General History of Ecuador,* one of the first scholarly works on Ecuador's history, still considered a classic, to school and other libraries throughout the country. Public works projects included potable water projects for Guayaquil, Manta, Jipijapa, and Bahía de Caraquez, procurement of firefighting equipment for Manabí, upgraded port facilities at Puerto Bolívar, and construction of highways. He also revised the civil law codes, attempted to service the foreign debt, and initiated monetary reforms, including chartering the National Bank of Quito.

Flores vigorously supported the missionary work of the Catholic Church in the Oriente and its role in education but was more moderate in other aspects of church-state relations. One of the president's pet projects was to have an exhibit at the Universal Exposition in Paris commemorating the centenary of the French Revolution. Conservatives in Congress temporarily blocked the project by refusing to fund the exhibit based on objections presented by the Ecuadorian episcopate, which stated that the French Revolution should not be honored in light of its anticlerical nature.

Flores's idea of a *media via* never took hold in Ecuador and he soon found opponents from both ends of the political spectrum. Liberals found fault with his modest support of the church and continued to foment insurrections. Conservatives charged him with nepotism in his government appointments and the awarding of lucrative contracts for public works. The president was assailed more because he came from the powerful Flores-Jijón clan than for his progressive ideals. *Personalismo* (personal politics) remained at the center of Ecuadorian political life. Despite these difficulties, Flores served out his term.

LUIS CORDERO AND THE END OF CONSERVATIVE RULE

Flores's Republican Party hoped to retain the presidency and nominated General Francisco Javier Salazar, but he died of yellow fever and was replaced by Dr. Luis Cordero of Cuenca, an associate of former president Caamaño. Cordero was a noted poet, educator, and journalist. The Conservatives nominated Dr. Camilo Ponce, a lawyer, diplomat, and long-serving member of both the House of Deputies and the Senate. No Liberal candidate ran in the 1892 presidential race. The election was fairly free of fraud and closely contested. Cordero won with 32,467 votes to Ponce's 27,842.

Cordero continued the moderate polices of his predecessor, emphasizing education, debt service, improved government services, and public works. During his first two years in office, enrollments in public schools increased from 74,000 to 83,000 and new schools were constructed. For the first time in Ecuador's history more funds were allocated for education than the military. At first Cordero continued to pay the interest on Ecuador's foreign debt, but a downturn in the economy forced a suspension. Like most presidents in this period, Cordero launched a number of public works projects including highways, communication systems, hospital construction, and electrification.

Cordero was really a Conservative when it came to church-state relations. Although his candidacy had been opposed by most clerics, Cordero turned out to be their best friend. He announced that he would side with the Roman Catholic Church in any conflict with the state. He also approved of the consecration of the republic to the Most Pure Heart of Mary and promised to strictly enforce the Papal Concordat. This departure from Flores's *media via* would be one of the factors in Cordero's downfall, as he greatly inflamed Liberals who had once accepted him as the lesser of two evils.

A more important factor in Cordero's demise was his activity in the *Esmeralda* Affair. Ecuador and Peru had attempted to resolve their long-standing territorial dispute through both arbitration and bilateral negotiations. A draft treaty, the Herrera-García treaty, was signed on May 2, 1890, but failed to be ratified by either nation's Congress. Arbitration by the king of Spain also failed to yield a settlement. In October 1893, public frustration in both countries resulted in violent demonstrations at each nation's consulates. Ecuador, fearing war, entered into an arms agreement with Chile for the purchase of rifles, artillery, ammunition, and a warship. When the crisis eased, the agreement was left dormant. However, a war between China and Japan in 1894 would strangely revive the contract with Chile. During the First Sino-Japanese War, Japan sought a way to rapidly increase its naval power and sought to purchase the *Esmeralda,* a state-of-the-art Chilean cruiser. Because Chile had declared neutrality in the dispute, it could not directly sell the ship to Japan. An alternate plan was concocted whereby Chile would transfer the ship to Ecuador. Ecuador would then sail the ship to Hawaii and transfer ownership to Japan. The Cordero government agreed to the arrangement and the *Esmeralda* was delivered to Japan under the Ecuadorian flag. The entire deal had been conducted in secrecy and allegedly some Ecuadorian officials were rewarded monetarily for their cooperation in the transaction. When the veil of secrecy was later lifted, Cordero's Liberal and Conservative opponents saw an opening to depose him by claiming that he and his supporters had sold the Ecuadorian flag for personal profit. From December 1894 until April 1895 Liberals mounted an unrelenting campaign against Cordero and his government over the *Esmeralda* Affair. On April 16, Cordero resigned, ending the period of Conservative rule and marking the beginning of the Liberal Revolution.

AN ASSESSMENT OF CONSERVATIVE MODERNIZATION

García Moreno's ambitious vision to modernize Ecuador by improving infrastructure, reforming government, expanding educational opportunities, and promoting commerce was a qualified success. For example, the Quito-to-Guayaquil wagon road united Ecuador's two largest cites. In addition, he introduced the telegraph, started a railroad, constructed a state-of-the-art stellar observatory and many other public works projects, and brought the latest technology to the republic. The Ecuadorian government was relatively free of corruption because the president introduced modern methods of public administration. Public schools were built and staffed throughout the country and higher education received more funding than ever before. Ecuadorian products were promoted at international exhibitions and trade was vastly expanded. García Moreno's successors moderated his pro-church policies, but otherwise continued the modernization project. These projects unquestionably improved the lives of many Ecuadorians but failed to rid Ecuador of the scourge of poverty that the vast majority of its citizens continued to experience.

On the other hand, García Moreno's vision to use the ultramontane philosophy of conservative Catholicism to unite Ecuador did more harm than good. His alliance with the Vatican in the form of the most generous Papal Concordat in history only served to unite and inflame the Liberals, who considered themselves faithful Catholics. The *caudillo's* repressive tactics, which included censorship, banishment, and occasional executions, coupled with the church's condemnation of Liberals and their agenda, revived old animosities. Thus Ecuador continued to suffer the effects of regionalism, personalism, and dictatorship that had plagued the republic from its inception.

NOTES

1. Frank MacDonald Spindler, *Ecuador in the Nineteenth Century* (Fairfax: George Mason University Press, 1987), 53–60. The best recent biography of García Moreno is found in Peter Henderson, *Gabriel García Moreno and Conservative State Formation in the Andes* (Austin: University of Texas Press, 2008).

2. Panama at the time was a province of Colombia. Apparently Colombian officials felt it was remote enough to exile the Jesuits there.

3. Henderson, *Moreno and Conservative State Formation*, 73.

4. Ibid., 26.

5. Friedrich Hassaurek to William Seward, February 18, 1863, *Diplomatic Despatches from United States Minister to Ecuador, 1848–1906* (Washington, DC: National Archives and Record Service, 1956), microfilm, reel 6.

6. George Frederick Howe, "Garcia Moreno's Efforts to United Ecuador and France," *Hispanic American Historical Review,* 16 (1939): 257–58.

7. Mark J. Van Aken, *King of the Night: Juan José Flores and Ecuador, 1824–1864* (Berkeley: University of California Press, 1974), 264.

8. Hassaurek to Seward, December 17, 1863, *Despatches Ecuador,* microfilm 6.

9. Ibid.

10. Spindler, *Ecuador in the Nineteenth Century,* 65.

11. Hassaurek to Seward, January 4, 1865, *Despatches Ecuador,* microfilm 5.

12. Ibid.

13. Ibid.

14. Henderson, *Moreno and Conservative State Formation,* 146.

15. Spindler, *Ecuador in the Nineteenth Century,* 77.

16. Henderson, *Moreno and Conservative State Formation,* 179–83.

17. Ibid., 169.

18. Ibid., 179.

19. Spindler, *Ecuador in the Nineteenth Century,* 89.

5

The Liberal Revolution

The Liberal Revolution of 1895 heralded significant changes for Ecuador's domestic system as the Liberals sought to separate church and state; enforce religious toleration; provide for civil registration of births, marriages, and deaths; secularize cemeteries; provide universal public education; professionalize the armed forces; and construct railroads to unify the country. The Revolution of 1895 also brought to power the most dominant personality of the age, General Eloy Alfaro Delgado, the third great *caudillo* in Ecuador's history. Alfaro and another liberal general, Leonídas Plaza Gutiérrez, implemented many reforms but also engaged in a fierce rivalry for control of the Liberal Party and the nation.

THE CACAO BOOM

Ecuador became the world's leading producer of cacao, the most important ingredient in confectionery chocolate, during the third quarter of the 19th century.[1] Cacao accounted for up to 70 percent of Ecuador's exports in the period 1885–1922 and was called *pepa de oro* (golden seed). Swiss and American companies that made milk chocolate bars and other treats available for mass consumption drove the demand for cacao. Ecuador's coastal areas provided ideal climatic and soil conditions for the production of the golden seed. Cacao production was capital-intensive and was most economically produced on plantations. Initial investment costs, while high, could be met by Ecuadorian entrepreneurs, and the cacao profits ended up in the hands of the 20 families who owned the largest plantations. The cacao boom also generated tax revenues that Liberal governments used to finance modernization projects. The boom benefited Ecuador's coastal elite, expanded the wage-earning labor class, and led to migration from the highlands to the coast.

ELOY ALFARO

Eloy Alfaro, Ecuador's 20th president, was born on June 25, 1842, in humble surroundings to a Spanish father and a mestiza mother in the littoral village of Montecristi in the province of Manabí. His education was rudimentary, but he developed an acumen for politics, and as a young man became the leader of two failed insurrections against García Moreno.

After his second attempt to remove García Moreno in 1871, Alfaro was exiled to Panama. Time in exile proved to be beneficial for the erstwhile revolutionary because he married Ana Paredes Arosemena from a prominent Panamanian family and entered into successful milling and mining ventures. From the safety of Panama, Alfaro continued plotting to overthrow García Moreno. He financed the publication of Juan Montalvo's pamphlet, *The Perpetual Dictatorship*. When García Moreno was assassinated on August 6, 1875, Alfaro expected a reward for his support of the dictator's overthrow. He was disappointed when he was not given the governorship of Manabí and immediately joined the opposition to the regime of Antonio Borrero. On September 8, 1876, Alfaro returned to Ecuador as an ardent supporter of General Ignacio Veintemilla, who soon deposed Borrero and became president (1878–83).

Veintemilla rewarded Alfaro by naming him political chief of Portoviejo and promoting him to colonel. However, Alfaro soon became disillusioned with his mentor's policies and began agitating for his removal. Over the next six years, Alfaro attempted to oust Veintemilla by leading revolts or fomenting opposition through his writings during his frequent exiles in Panama. In 1882 Alfaro participated in the War of the Restoration that ousted Veintemilla, and then became supreme chief of Esmeraldas and Manabí provinces. His participation in the campaign to oust Veintemilla earned him international acclaim as a champion of liberalism.

In 1884 Alfaro led a revolt against President José María Plácido Caamaño, who, Alfaro claimed, had deserted the Liberal cause and was, in fact, suppressing it. Caamaño's navy and troops defeated Alfaro at Bahía on December 6, 1884, and *el viejo luchador* (old campaigner), as Alfaro had come to be known, narrowly escaped capture and certain execution by escaping to Panama on February 7, 1885.

Alfaro remained in exile for the next 10 years but made good use of his circumstances to promote the liberal cause throughout Latin America. He wrote two polemics, *Dinastía mastuerza* (Stupid Dynasty) and *Deuda Gordiana* (The Gordian Debt), which condemned the conservative governments of Ecuador. His revolutionary exploits earned him the veneration of the opposition within Ecuador and the respect of liberal governments throughout the Americas.

In early 1895 Ecuadorian Liberals mounted a revolt against the government of Luis Cordero. Cordero resigned in April, but the Conservatives managed to retain power under the direction of President Vicente Lucio Salazar. On June 5 insurgents gained control of Guayaquil and proclaimed Alfaro supreme chief of the republic and general in chief of the army. Alfaro returned to Guayaquil on June 18, assumed command of rebel forces, and launched his campaign to gain control of all of Ecuador.

Alfaro and his troops stormed into the sierra, and it soon became evident that this was a social, rather than merely a political, revolution. At the town of Riobamba one observer noted that the indigenous population had sided with the Alfaristas. Shouts of "Long live Alfaro! Down with the Friars! Death to Jesus Christ!" could be heard as government troops and priests fled the city.[2] On September 4, 1895, Eloy Alfaro entered Quito in triumph. Ecuador would never again be the same.

THE RADICAL DECALOGUE AND CONSTITUTION NUMBER ELEVEN

Alfaro ruled as supreme chief in the aftermath of the revolution and published a manifesto, *The Radical Decalogue,* outlining the Liberals' 10 goals for transforming Ecuador into a modern nation. These included (1) a decree on mortmain, (2) suppression of convents, (3) suppression of monasteries, (4) obligatory laic education, (5) freedom of the Indians, (6) abolition of the Vatican Concordat, (7) ecclesiastical secularization, (8) expulsion of foreign clergy, (9) a strong and well-paid army, and (10) railroads to the Pacific.[3]

In an attempt to gain legitimacy, Alfaro ordered the convening of a national convention to draft a new constitution. However, he rigged the election of delegates by excluding the clergy but allowing government employees to vote for convention delegates. The Conservatives boycotted the election and no Progressives or Independents won seats. Thus Alfaro's cronies totally dominated the national convention. One interesting aspect of the new constitution was a statement on religion that proclaimed Roman Catholicism as "the religion of the Republic . . . with the exclusion of every cult to the contrary to morality."[4] Yet at the same time the constitution also stated, "The state respects the religious beliefs of the inhabitants of Ecuador and will cause to be respected the manifestations of them. Religious beliefs do not hinder one in the exercise of his political and civil rights." This was the first declaration of freedom of religion in Ecuador's history and it was met with a storm of protest from the Catholic clergy. Another restriction excluded foreign clergy from holding church offices. On January 13, 1897, the convention dutifully elected Alfaro as the constitutional president of Ecuador.

FIRST ALFARO PRESIDENCY

Alfaro was a mestizo and openly acknowledged his ethnic background. He was the first self-acknowledged mestizo to become president of Ecuador and this greatly bolstered this group's standing in Ecuadorian society as Ecuador began to identify as a mestizo nation. This is ironic as mestizos comprised the largest segment of Ecuador's population in 1897 as well as today. Alfaro's economic policies also encouraged the growth of a middle class.

One of the main objectives of Alfaro's liberal program was to greatly diminish the power of the Ecuadorian Catholic Church in national life. To that end, a new *Ley Patronato* (Patronage Law) was enacted to make the state supreme over the church. The law clearly defined the relationship between church and state by stating that church laws, appointments, and activities could only be exercised "when not in opposition to the institutions of the republic." The Vatican was denied rights of jurisdiction unless it was specifically granted by executive power. Moreover, all clergy were required to take an oath of allegiance to the government before assuming ecclesiastical offices. Only Ecuadorian citizens could be parish priests and likewise high church offices could only be held by natural-born Ecuadorians. The country that had once been dedicated to the Sacred Heart of Jesus broke diplomatic relations with the Holy See. The government reviewed the creation of new parishes and regulated mission areas. No person could enter a religious order before the age of 18 and final vows could not be taken until the age of 21. No additional religious orders could be established.

The prohibition on charging for services or direct collection of tithes significantly reduced the financial power of the church, thus making it dependent on the state for funds. In addition, the church could not sell or mortgage property without state approval. The government now audited church accounts, including those of the cathedral chapters and *cofradias* (religious lay organizations), and conducted inventories of all church properties with particular attention directed to mortmain holdings (properties bequeathed to the church). The religious orders became subject to government inspections of their communities under the pretense of sanitation but also to ferret out abuses such as austere living conditions.

THE GUAYAQUIL AND QUITO RAILWAY

Alfaro launched ambitious modernization and infrastructure improvement plans including new water systems, expansion of electrification and telephone grids, construction of streetcar lines, and the founding of additional vocational and normal schools. However, the centerpiece of his modernization scheme was to complete the Trans-Andean Railroad begun by his old adversary, García Moreno. The need for an economical and dependable transportation system to link the littoral with the sierra and foster economic growth had been obvious for decades. The project caught the imagination of the Ecuadorian people, who named it *la obra redentora*—the redemptive work.[5]

However, the obstacles to such a transportation system were enormous. Foremost were the natural barriers of mountains, white-water rivers, and rain forests. Ecuador's record of political instability, coupled with its empty treasury and burdensome foreign debt, were added hindrances. Despite the apparent drawbacks, Alfaro was determined to have his railroad. He rightly concluded that state-of-the-art railroad technology could overcome the natural barriers. Moreover, he intended to provide Ecuador with political stability by maintaining his presidency for as long as possible. Ecuador's impoverishment was more problematic, but Alfaro reasoned that the subsequent economic boom from the railroad would provide the prosperity that would end the nation's financial woes. He instructed Luis F. Carbo, Ecuador's minister to the United States, to search for entrepreneurs to provide financial backing and engineering expertise for the venture.

Carbo soon found Archer Harman, a Virginia railroad man, and his brother John, a U.S. Army engineer, and interested them in the project. Within weeks Archer Harman attracted a group of investors and formed a syndicate to negotiate for the railroad contract. He arrived in Quito in March 1897 and began negotiations. Alfaro and Harman soon found they were kindred spirits. Each was restless, energetic, and highly intelligent. Both men envisioned the railroad project as the culmination of his life's work. They overcame obstacles that would have thwarted lesser men. General Alfaro used his dynamic personality, immense persuasive powers, and, when needed, repressive tactics to quell internal opposition to the project. For his part, Harman obtained innovative financial backing for the project and used his prodigious organizational skills to assemble the experts, labor, and materials that turned the vision of a trans-Andean railroad into a reality.

Work commenced on the railway in 1899. The political and financial conditions that confronted Alfaro and Harman paled in comparison to the daunting task of construction that faced the chief engineer, Major John A. Harman. In a distance of only 100 miles, the railroad rose from sea level to 10,000 feet, passing from torrid jungle to everlasting snow. From its terminus at Durán, on the banks of the Guayas River opposite Guayaquil, the rail bed proceeds northeast through 55 miles of tropical lowlands. This stretch, though relatively flat, presented problems because of soft soil, swampy conditions, and tidal flooding. A gradual incline brought the line to the foothills of the Andes at Bucay, an elevation of 1,000 feet. From Bucay to Sibambe the train ascends 7,000 feet in only 25 miles. Just 5 miles from Sibambe at Pistichi, the railway encounters its most imposing obstacle, the famed Nariz del Diablo (the Devil's Nose), an apparently insurmountable mountain of sheer rock. A switchback arrangement allowed the train to overcome nature and an arduous climb of 110 feet per mile on a 5 percent grade. The great Alausi loop afforded an ascent of 290 feet per mile. From Alausi the train continued its dizzying climb until Palmira Pass (10,648 feet) and then descended 1,500 feet to Riobamba. On the other side of the Riobamba Valley, the railroad climbed steadily until the Chimborazo Pass, the highest elevation on the line (11,840 feet above the Pacific), was surmounted. The line then descended suddenly to Ambato at 8,340 feet. The Latacunga Valley is relatively flat and offered little resistance before the last towering climb to 11,650 feet elevation, over the base of the world's highest active volcano, Cotopaxi. From the foot of Cotopaxi, the line followed the inter-Andean valley until it finally arrived at Quito, 9,000 feet above the level of the sea. John Harman and his men had a difficult task to say the least.

The "Redemptive Work" was completed on June 15, 1908, when Eloy Alfaro's daughter, América, drove the commemorative golden spike. The railway was the largest and most controversial development project that Ecuador had ever undertaken up until that time. Opponents of the venture objected to the cost, which exceeded $17 million. There were accusations that the railway company overstated its costs and that the Ecuadorian government had assumed unreasonable risks in guaranteeing the stocks and bonds issued to investors. At times the controversy strained relations with the United States government, which supported the company's point of view. However, the railroad created a national market, led to economic growth, and began to mitigate regional tensions. The government nationalized the line in 1925. In 2008 Ecuador commemorated the G&Q Railway's centennial with celebrations and currently plans to renovate the line as a tourist attraction.

THE FIRST ALFARO ADMINISTRATION: CONCLUSIONS

Alfaro succeeded in implementing a portion of the Liberal agenda. This included reforms restricting the power of the Catholic Church in secular affairs and modernization projects such as the Guayaquil and Quito Railway. However, Alfaro used repression whenever he encountered opposition to his plans. He created a secret police force and a group of enforcers known as the *garroteros* to intimidate his opponents. The presses of opposition newspapers were demolished and editors threatened. The *garroteros* roughed up congressional opponents and harassed their families. In addition, opponents were exiled or imprisoned without charge, their private property confiscated, and, in extreme cases, they were murdered. Alfaro was a Freemason, which further exacerbated the resentment of Conservatives. His policy of separation of church and state differed from the model of the United States in that Alfaro sought to control the Catholic Church.

The most disturbing aspect of Alfaro's program was personalism, or his belief that only he could lead Ecuador into modernization. However, his constitutional term ended in August 1901. His plan was to have a sycophant become president in order to rule from behind the scenes, much as García Moreno had done. His handpicked successor, General Leonidas Plaza Gutíerrez, easily won the 1901 presidential election. To Alfaro's chagrin, it turned out that Leonidas Plaza was his own man.

LEONIDAS PLAZA GUTÍERREZ: ECUADOR'S MODERATE LIBERAL PRESIDENT

Like his predecessor, Leonidas Plaza was born in the coastal province of Manabí. He was born on April 18, 1865, in the small town of Charapotó; his parents were Colombian immigrants. At age 18 Plaza chose a military career and served in Alfaro's rebel army during the War of the Restoration in 1883. He later participated in the rebellion against the Caamaño government and fled the country when it failed. Plaza became a professional soldier in Central America, serving at various times in El Salvador, Nicaragua, and Costa Rica. While serving in the Costa Rican army he obtained the rank of major general. Plaza returned to Ecuador in 1895 to serve in Alfaro's Liberal army. He was assigned to important military commands and was named the governor of Azuay Province when Alfaro became supreme chief. Plaza served as a member of the National Assembly that confirmed Alfaro as president of the republic and drafted the new liberal constitution. The National Assembly appointed him a general and he became commander in chief of the Coastal Army during Alfaro's first presidency. Only Liberals ran in the 1901 presidential election and Plaza, as the party's official candidate, won 65,781 votes out of the nearly 75,000 ballots cast. Alfaro soon had doubts about Plaza and plotted to retain the presidency. Plaza used his control of the army and his popularity in congress to thwart Alfaro's attempts to remain in power. This feud resulted in a split in the Liberal party that would ultimately have deadly consequences.

Leonidas Plaza was a true Liberal who ended Alfaro's repressive tactics. He terminated systematic persecution of the Conservatives and abolished the secret police. Believing in freedom of the press, Plaza not only ended official harassment of the opposition press, he withdrew funding for the progovernment newspapers. Plaza's style was unpretentious and he was easily approachable by average citizens. He insisted upon an honest government and was scrupulous in the administration of public funds and projects. He continued the railroad contract with Archer Harman but served notice that the contract would be strictly enforced to Ecuador's satisfaction.

Plaza continued the Liberal program of secularization. He implemented civil marriage procedures and Ecuador became one of the first countries in Latin America to allow divorce. The *Ley de Cultos* (Law of Religions), implemented on October 13, 1904, is an example of Plaza's efforts to extend state control over the Catholic Church. This law abolished life vows and civil death that some religious orders required of their participants. In Plaza's view these vows were a type of slavery, albeit voluntary, which was prohibited under Ecuador's constitution. The law expanded upon the Law of Patronage, and was intended to suppress the religious orders. Not surprisingly, Conservatives protested and then plotted a revolution. Plaza expertly defused the crisis before it became an open revolt.

Plaza provided Ecuador with a four-year respite from Alfaro's machinations and honored the constitution by stepping down when his term ended in September 1905. The Liberal Party had split into two factions, the Plazistas and the Alfaristas. Plaza was not above political maneuvering and selected Lizardo García as the official candidate of the Liberal Party. The Alfaristas launched a protest and attempted to nominate Eloy Alfaro's nephew, Flavio, as the Liberal candidate. This tactic did not work and they then nominated Ignacio Robles, who promptly declined the nomination. This assured García's election as Conservatives did not participate. After García was inaugurated on September 1, 1905, Leonidas Plaza left Ecuador to serve as minister to the United States.

THE RETURN OF ELOY ALFARO

Furious that Plaza had outmaneuvered him for a second time, Alfaro's lust for power could not be constrained and he was determined to seize control of Ecuador at the earliest opportunity. On December 1 some of Alfaro's political operatives met and formed a directory to plan a *golpe de estado*, or coup d'etat, that would bring the Old Warrior to power once again. The insurrection began a month later in the central highland cites of Riobamba and Guaranda when rebels audaciously proclaimed Eloy Alfaro supreme chief. The ensuing Campaign of 20 Days proved a bloody event that resulted in

1,000 Ecuadorians being killed or wounded. Outside observers were astounded that Alfaro orchestrated the revolt because the Liberal García had continued the party's agenda. The American minister resident, Joseph W. J. Lee, termed it "a revolution without reason."[6] Alfaro took command of rebel forces and defeated a government army at the Battle of Chasquí on January 13, 1906. This victory resulted in the surrender of most government forces in the sierra and President García abandoned Quito for Guayaquil. In a vain attempt to calm the crisis, García resigned and relinquished the presidency to his vice president, Dr. Baquerizo Moreno. Moreno was soon overwhelmed when Alfarist supporters took control of Guayaquil on 20 January. Once again, Eloy Alfaro took power and resided in the Carondelet, Ecuador's executive mansion.

THE SECOND ALFARO PRESIDENCY

Alfaro again ruled as supreme chief and the *garroteros* backed up the dictatorship by using brutal methods to quell dissent. Lee, the American diplomat, summed up the disillusionment that followed Alfaro's triumphant return: "The Supreme Chief desires to remain in power as long as possible. There is much discontent in Guayaquil, on the Coast, and the people in that section seem to have changed their opinion of the Supreme Chief since the late political transformation."[7] Eventually Alfaro legitimized his dictatorship by convening a national assembly made up entirely of Liberals from his faction. The assembly drafted yet another constitution, Ecuador's 12th, which declared Alfaro interim president and in, 1907, the constitutional president, with a term to end in August 1911. The new constitution proclaimed Ecuador to be a democracy with a government that was "representative, alternative, elective, democratic and responsible." The reality proved quite different. General Antonio Vega instigated one of the first revolts against the dictatorship in late November, 1906. Vega was defeated, captured, and executed without trial. His death was covered up as a suicide. Alfaro's second regime proved to be more repressive than the first.

Alfaro imposed additional restrictions on the Catholic Church with the implementation of the *Ley de Beneficencia* (Law of Charity). All church properties held in mortmain were nationalized. The state used half of the income from the properties to pay clerical salaries and the other half to support charities. State inspection of monasteries was reinstated.

Alfaro presided over the completion of the Guayaquil and Quito Railway in 1908 and, the following year, hosted an exposition to celebrate the centennial of independence from Spain. A special complex housed displays from the United States, France, Chile, Peru, Colombia, and Nicaragua. Today the Ministry of Defense occupies the original buildings.

In the latter years of Alfaro's second presidency, Ecuador's fiscal health began to decline. The foreign debt soared to 27,950,000 sucres and the internal debt reached 11,000,000 sucres, while the national income was only 12,000,000 sucres. Ambitious public works projects and excessive spending on the military resulted in a financial crisis. The government was often in arrears in paying its employees and the private sector also suffered. There was growing labor unrest and Alfaro responded to student demonstrations with an iron fist. On July 19, 1907, disgruntled army officers attempted to assassinate Alfaro. The plot failed but was exceedingly bloody with scores killed and many wounded on both sides. Alfaro captured 15 of the plotters and ordered 8 to be executed by firing squad. Alfaro faced continuing protests and riots in the remaining years of his presidency. There was a period of calm in 1910 when war with Peru seemed imminent but, when this crisis passed, opposition to Alfaro continued to flourish primarily from within the Liberal Party.

In 1911 Alfaro handpicked an old friend, Emilio Estrada, to succeed him as president with the intention of again ruling through a surrogate. The plan backfired as Estrada refused to step aside before taking office. Estrada's supporters decided not to allow Alfaro to initiate another *autogolpe*. On August 11, Alfaro was deposed and offered political asylum in the Chilean Legation. He left the country for Panama in September under an agreement not to return for at least two years. The Estrada presidency was short-lived as the new president died of heart failure on December 24. Estrada's death plunged the country into chaos as various generals declared themselves supreme chief. Alfaro returned to Ecuador on January 4, 1912, claiming to offer his services to mediate between the rival factions. This plan was rejected and Ecuador plunged into a brief but bloody civil war. Former president Leonidas Plaza took command of government forces and quickly defeated Alfaro's rebel army. Alfaro surrendered to Plaza through a truce agreement brokered by the British and American consuls that provided for his personal safety. Nevertheless, the government broke the agreement and sent Alfaro via the railroad to Quito to stand trial. Soon after Eloy Alfaro had been incarcerated in Quito's Panóptico prison, an angry mob entered the prison and brutally murdered him.

Alfaro's death paved the way for Leonidas Plaza to take control of the Liberal Party and he returned to the presidency in 1912. Liberal internecine strife continued but Plaza was able to orchestrate constitutional transfers of power to his successors, Alfredo Baquerizo Moreno (1916–20) and José Luis Tamayo (1920–24). Plaza continued the Liberal program of infrastructure improvements, most notably railroad construction. Military expenditures also increased. Plaza believed in these programs but he also used them to assuage regional demands and to insure the support of the military. Unfortunately, Ecuador's cacao boom waned and tax revenues from the import sector sharply declined. World War I further diminished revenues from cacao as the European market was no longer available. Ecuador's international credit rating, never strong, dropped lower. Therefore, the post-Alfaro liberal governments borrowed heavily from domestic banks in Guayaquil to finance public works projects. The Banco Comercial y Agrícola (Commercial and Agricultural Bank) held much of Ecuador's internal debt and exerted great influence over the government. Ecuador's working class and intelligentsia derisively labeled the coalition of banking interests and the coastal oligarchy the ring (*la argolla*). Ultimately, the failure of the Liberals to deliver real change and the perception that *la argolla* was running the country led to a reform movement that came from an unexpected source: junior officers in the Ecuadorian army.

NOTES

1. David Schodt, *Ecuador: An Andean Enigma* (Boulder, CO: Westview Press, 1987), 36–41.

2. Frank MacDonald Spindler, *Ecuador in the Nineteenth Century* (Fairfax: George Mason University Press, 1987), 163.

3. Ibid., 169.

4. Ibid., 172.

5. There are several books that cover the G&Q Railway, including A. Kim Clark, *The Redemptive Work: Railway and Nation in Ecuador, 1895–1930* (Wilmington, DE: Scholarly Resources, 1998) and Elisabeth Harman Brainard and Katharine Robinson Brainard, *Railroad in the Sky* (Quito: Corporación para el Desarrollo de La Educación Universitaria, 2007).

6. Spindler, *Ecuador in the Nineteenth Century,* 193.

7. Ibid.

6

Revolution, Reform, Chaos, and War, 1925–48

The Liberals, under the presidential leadership of Leonidas Plaza Gutierrez (1912–16) followed by Alfredo Baquerizo Moreno (1916–20), José Luis Tamayo (1920–24), and Gonzalo S. Córdova (1924–25), provided Ecuador with an unprecedented period of political stability. However, with the exception of Plaza, the presidents of this period did not exercise real power in Ecuador. Instead, power was wielded by a coastal-based plutocracy with interests in banking and export agriculture which became known as *la argolla* (the ring). The ring's center of operations was the Banco Comercial y Agrícola (Commercial and Agricultural Bank).[1] This combination of agricultural exporters and bankers, often described as the *bancocracia*, dominated finances as well as politics and allegedly designated who would be president, cabinet members, and even lesser office holders.[2] The bank made large loans to the government to underwrite public works projects. Not unexpectedly, these pork-barrel projects included graft and kickbacks at the expense of the general welfare of the vast majority of Ecuadorians. By the early 1920s it was clear that the party of Eloy Alfaro and Leonidas Plaza had lost its way.

There were other developments that resulted in changes to the Ecuadorian political and social tapestry. An organized urban-based working class emerged and sought redress for low wages and deplorable working conditions via a number of strikes and protests. A larger middle class was apparent after World War I and some of this group found military service to be an attractive career. The Conservatives and Liberals were challenged by new ideologies including socialism and populism. Thus Ecuadorian politics became even more fragmented and the result was a kaleidoscopic change of governments in the 1930s.

There were also dramatic developments in Ecuador's foreign affairs that had long-term consequences. Diplomatic attempts to resolve the territorial dispute with Peru over the Oriente failed. In July 1941 Peru invaded Ecuador, soundly defeated the Ecuadorian army, and was granted almost all the disputed portion of the area in the 1942 Río Protocol. This humiliation would impact Ecuadorian politics until 1998. World War II also brought change. Ecuador cooperated with the United States by allowing American military and naval bases at Salinas on the Pacific coast and in the Galápagos Islands. Ecuador also expelled German and Italian aliens, declared war on Japan, and became a charter member of the United Nations.

THE JULY REVOLUTION

For the 1924 elections the Liberals and the ring made an ill-fated choice when they selected Gonzalo S. Córdova as their presidential candidate. Córdova was a sickly man, suffering from heart disease, a condition that necessitated his frequent departure from Quito's dizzying altitude. Córdova spent most of his presidency in Guayaquil, and this only intensified accusations in the sierra that he was a puppet of the coastal ring. Córdova's illness and ineptitude masked the underlying causes of economic complaints and regional interests, which resulted in a bloodless military coup that removed him from office on July 9, 1925.[3]

The July or Julian Revolution, as the ouster of Córdova became known, was unique because it was instigated by the Liga Militar (Military League), a group of junior army officers who proposed a reform agenda. Moreover, the young officers launched a corporate coup, insisting that they were taking power to serve the national interest rather than to install a new *caudillo*. As evidence of their sincerity, the officers established a junta instead of a dictator. On the surface the July revolution appeared to offer Ecuador radical alternatives, proclaiming goals of equality and protection of the "proletariat."[4] The Liga Militar was an outgrowth of Alfaro's and Plaza's program to professionalize the army. The Escuela Militar (Military Academy) was founded in 1901 and its graduates constituted a new breed of officers who were loyal to the army as an institution rather than to one general or politician. About 90 percent of the new officers were from the sierra, a trend that continues to the present. An attempt had been made to keep the officer corps apolitical

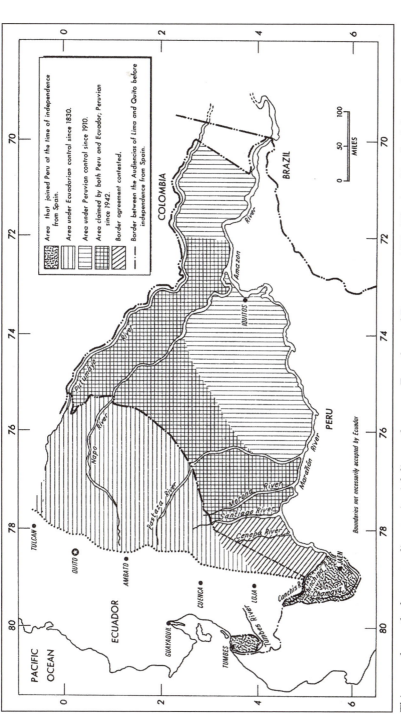

This map shows the long-standing territorial dispute between Ecuador and Peru up to 1973. (*The Area Handbook for Ecuador*, Department of the Army Pamphlet 550–52, 1973)

by prohibiting officers from joining political parties. In the end, however, the officer corps became highly politicized and since they could not join the traditional parties they constituted a movement of their own and, in time, became a force to be reckoned with. The officers were also strongly influenced by two newspapers: *La antorcha,* a socialist publication, and *El abanderado,* a paper that proposed that only the military could save the country from the clutches of corrupt politicians of any stripe.[5] While the junior officers started the July Revolution, they soon relinquished control to senior officers, who formed a temporary military junta.

On April 3, 1926, Isidro Ayora, rector of the Central University, minister of social welfare under the junta, and a prominent physician, was granted dictatorial power. Ayora would rule as dictator until April 1929, when he was installed as president under Ecuador's 13th constitution.

THE JULIAN REFORMS

Ayora invited Dr. Edwin Walter Kemmerer, professor of economics at Princeton University and one of the foremost experts on government finance, to evaluate Ecuador's banking system and to offer proposals to restructure the country's financial and monetary institutions. When the Kemmerer Mission arrived on October 18, 1926, it was a rare moment in Ecuadorian history because the elite of the coast and sierra, Liberals and Conservatives, the press, the government, the military, bankers, and agro-businessmen all seemed to be in agreement. All saw Kemmerer as the money doctor whose reforms would stimulate the economy and attract foreign capital. The money doctor's prescription for Ecuador's poor financial health included the establishment of a central bank, adoption of modern financial and fiscal institutions, and adherence to the gold standard. In addition, Kemmerer recommended the enactment of sound customs collection and taxation laws to make Ecuador attractive to foreign investors. The Kemmerer Mission completed its work in March 1927 and presented the government with 2,000 pages of proposed laws.[6] The Kemmerer mission provided Ecuador with new institutions, most notably the Banco Central (Central Bank), a reformed customs system, the Office of Comptroller General, and the Superintendent of Banks. While the reforms and new institutions were indeed steps toward modernization, special-interest groups soon found ways to work around them.

In addition to financial and monetary reforms, the Ayora government implemented programs that were quite progressive for this period. Ecuador was the first country to grant women the right to vote. In addition, government pensions and protective labor laws were enacted.

A CHAOTIC DECADE

The euphoria produced by the Julian reforms proved to be ephemeral. The October 1929 Wall Street crash caused a further drop in the demand for cacao and other Ecuadorian export crops. The global Great Depression brought unemployment and misery to Ecuador. The Kemmerer reforms were soon subverted and the newly created Central Bank and other institutions succumbed to the traditional way of doing business in Ecuador. Ayora was assailed for adopting a program that contracted the money supply at a time when growth was needed to combat the ravages of the Depression. Mass demonstrations in Quito and pressure from the military convinced Ayora to resign on August 24, 1931. Ayora's departure marked the beginning of a turbulent decade during which 15 men served as chief magistrates of the republic. In addition to the economic downturn, a key explanation for this political turbulence was a growing expectation by the population that the state could solve the nation's economic and social problems.[7] However, the masses had not yet found a political organization through which they could express their demands. Therefore the people used street demonstrations and strikes to express their frustration with the hapless men who had the ill fortune to be president.

THE FOUR-DAY WAR

Colonel Luis Larrea assumed power as minister of government until elections could be organized. In the highlands, conservative large landowners formed a new political coalition, Compactación Obrera Nacional (National Consolidation of Workers). The name was a subterfuge as the group did not represent the interests of the working class but rather merely pretended to be democratic and mass-oriented. The Compactación was quasi-fascist and, in addition to the *hacendados* (large landowners), included artisans and the serrano lower classes.[8] The Compactacíon supported the candidacy of Neptalí Bonifaz, a past president of the Central Bank and a member of the highland elite. The Liberals were divided and two candidates emerged: moderates Modesto Larrea Jijón and Ildefonso Mendoza. The bifurcation of the liberals enabled Bonifaz to win decisively with 48 percent of the vote.[9]

As is so often the case in Ecuadorian electoral politics, the losers, divided during the election campaign, unified to deny the winner the fruits of victory. The Liberals claimed that Bonifaz was Peruvian and therefore should be disqualified. To his great regret, Bonifaz as a young man had boasted about his Peruvian roots. Bonifaz was born in 1870 in Quito. His father was a Peruvian diplomat and his mother, Josefina Ascázubi y Salinas, was Ecuadorian. After studying in Europe, Bonifaz returned to Ecuador and managed his extensive agricultural properties. To his dismay, the Congress of 1932 debated the issue of his citizenship and nullified Bonifaz's election.

Outraged, Compactación thugs took to the streets of Quito in angry protests that turned into violent riots. Liberal paramilitary forces arrived from the coast and the north and clashed with armed Conservatives. Street battles raged between August 29 and September 1, 1932, as the various factions barricaded city blocks. As the death toll and property damage mounted, the foreign diplomatic corps intervened and the bloody affair, with its toll of at least 1,000 lives, came to an end.[10]

Ecuador's severe political fragmentation was apparent in the aftermath of the Four-Day War. The middle class feared the urban laboring masses but found comfort in its over-representation in the military officer corps. However, the army was impotent in preventing the violence of the Four-Day War and by no means had control of the entire nation. Obviously the long-standing Liberal-Conservative feud had not abated. A provisional government, headed by Alberto Guerrero Martínez, was tasked to maintain order until new elections could be organized.

JOSÉ MARÍA VELASCO IBARRA: THE ADVENT OF ECUADOR'S STORMY PETREL

In October 1932, Juan de Dios Martínez Mera, the candidate of a Liberal coalition, prevailed in a presidential election that was widely viewed as fraudulent by his opponents and the urban masses. In addition to allegations of fraud, Martínez Mera faced growing criticism over his decision to remain neutral in the dispute between Colombia and Peru over the territory of Leticia. The opposition proposed supporting Colombia in order to harm Peru, Ecuador's traditional adversary. Martínez Mera's firm stand on neutrality played into the hands of his opponents, who claimed that they were patriots and the president was something less. The Leticia crisis paled in comparison to the attacks the president had to endure from José María Velasco Ibarra, a fire-eating populist orator who would cast a long shadow over the Ecuadorian political scene for the next five decades.

Velasco Ibarra was born into a upper-middle-class Quiteño family in 1893. He most likely acquired his political instincts and volatile personality from his father, Juan Alejandrino Velasco, an engineer who was active in conservative causes and participated in several revolutions. From his mother, Delia Ibarra, he inherited the traits of a keen intellect, stubbornness, and strict discipline. Velasco excelled in his studies at the prestigious Jesuit school, Colegio San Gabriel. Upon graduation from San Gabriel he was admitted to the Central University. He was the top student in his law school class, earning a doctorate of law in 1922. He used the title "doctor" to great effect through-out his life in a society that valued titles. Like many well-educated Ecuador-ians of the 1920s, Velasco at first did not limit himself to any one career. He accepted a teaching position at the Central University and also was appointed to various government positions. However, his real passion was journalism and he soon began writing political commentary under the pseudonym Labriolle for two Quito dailies, *El comercio* and *El día*. In 1931 Velasco trav-eled to Paris and enrolled in the Sorbonne. A year later he was surprised to learn that he had been elected in absentia to Congress.

At first he was reluctant to interrupt his European education, but was con-vinced by the Mexican revolutionary and intellectual, José Vasconcelos, that it was his destiny and duty to return to his native Ecuador and enter politics.[11]

Velasco entered the Congress in 1933 and soon became the leader of the opposition. He had been elected without affiliating with any political party and this enabled him to solicit broader support. Although his family background was conservative, he gained the support of the radical left. His spellbinding oratory coupled with his emphatic gestures made congressional debates the hottest ticket in town. He attacked Martínez Mera relentlessly. Velasco charged the president with being unpatriotic for his refusal to support Colombia in the Leticia dispute. He challenged the legitimacy of the government, citing electoral fraud. He railed at the failed economic policy and claimed that cor-ruption was rampant.[12]

Velasco's exhortations had an impact outside the Congress as street dem-onstrations organized by the Compactación intensified. Finally, the Congress demanded that Martínez Mera resign. The besieged president resisted and attempted an *autogolpe* (self-coup) to make himself dictator, but lacked the support of the military. Martínez Mera appointed Abelardo Montalvo as min-ister of government and left Quito. On October 17, the Senate appointed Mon-talvo as interim president and called for new elections.[13]

Velasco's part in bringing down the Martínez Mera government, while important, was only a prelude to his starring role in the 1933 presidential elections, which brought fundamental changes to Ecuadorian politics. Once again, Velasco's candidacy was launched without an affiliation with a tradi-tional political party. He was the overwhelming choice of a new coalition, the Junta Nacional de Sufragio Libre (National Committee on Free Suffrage). The support of this organization, which on the surface appeared to be civic-minded, freed Velasco from the taint of past political intrigues associated with both the Liberal and Conservative parties. It also gave the appearance that Velasco was not seeking the presidency but rather responding to a pop-ular call.

After accepting the nomination, Velasco outlined the objectives of his can-didacy, promising a true democracy that would center on educational and economic reforms. Public works including new schools, roads, hospitals, and irrigation and sanitation projects would be undertaken. In addition, opportunities for small businesses would be expanded and corruption ended through honest and transparent government. He refused to affiliate with any party but announced he would accept support from any organization that agreed with his platform. The Conservative Party soon endorsed his candidacy.

Velasco next launched the first modern political campaign in Ecuador's history by taking his cause directly to the people, personally campaigning throughout the country. Never before had a presidential candidate delivered speeches in small villages and hamlets in the remote regions of the country. Velasco flattered average Ecuadorians with his appeal for their support and he exhorted the crowds to vote for change that only he could bring about. He was an imposing figure: tall, gaunt, impeccably dressed in a three-piece suit even in tropical locales. His thick glasses and mustache coupled with his title of "doctor" caused the masses to assume that an intelligent, strong, and compassionate leader had arrived to rescue them from poverty and despair. As one observer noted, "He loves the people, he understands them, and he knows how to lead them to greatness."[14]

Velasco's populist campaign caught the traditional parties by surprise. The Conservatives did not field a candidate and endorsed Velasco. The Liberal Party dithered and ultimately did not nominate a candidate. The Socialist Party and the Communist Party provided the only opposition. Velasco Ibarra won by the greatest margin in Ecuador's history, winning 81.4 percent of the vote in an open and fair election. He would soon find out what a difficult country he was about to govern.

THE FIRST VELASQUISMO, 1934–35

José María Velasco Ibarra donned the presidential sash for the first time on September 1, 1934. He immediately launched an ambitious public works program that resulted in a 33 percent increase in spending. New roads were started and existing ones repaired. New docks, customs facilities, and police barracks were erected in Guayaquil and potable water systems installed in Riobamba and Cuenca. Education projects included the introduction of experimental rural schools, an Indian school, a teacher training academy, an all-female high school, and a school of radio technology. The long-neglected Polytechnic School was rechartered and properly staffed. Unfortunately, these projects were often undertaken without proper planning, resulting in waste and corruption.

Velasco courted the support of the armed forces by doubling the defense budget, improving the lot of the common soldier, and upgrading the navy and the fledgling air force. He started the first civic action programs by ordering the army to assist in the building of roads and irrigation projects. The military was also charged with developing agricultural colonies in the remote Oriente.

Velasco was a diligent and tireless worker and he demanded the same from the government bureaucracy. He was famous for making impromptu inspections of government offices to determine if the employees were reporting to work on time and conducting the business of government properly. He summarily dismissed workers if he decided their performance was lacking. While some employees deserved to be fired, others were let go with no evidence of any wrongdoing other than being disrespectful to the president.

While his objectives of reforming Ecuador and improving the lot of the common people were noble, Velasco exhibited traits that explain why all but one of his five presidencies were short-lived. One characteristic was his confrontational relationship with Congress, manifested even before he assumed office when he denounced the Ecuadorian Congress as a do-nothing chamber.[15] He threatened to turn the people loose if Congress dared to block his agenda. Not surprisingly, the Ecuadorian Congress soon opposed his financial recovery plan and other policies. Velasco soon unleashed his followers, who stormed the legislative palace and roughed up members of the not-so-loyal opposition. Congress responded with votes of no confidence and forced the resignation of some cabinet members. When the press critiqued his policies, Velasco responded with repression, jailing journalists, politicians, army colonels, and students. In time, Velasco lost popular support, his heretofore most potent weapon in his fight with the opposition. His erratic behavior, the breakup of his marriage, the murder of his official chauffeur, and Ecuador's deteriorating economy plunged his administration into crisis in August 1935. Velasco decided that the only solution to the impasse with Congress was to establish a dictatorship. On August 20, 1935, Velasco announced the dissolution of Congress and his intention to rule as dictator. As usual, he acted without fully considering the consequences or the advice of trusted advisors. He was warned by his military aide that the full support of the military for his *autogolpe* had not been consummated. Key commanders rejected Velasco's call for a dictatorship and arrested the president. Velasco resigned the following day and went into the first of many exiles, this time to Colombia.

Velasco's brief first presidency was a turning point in Ecuador's political history. He was the first man to win the highest office through an authentic popular election. He had awakened the masses and mobilized the participation of the common man and woman. The old Liberal-Conservative political system, dominated by the oligarchy, had temporarily been thwarted. He had introduced a rare moral authority through his examples of hard work, devotion to duty, and scrupulous personal honesty. His actions, however, did not always match his ideals. His impetuous personality, his firm belief that only he could bring about reform, his bewildering failure to properly assess the strength of his opposition, and the fact that he was impervious to sound advice all contributed to his downfall. More important, Velasquismo inhibited Ecuador's social and political progress. Velasco Ibarra soon became known as *el gran ausente* (the great absentee) because of frequent and lengthy periods of exile. From exile he declared himself the national personification and initiated a relentless campaign to return to power. He had indeed become the stormy petrel of Ecuadorian politics.

THE RETURN OF THE OLD POLITICS

The military leadership had refused to allow Velasco Ibarra to establish a dictatorship, but they had no reservations against installing one of their own choosing. Antonio Pons, the erstwhile minister of government, served as head of the government for 36 days. Pons's replacement was Federico Páez, a jovial former senator and engineer whose main qualification was that he had never been very serious about politics. Páez's modus vivendi was to not rock the boat, as he disavowed all political parties. However, he exhibited leftist sympathies and appointed several Socialists to his cabinet, closed down the conservative paper *El debate*, and sent Jacinto Jijón, the leader of the far right, into exile. Páez pampered the officer corps through salary increases and boosted military expenses to 22.5 percent of the national budget.[16] When Páez lost the support of the Socialist Party he aligned with the Liberal Party. When this proved unpopular he courted the Conservative Party. As pressure from the left grew, the dictator resorted to repression, jailing or exiling has opponents and closing down labor unions and universities. The military decided to end the charade and ousted Páez on October 23, 1937.

General Alberto Enríquez Gallo, the minister of defense in the Páez government, now became supreme chief. Enríquez proved to be a progressive social reformer. He abolished the Social Security Law,[17] which had been used by Páez to quell the opposition, enacted the Labor Code of 1938, which restored the rights of labor unions, improved public and higher education, and ended the tax-exempt status of the South American Development Company, a firm that was largely owned by U.S. investors. He also constituted a parliament with equal numbers of representatives from the Conservative, Liberal, and Socialist parties in an attempt to create a consensus. Enríquez voluntarily stepped aside in 1938. The political balance that Enríquez thought would resolve Ecuador's political infighting backfired as the parliament became deadlocked on naming his successor. Manuel María Borrero became provisional president. The Liberals eventually selected Aurelio Mosquera Narváez, who assumed office on December 2, 1938. When Mosquera suddenly died of natural causes in November 1939 he was succeeded by the president of the senate, Carlos Arroyo del Río.

Arroyo del Río, a longtime leader of the Liberals, called for new elections in January 1940. The 1940 presidential election was a three-way race between Arroyo del Río, the candidate of the Liberals, Jacinto Jijón representing the Conservatives, and Velasco Ibarra, the champion of the masses. As usual Velasco wowed the masses and, if political polling had been available in Ecuador in 1940, it would have indicated that he had an insurmountable lead. Initial returns indicated a Velasco victory but on the morning after the election the government declared Arroyo del Río the winner. Velasco's supporters realized that they had been cheated and took to the streets of Guayaquil. It was clear that Arroyo del Río had resorted to fraud as observers documented many voting irregularities. The government broke up the demonstrations. Several people were killed and scores wounded. Velasco was arrested and sent into exile in Colombia. Arroyo del Río would rule for four controversial and turbulent years until he was deposed by a coup in 1944.

ECUADOR DURING WORLD WAR II

Ecuador's strategic location on the westernmost point of South America and its possession of the Galápagos Islands left little doubt that it would become involved in World War II. The United States was interested in the Galápagos as they offered an excellent location for the forward defense of the Panama Canal. The United States was concerned that Germany or Japan could use the Galápagos to launch a bombing attack on the canal. In addition, Germany hoped to gain influence in Ecuador by developing a commercial airline and nurturing an intelligence network using German immigrants who resided in Quito and Guayaquil.

Ecuador's own security concerns in 1939–41 were not focused on Germany, Japan, or the United States but were, rather, directed at Peru. Ecuador and Peru were in dispute over a vast region of the remote upper Amazon basin known to Ecuadorians as the Oriente. The area included a triangular section east of the Andes bounded on the south by the Marañón and Amazon rivers and on the east and north by the Putumayo. All previous attempts to resolve the dispute through bilateral or multilateral negotiations had met with failure, including the 1936–39 Washington Conference hosted by the United States.

On July 5, 1941, hostilities erupted near the towns of Huaquillas and Charcas on the Zaramilla River. Peru opened a major offensive on July 22, and the Ecuadorians, outnumbered four to one with no tanks or air support, were quickly overwhelmed. A relentless Peruvian air campaign destroyed Ecuadorian resistance. The Peruvian army broke through Ecuadorian defensive positions and occupied El Oro Province while its navy blockaded

Guayaquil and shelled the coastal town of Puerto Bolívar. On July 31, Ecuador accepted Peru's terms for a cease-fire. As Ecuador's foreign minister, Dr. Julio Tobar Donoso, wrote, "Disarmed and annihilated Ecuador resigned herself to this measure which constituted the amputation of her sovereignty."[18]

The brief Peru-Ecuador War threatened to break the hemispheric solidarity that the United States had crafted under the Good Neighbor Policy. Ecuador, on the other hand, was confronted with Peruvian occupation of El Oro Province as well as the loss of any claim to the disputed territory. Ecuador's tenuous position did not improve when the United States entered World War II on December 7, 1941. The United States was determined to present a united hemispheric front against Germany, Italy, and Japan and sought a resolution to the Ecuador-Peru dispute at the January 1942 meeting of foreign ministers in Río de Janeiro. Brazil also wanted the dispute resolved and the Brazilian foreign minister, Oswaldo Aranha, played a pivotal role in the negotiations.

Aranha took the lead in convincing Ecuador to relinquish its claim to the disputed area in exchange for the withdrawal of Peruvian troops from its soil. Aranha bluntly told Tobar Donoso: "A country that doesn't have borders is like a man without skin. If you do not settle now, Peru will continue the invasion. It is not possible to have preliminary terms, it is better to lose a limb than the whole body."[19] At this point, Ecuador realized that neither the United States, Argentina, Brazil, nor Chile would intervene on its behalf. Ecuador, with great reluctance, signed the Protocol of Peace, Friendship, and Boundaries, which became known simply as the Río Protocol. Ecuador agreed to rescind its claim to most of the long-disputed area in exchange for the removal of Peruvian forces from El Oro Province. In addition, Peru and Ecuador agreed to allow the United States, Argentina, Brazil, and Chile, the guarantors of the treaty, to demarcate the boundary through an international commission.

The Río Protocol was the most significant outcome of World War II for Ecuador. The Río Protocol became a controversial and inflammatory issue, used by Ecuadorian populist politicians to discredit sitting governments. For example, President Carlos Arroyo del Río was ousted by a coup in 1944, in no small part due to his alleged sellout at the Río Conference. Later, José Maria Velasco Ibarra declared the protocol null and void and used the issue to stir Ecuadorian patriotism and deepen enmity toward Peru.

Ecuador cooperated with the United States throughout World War II despite the outcome of the Río Protocol, due to number of factors. Ecuador obtained funding for the modernization of its armed forces with an initial allocation of $17 million from the U.S. Lend-Lease program. The United States established and funded naval and aviation training missions and constructed training facilities at Quito and Salinas.[20] In return, Ecuador allowed the United States to build air bases at Salinas and on Baltra Island in the Galápagos.

The U.S. bases served as a deterrent to possible renewed Peruvian aggression and also demonstrated that Ecuador was making a positive contribution to the defense of the hemisphere.

In addition to military assistance, Ecuador received a comprehensive U.S. assistance package to compensate for damages from the Peruvian War. Twenty million dollars was granted for the rehabilitation of El Oro Province to provide food, tools, and other necessities. Guayaquil's water system was improved with an $8 million grant and the Export-Import Bank extended credits of $5 million to the Ecuadorian Development Company to oversee improvements in mining, transportation, and farming. Additional loans of $7 million helped stabilize the sucre and fostered health projects throughout the country.

Ecuador viewed its wartime cooperation with the United States as the lesser of two evils. One option was to walk out of the Río Conference, shatter hemispheric unity, and wait to see if Peru would make further military advances. Instead Ecuador chose to support the U.S. quest for solidarity and accept the loss of a century-old aspiration to become an Amazonian nation in exchange for the guaranteed security of the area and populations that had traditionally been Ecuadorian. By choosing the latter option it achieved a measure of national integrity, but at a bitter price.

THE FALL OF THE ARROYO GOVERNMENT

President Carlos Arroyo del Río proved to be one of the most popular politicians in the Western Hemisphere during World War II—except in Ecuador. Because of his cooperation with the United States and its Allies in defense of the hemisphere, Arroyo was known as the "Apostle of Pan-Americanism." However, in Ecuador he was loathed as the man who had stolen the 1940 presidential election through fraud, lost the 1941 war with Peru, and worse yet, signed off on the 1942 Río Protocol, regarded as a great national humiliation. Despite his unpopularity, Arroyo was determined to complete his term and hand over power to a handpicked successor from the Liberal party. Arroyo, aware of his precarious standing with the public, created the Fuerza de Carabineros, a national police force made up of former military men and professional thugs, to counter the influence of the army and to serve as his personal enforcers. He used his influence in the Radical Liberal Party to secure the nomination of Miguel Angel Albornoz, the 70-year-old president of the Senate, to be the party's candidate for president in the 1944 elections. He also schemed to make Albornoz the only "official" candidate. Arroyo later justified his actions saying, "I hated Velasco Ibarra, I knew that if he were to come to the presidency, he would ruin the country."[21]

Opposition to Arroyo's manipulations came from three directions. First was Velasco Ibarra, who announced his candidacy from exile in Chile and rightfully boasted that he would receive at least 80 percent of the vote in the upcoming election. The second group to oppose Arroyo was the Alianza Democrática Ecuatoriana (Ecuadorian Democratic Alliance) or ADE, a coalition created by Camilo Ponce Enríquez and others who feared that Arroyo had established a dictatorship to keep the Liberal Party in power. As Ponce had been Velasco's campaign manager in 1940, many assumed that ADE was formed to promote Velasco Ibarra's quest for the presidency; but this was not the objective of the group in the beginning. The ADE was broadly based and had the support of the Ecuadorian Socialist, Communist, and Revolutionary Vanguard parties and, eventually, even the Conservatives. When Arroyo refused to listen to the pleas of moderate factions of the Liberal Party to nominate Colón Alfaro, the son of Eloy Alfaro, as an alternative to Albornoz, they also joined forces with the ADE. The third and most important group was a coterie of junior army officers led by Captain Sergio Enrique Jirón. These officers were dismayed that Arroyo blamed them for the Peruvian defeat and disliked his favoritism toward the *carabineros.* In the early months of 1944 ADE decided to support Velasco's candidacy primarily because they had no other alternative. Only Velasco could command the support of the masses and he was sure to win the upcoming election if he were allowed to be on the ballot. Jirón and his followers arrived at the same conclusion and entered into negotiations with ADE. The officers and ADE feared that Arroyo would rig the election or declare a dictatorship. Contingency plans were made to launch a coup in the event of fraud, the arrest of any conspirator, or violent acts against the masses by the government.

On May 27 an ADE conspirator was arrested, touching off a *golpe* by Jirón and his men the following evening in Guayaquil. Army units surrounded the headquarters of the Guayaquil *Carabinero* unit. A firefight ensued and lasted for several hours until the surviving *carabineros* surrendered. The army then allowed a mob to destroy the building. Other army units in other cities soon joined the cause. In Quito the *carabineros* deserted Arroyo and joined in with the army. Arroyo fled to the Colombian Embassy and later went into exile. Velasco Ibarra had relocated to Colombia and awaited the call of the army and ADE to assume the presidency.

THE SECOND VELASQUISMO, JUNE 1, 1944–AUGUST 23, 1947

On May 30, Velasco Ibarra, a man who firmly believed that he had become the "National Personification" and that "my destiny is indestructibly tied to the destiny of my country," triumphantly crossed the border into his homeland.[22] He was the at the height of his power as a spellbinding orator and had a hypnotic effect on the crowds that thronged the route from Tulcán to

Quito. At every town and hamlet the man of the hour mesmerized his audiences as he promised to work tirelessly for the people, end corruption, defeat the oligarchy, and lift the country to prosperity. As one army officer later commented, Velasco was "a man of the people, a pure man . . . the soul of Ecuador . . . a force of nature."[23] When he finally arrived in the capital the following day, he was deliriously greeted by 60,000 citizens braving a dreary drizzle to catch a glimpse of Ecuador's political messiah. Velasco Ibarra's portrait, draped in the Ecuadorian tricolor, adorned houses, commercial enterprises and public buildings. Few chose to remember that the previous Velasquismo had been an unmitigated disaster, nor did the vast majority of Ecuadorians have any sense that the second one was about to follow the same course.[24]

Soon after Velasco Ibarra was sworn in on June 1, a constituent assembly was formed to write yet another constitution and to confer legitimacy on the new government. Not surprisingly, the assembly was dominated by the ADE. Problems soon emerged. Velasco Ibarra had been brought to power by the ADE but he felt no obligation to cooperate with it, stating: "I will not serve any particular party, I will be the Leader of the Nation, I will be the servant of the people."[25] His petulant stance stemmed from strong convictions. If Velasco Ibarra cooperated with the ADE he would be seen as an ordinary politician and thus lose his appeal as a man of the people. He also realized that the ADE would not last long as it was made up of too many disparate elements. Velasco Ibarra was astute in his assessment of the ADE; partisan interests led to its demise soon after the 1945 constitution was drafted. However, by failing to find a way to cooperate with ADE or any other political group, Velasco Ibarra unwittingly sowed the seeds of destruction that ultimately doomed his second presidency. One early sign of a break with ADE was the president's objection to the 1945 constitution, which he signed "against my personal convictions and only to save the country from evil times."[26] His main objection was the elaborate system of checks and balances that curbed the power of the president by creating the Tribunal of Guarantees. Like most of his predecessors, Velasco Ibarra intended to follow the constitution only when it was convenient, which, in the populist *caudillo's* view, it seldom was.

THE ACHIEVEMENTS OF THE SECOND VELASCO GOVERNMENT

Some successful reforms and modernization programs were initiated during Velasco Ibarra's second administration despite the president's erratic behavior and the political acrimony that soon engulfed the country. Significant progress was made in education and public works. The government also attempted to initiate centralized national economic planning to spur development and to curb the scourge of inflation.

Velasco Ibarra believed that improved education was the key to improving the life of the poor. The main focus of his second administration was on building primary schools in areas that had few. In two years 143 new elementary schools were completed and ground was broken for an additional 155. Special consideration was given to Loja Province in the southern highlands and to El Oro Province on the southern coast. Loja had long suffered neglect by the central government and El Oro was recovering from destruction that had occurred during the Peruvian war. In addition to these, an Indian school was started in Otavalo and an effort made to bring schools to remote rural areas. The secondary education system was reformed with changes in the curriculum that moved from vocational specialization to a broader arts and sciences approach. In addition, private schools now could administer comprehensive graduation exams, alleviating the frustration of many students who previously were required to take them at public high schools. In higher education, the Velasco government introduced competition through a law that permitted the chartering of private universities. This opened the way for the later founding of the Catholic University in Quito and other private universities and technical colleges. Velasco Ibarra's early career as a journalist made him determined that future journalists would have opportunities that he did not. Therefore he funded the creation of journalism schools at the state universities in Quito and Guayaquil. Adult education was also a priority and the government established the League for the Teaching of Illiterates and supported the existing literacy effort of the National Union of Newspapermen. These campaigns taught 80,000 Ecuadorians to read and write and at least attempted to deal with this critical problem that affected more than 2 million people. The government also supported the construction of a building for the National Academy of History and started the Casa de la Cultura, the Ecuadorian version of the Smithsonian Institute.

Public works were another hallmark of the second Velasquismo and centered on road building. More than 30 projects were undertaken throughout the country as part of Velasco's vision to bring progress to areas besides Quito and Guayaquil. Perhaps the most significant highway linked Quito to the coastal city of Esmeraldas, providing an outlet for highland products to a port other than Guayaquil. The government also started to expand the rail system with the construction of a line from Quito to Ibarra and on to San Lorenzo on the northwest coast. Other public works initiatives included a national irrigation fund and the building of hospitals.

Velasquista economic reforms were more problematic but, nevertheless, represented a sincere attempt to improve the human condition in the impoverished republic. The Ministry of Economy was created and tasked with centralized national economic planning, regulation of industry and commerce, and the promotion of various development schemes. One tangible result was the establishment of the National Development Bank. Loans from this bank to the agricultural sector resulted in significant increases in the production of rice, sugar, and potatoes. Funding was provided to ranchers to bring in new strains of cattle that quickly improved both the availability and quality of beef. Loans to mid- and small-sized banana producers would abet Ecuador's banana boom, which was about to take off. Inflation was a major problem in the aftermath of World War II and Velasco tried to bring it under control. However, his attempts to initiate increased food production and price controls did little to ameliorate the impact of inflation.

THE FALL OF THE SECOND VELASCO GOVERNMENT

Despite the tangible accomplishments of his second administration, Velasco Ibarra was a polarizing force in Ecuadorian politics and his refusal to compromise with the power structure led to his downfall. His falling out with the ADE was predictable as he easily destroyed the organization by banishing various factions from his government. Ironically, the first of his supporters to leave the coalition were the Communists and Socialists, the parties that had been most fervent in supporting his return to Ecuador. On March 30, 1945, Velasco eliminated his other nemesis, the Tribunal of Guarantees, which had constantly blocked his programs on constitutional grounds, by declaring himself dictator. He then called for national elections to select delegates for a constituent assembly to write a new constitution. All political parties except the Conservatives and the Unión Popular Republicana (Popular Republican Union), made up mostly of government employees, boycotted the elections. Thus, Velasco Ibarra, brought to power by the Left, became the darling of the Right. The first task of the constituent assembly was to appoint a new president. When the assembly decided to debate this issue and to possibly select a Conservative, Velasquista politicians consulted with the army. The assembly soon found itself surrounded by tanks and was persuaded that Velasco Ibarra should be confirmed as president with a term expiration date of September 1, 1948. The assembly then drafted a constitution that was more to Velasco's liking.

Velasco's plan to govern Ecuador without being beholden to any political group or faction seemed to have succeeded, at least for the moment. The ADE had fallen apart, the Communists and Socialists had been forced underground, the Radical Liberal Party was in disarray, and the army had kept the Conservatives in check. However, these measures led to a rise in popular opposition to the regime. Moreover, Ecuador's economic problems, most notably inflation, were contributing to widespread discontent. Velasco's frequent changes of department heads (29 different men held the eight posts in a two-year period) caused some to believe that if he was not crazy he was certainly erratic. By 1947 Velasco was hanging on to power mostly due to the support of the army. A gross miscalculation over several petty issues resulted in the end of army support.

In 1944 Velasco had appointed army Colonel Carlos Mancheno Cajas minister of defense. Mancheno had served as one of Velasco's aides-de-camp in 1934 and the president had been impressed with his loyalty. At first the relationship was cordial and it was Mancheno who had ordered army units to support Velasco during his brief dispute with the recent constituent assembly. The relationship began to sour in late 1946 when Velasco began excluding Mancheno from high-level cabinet meetings. The rift was further exacerbated by a dispute over the president's white gloves. Velasco accused a lieutenant of stealing his gloves. Mancheno stood up for the lieutenant and Velasco was enraged. Mancheno realized that the volatile Velasco was about to sack him so, on January 7, 1947, he resigned and retired to civilian life. In June, Velasco decided he needed Mancheno and called him out of retirement to once again be minister of defense. Velasco failed to understand that Mancheno accepted not out of loyalty but because he saw an opportunity for revenge. When Velasco harassed one of Mancheno's favorite officers, Mancheno initiated a *golpe de estado.* On the night of August 23 infantry units in the Quito Garrison started the rebellion. Velasco rushed to a unit of the tank corps that he believed would support him. He was arrested and forced to resign as president. Mancheno declared himself president but soon found himself in a struggle for power with Mariano Suárez Veintemilla, then Ecuador's vice president. Mancheno held power until September 2 and then turned over the reins to Suárez, who promised to serve only until Congress would appoint a new president. Congress selected Carlos Julio Arosemena Tola, who promised to only serve out the remainder of Velasco's term. In the meantime new elections could be organized. Arosemena Tola brought a much-needed respite to the political chaos that had swept Ecuador. His steady hand was a preface to a 12-year period of stability and the peaceful transfer of power between three duly elected constitutional presidents.

AN ASSESSMENT OF THE SECOND VELASQUISMO

Ecuador had never had a more popular president than José María Velasco Ibarra. Even his opponents admitted that he was the choice of more than 80 percent of the voters. However, his popularity did not translate into effective government and the same people who supported him were relieved when the army sent him into exile a second time. Velasco failed because he was Velasco. His greatest strength was his firm belief that only he could deliver Ecuador from the chaos and ruin that lesser men had bestowed upon her. This was also his greatest weakness. The notion that he was above politics was noble but unrealistic. While it gave him power with the masses it ignored the traditional political party structure. His refusal to work with existing parties or even to form a new one meant that he did have the political structure needed to remain in power. He also did not address Ecuador's long-standing problem of regional differences between the highland and coastal elite. Additionally, he failed to realize that the army was the final arbiter of power in Ecuador. He alienated General Mancheno, a man that he handpicked to run the Ministry of Defense. In the end he sacrificed his government for a pair of white gloves.

On the other hand, he stirred the interest of ordinary Ecuadorians in politics and in doing so broadened the electorate and ushered in an essential element of democracy: the participation of the people. By 1979 this participation extended to every Ecuadorian who was 18 years of age, regardless of his or her ability to read. Though his public works projects were often ill-conceived and wasteful, some demonstrated to the people that the government was at least trying to provide them with basic services such as schools, roads, and hospitals. Thus his most significant contribution was to give the poor hope that there would be better days in the future. Of course, that future always depended on the return of the Great Absentee.

The period between the July Revolution of 1925 and the fall of the second Velasco government in 1947 was one of the most convoluted in Ecuador's turbulent political history. The old problems of regionalism, personalism, dictatorial inclinations, and military interference in politics impeded the nation's economic and social advancement. The lack of national unity and a realistic defense policy resulted in the loss of half the national territory to Peru.

Significant trends also emerged during this time. The July Revolution represented an attempt by some elements of the Ecuadorian army to create a more just and equitable government for Ecuador. This was a refreshing departure from the past practice of supporting an individual in his quest for personal power. Therefore, the Julian Rebels laid the foundation for the military to play a role in the development of the state and to hold politicians accountable. Another trend was the loss of power and prestige by the traditional elite-dominated Conservative and Liberal parties. In a sense, it was the beginning of the end for these parties that had dominated Ecuadorian politics. The emergence of populism, as represented by Velasco Ibarra demonstrated that there was a new force to be reckoned with and that politics was no longer the sole domain of the elite.

NOTES

1. Dennis M. Hanratty, ed., *Ecuador: A Country Study* (Washington, DC: Library of Congress Federal Research Division, 1981), 27.

2. Agustín Cueva, "El Ecuador de 1925 a 1960," in *Nueva historia del Ecuador,* vol. 10, ed. Enrique Ayala Mora (Quito: Corporación Editora Nacional, 1995), 89.

3. Paul W. Drake, *The Money Doctor of the Andes* (Durham, NC: Duke University Press, 1989), 135.

4. Cueva, "El Ecuador," 90.

5. David Schodt, *Ecuador: An Andean Enigma* (Boulder, CO: Westview Press, 1987), 51.

6. Linda A. Rodriquez, *The Search for Public Policy: Regional Politics and Government Finances in Ecuador, 1830–1940* (Berkeley: University of California Press, 1985), 142.

7. Ibid., 164.

8. Hanratty, *Ecuador: A Country Study,* 29.

9. Rodriquez, *The Search for Public Policy,* 165.

10. Oscar Efren Reyes, *Breve historia general del Ecuador,* vol. 3 (Quito: Imprenta del Colegio Técnico Don Bosco), 275.

11. Robert Norris, "José María Velasco Ibarra: A Charismatic Figure in Ecuadorean Politics, 1934–1961," PhD diss., University of New Mexico, 1969.

12. Ibid.

13. Ibid.

14. Ibid., 118.

15. Ibid., 137.

16. Agustín Cueva, *The Process of Political Domination in Ecuador* (New Brunswick, NJ: Transaction Books, 1982), 21–28.

17. The Social Security Law should not be confused with the Social Security Act in the United States, which is a government retirement plan. Ecuador's Social Security Law was designed to repress dissent and public demonstrations.

18. Julio Tobar Donoso, *La invasión peruana y el Protocolo de Río: Antecedentes y explicación histórica* (Quito: Banco Central del Ecuador, 1982), 216.

19. Ibid. 369.

20. "Memorandum: The Status of Measures of Cooperation which Have Been Agreed Upon between the Government of Ecuador and the United States, Agreed at the Río Conference, 1942–1943," Archive of the Ecuadorian Foreign Ministry.

21. George I. Blansten, *Ecuador: Constitutions and Caudillos* (New York: Russell and Russell, 1964), 43.

22. Ibid., 50.

23. Ibid.

24. Norris, "José María Velasco Ibarra," 216.

25. Ibid., 224.

26. Blansten, *Ecuador: Constitutions and Caudillos,* 52.

7

Ecuador, 1948–72: Bananas, Democracy, Populism, and Juntas

In the aftermath of World War II, Ecuador found a much-needed respite from the economic and political chaos of the 1930s, the humiliation of Río Protocol, the ineptitude of the Arroyo del Río government, and the erratic machinations of Velasco Ibarra. On a positive note, an economic boom based on the export of bananas increased revenues, provided opportunities for small and medium-sized entrepreneurs, and generally benefited various other segments of Ecuadorian society. Coupled with the improved economy was an extraordinary period of stable government know as the "Democratic Parenthesis" that saw three presidents elected in fair elections and, more importantly, complete their constitutional terms. Soon, however, other currents reversed the hopeful trends of prosperity and stability. Populism, by now perfected by Velasco Ibarra and adopted by others, offered great hope to the masses, but hope that had no basis in reality. In sum, it was an adaptation of old-fashioned Ecuadorian *personalismo* and *caudillismo* that promised a better future if the electorate vested power in one great man. It proved to be effective only in winning elections. The failure of Velasco Ibarra to deliver on his populist promises resulted in one military coup and the presidential prospects of Assad Bucaram, a new populist succeeding Velasco Ibarra, led to another. In addition, the Ecuadorian military assumed a new role in Ecuadorian politics. In addition to intervening and removing presidents, the military twice, attempted to govern and implement reforms.

THE BANANA BOOM, 1948-60

Prior to World War II bananas accounted for only 1 percent of the value of Ecuador's export crops. However, earlier developments explain the sudden emergence of Ecuador as the world's leading banana producer after the war. The United Fruit Company (UFCO) purchased the old Tenguel cacao plantation in 1933 and began experimenting with banana production.[1] While there was at first only a modest increase in banana exports, Tenguel proved that Ecuador had the potential to expand production. As supplies of bananas from Central America dropped, brought on by Panama disease and Sigatoka Leaf Spot, Ecuador replaced the traditional area of production. Finally, demand rose, mostly in Europe, with the end of World War II.

Ecuador proved an ideal alternative to Central America as it enjoyed a favorable climate, agreeable topography, and fertile land previously used for cacao production. Free of the banana blights that plagued Guatemala, Costa Rica, and Honduras, Ecuador did not suffer from the devastating hurricanes that frequently damaged plantations in the Caribbean basin. Convenient rivers linked the farms and plantations to the port of Guayaquil and this transportation system was soon augmented by new roads. Ecuadorian bananas were highly profitable, costing 70 percent less per pound to bring to market than from the traditional source.[2] These favorable conditions soon resulted in a dramatic increase in Ecuador's banana exports. For example, exports rose from 67,858 tons in 1947 to 602,968 tons in 1955, an 800 percent increase. Ecuador was the world's leading producer until 1983 and still is the largest banana exporter.[3]

The banana boom impacted Ecuador in primarily a positive way. It enabled the rise of small entrepreneurs in the coastal region as Ecuadorian bananas were mostly grown on small farms. Only a few large plantations existed but wealth was not concentrated in the hands of a few families or an international company, as in some other instances. Agricultural production in the highlands rose by 25 percent as demand by the coastal middle class increased. Some of the population shifted from the sierra to the coast as workers migrated in search of better wages. Finally, the boom ushered in an extraordinary 12 years of political stability. Eventually Ecuador had to confront the same problems that Central American producers had encountered. Ecuadorian producers were better prepared to face these threats with advanced spraying techniques and the introduction of the disease-resistant Cavendish variety. The boom ended with a slowdown in demand, a revival of Central American competition, and the emergence of new producers in Africa and Asia.

THE 1948 ELECTIONS

The caretaker government of Carlos Julio Arosemena Tola wanted to oversee free and fair elections and to provide the incoming president with a chance to complete a full four-year term. Arosemena Tola had no long-term political ambitions and did his country a great service by achieving that outcome. An ad hoc party, the National Civic Democratic Movement (MCDN), a largely Liberal group, was created to prevent the Conservatives or the radical left from winning the election. The MCDN countered the image of the Radical Liberal Party, which had lost most of its prestige in the 1941 debacle with Peru. The MCDN nominated Galo Plaza Lasso, a diplomat, senator, and son of President Leonidas Plaza, as their standard bearer. The Conservatives nominated Dr. Manuel Elicio Flor, a constitutional lawyer and president of the supreme court. The Radical Liberals and Socialists formed a temporary coalition and nominated the former dictator, General Alberto Enríquez Gallo. At the time it was the most democratic election in Ecuador's history. Plaza won by a narrow margin with 115,835 votes to 112,052 for Flor and 52,601 for Enríquez Gallo.[4] While often hailed as a landmark election, fewer than 9 percent of Ecuadorians voted.

THE PLAZA PRESIDENCY, 1948–52

Galo Plaza Lasso was born in New York City in 1906 while his father, General Leonidas Plaza Gutíerrez, was serving as Ecuador's minister to the United States. His father had just completed his first term as Ecuador's president (1901–5). His mother, Avelina Lasso, was from a prominent highland family. Galo Plaza returned to the United States in the 1930s to attend college. He first studied at the University of California at Berkeley, where he played American football, and he later attended the University of Maryland. While serving as an attaché at the Ecuadorian Embassy in Washington, D.C., Plaza completed a course of study at the Georgetown University School of Foreign Service. He took a job with the Grace Steamship Company and returned to Ecuador in 1933 to manage his family's highland haciendas. In 1938 he was appointed minister of defense and sports. He served as ambassador to the United States (1944–45) and was elected to the Senate in 1947. Upon his election he announced, "I believe that the essential task of government is to maintain and perfect the exercise of human rights and the fundamental human guarantees."[5] Plaza would attempt to practice these ideals as president and later as secretary general of the Organization of American States. His success in both these positions made him the most internationally respected of all of Ecuador's leaders.

Plaza wisely decided to tackle Ecuador's economic backwardness by improving production of existing resources including coffee, cacao, bananas, rice, and minerals rather than attempting import substitution schemes as many other Latin American countries attempted. He established the Coffee Institute to introduce modern methods of cultivation and production. He also focused on expanding land use, as Ecuadorian farmers cultivated only 15 percent of their arable land. He planned to use increased revenue from petroleum to fund land development, but this idea was derailed when Shell and Esso decided to discontinue oil exploration in the Oriente. He established the National Institute for Development and Production, which introduced improved seed strains, animal breeding stations, and soil conservation methods. The institute also started a modest land distribution program for small farmers. President Plaza accepted aid from the United States under the Point Four Program for health and education initiatives. Plaza, like most of his predecessors, sponsored transportation projects. A highway was started to link the northeastern port of Esmeraldas to Quito, the railroad received some upgrades, and airports were expanded. Plaza celebrated Ecuador's indigenous heritage by being frequently photographed at indigenous festivals and other events and including these images in tourist promotions. He fostered the promotion of indigenous weaving and encouraged the famous weavers of Otavalo to market their goods in the United States and Europe.

Plaza astutely included a broad representation of Ecuador's disparate political parties in his government, but he was not immune to political opposition. Early in his administration he thwarted an attempted coup by General Mancheno primarily because most officers and enlisted personnel refused to join the effort. He reopened Ecuador's claim to unfettered access to the Amazon River when discrepancies in the details of the Río Protocol were revealed by improved photo mapping of a portion of the border area by the United States Air Force.

Plaza was not, however, immune from criticism from a wide variety of sources. Academics and the far left pointed out that he was a member of the oligarchy who owned several large haciendas where he employed many indigenous workers at extremely low wages. They depicted his celebration of Ecuador's indigenous heritage as shallow photo opportunities. His development programs, his detractors claimed, did little to alleviate the extreme poverty that the majority of Ecuadorians experienced. To his credit, Plaza did not overreact to these charges and the Ecuadorian press enjoyed more freedom than ever before. The most serious political opposition to Plaza came from a new left-wing populist political party, the Concentración de Fuerzas Populares (Concentration of Popular Forces or CFP). The leader of CFP was Carlos Guevara Moreno, a radical leftist, once a student activist at the University of Guayaquil, a veteran of the Spanish Civil War, and a former member of a European Communist Party. Guevara Moreno briefly served as minister of government during the second Velazquista but soon split with the populist *caudillo.* In 1950 Guevara Moreno attempted to overthrow the Plaza government and this abortive coup resulted in his imprisonment for 14 months. Elected mayor of Guayaquil in 1951, he used this office to promote the CFP agenda and to offer a populist alternative to Velasco Ibarra. The CFP became a major force in coastal politics but Guevara Moreno was unable to spread its influence into the sierra.[6]

Plaza's greatest contribution to Ecuador was his uncanny ability to navigate the minefield of Ecuadorian politics. He became the first president in 28 years to complete a constitutional term. He was also determined to hand over the presidency to his successor through the electoral process.

THE ELECTION OF 1952: THE RETURN OF THE GREAT ABSENTEE

As the 1952 campaign began, three colorless candidates emerged. The Conservatives nominated Ruperto Alarcón Falconí, president of the Chamber of Deputies, while the Liberal Party put forth José R. Chiriboga Villagómez, the incumbent mayor of Quito. As usual, the traditional parties were not very unified and some Liberals joined with the Socialists to form the Alianza Democrática Nacional (National Democratic Alliance or ADN) to support the candidacy of Eduardo Salazar Gómez, the minister of government under Plaza.

Following his removal from the presidency in 1947, Velasco Ibarra had gone into self-imposed exile in Argentina, where he lived an austere existence as an adjunct professor surviving on additional income from lectures and occasional meager payments from the regime of Juan Perón. During this period he became known as *El Gran Ausente* (The Great Absentee), or the "political cadaver," as it appeared he had little hope of regaining power in Ecuador for a third time. This assessment proved to be far off the mark. Simón Cañarte, a wealthy newspaper publisher from Guayaquil, considered a bet from a friend that Velasco Ibarra could easily defeat the three candidates. Intrigued, Cañarte not only accepted the bet of five dollars, he announced it in *La nación,* his widely circulated Guayaquil newspaper. When favorable responses flooded the paper's mail room, Cañarte decided to support Velasco Ibarra by financing his campaign. He also used his newspapers to push the Great Absentee's platform. The ultra-right-wing party, Acción Revolución Nacionalista Ecuatoriana (Ecuadorian Nationalist Revolutionary Action party or ARNE), modeled after the Spanish Falange, became another source of Velasco Ibarra's support despite his denunciation of all political parties. Guevara Moreno, who had his own presidential ambitions, decided to throw the support of CFP behind the man who now claimed to be "The National Personification."

Velasco Ibarra returned and once more proved that he was a master campaigner. He traveled throughout the country, appearing in small hamlets as well as the larger towns and cities. He promised to transform Ecuador by providing honest government and public works. In one town he promised to build a school, a hospital, and a bridge. When a member of the audience reminded him that the town did not have a river, Velasco Ibarra responded, "My dears, you shall have a river, too!" Velasco Ibarra won the election handily with 153,934 votes to Alarcón's 118,165 and Chiriboga's 67,306.

THE THIRD VELASQUISMO

The third presidency of José María Velasco Ibarra was unique, primarily because he actually completed his constitutional term. Despite this accomplishment, the popular *caudillo* encountered many problems during his four years as president. As his principal biographer states, "Peace and unity did not come during Velasco's third administration. It was not due to unrest among the masses, however, but rather to the ambitions of their would be *caudillos*. The next four years were characterized by constant political infighting which provoked numerous ministerial crises and led to the alienation of popular support. Political imprisonment, the closing of newspapers, attempted coups, and other types of violence seemed to be the order of the day."[7] Among Velasco Ibarra's problems was his refusal to form a political party or to acknowledge that he owed his election to conservative Velasquistas of the highlands, ARNE, the liberal Velaquistas of the coast, and the CFP, groups that hated each other.

Once in office, Velasco Ibarra began to settle old scores. His first target was Guevara Moreno, who in the final days of the campaign had withdrawn his support. Anti-Velasco street demonstrations in Guayaquil were used as a pretext to send Guevara Moreno and many of his lieutenants into exile. The disproportionate influence of ARNE within the administration soon drew the ire of the Liberals. These conflicts resulted in a revolving-door cabinet that experienced numerous resignations, firings, and hirings. In a strange turn of events, Velasco Ibarra turned to Camilo Ponce Enríquez, leader of the Partido Democrático Cristiano (Christian Democratic Party or PDC) to be minister of government. Ponce and the minister of defense, Carlos Julio Arosemena Monroy, disagreed on almost every issue and contributed to the constant state of turmoil that engulfed the government.

Velasco Ibarra was intolerant of criticism, especially from the press, and he soon reversed the freedom that had been enjoyed during the Plaza government. He even turned on Cañarte, when his former sponsor dared to criticize him, by closing down *La nación* and *La hora*. Even Quito's venerable daily,

El comercio, was shuttered after refusing to publish a government manifesto denouncing the paper and journalists in general. The censorship of *El comercio* resulted in worldwide condemnation in numerous newspapers and by the Inter-American Press Society. The most egregious offense occurred in 1955 when Alejandro Carrión, a columnist who wrote under the pen name Juan Sin Cielo for *El universo,* the popular Guayaquil paper, was severely beaten after penning a series of exposés revealing widespread corruption in the national police. The government did virtually nothing to track down and prosecute the perpetrators.

Velasco Ibarra also had opponents in the military and survived a serious coup attempt by his minister of defense, Lieutenant Colonel Reinaldo Varea Donoso, in late December 1953. Numerous student demonstrations and street protests disrupted his third administration. These were often dealt with harshly by the police and resulted in a number of shootings.

Despite the political turmoil there were also accomplishments during the third Velasquismo. Velasco expanded the highway system with the addition of 835 miles of new roads and another 634 miles of existing roads that were improved, including 378 miles that were paved. His administration completed 311 new schools and started 104 more, a significant increase over Plaza's 123. The Junta Nacional de Planificación (National Planning Committee or JNP) was Velasco Ibarra's most long-lasting achievement. The JNP coordinated national development plans for electrification, land reform, and promotion of commerce and industry.

Velasco Ibarra increased military spending from 15 percent of the national budget to 22 percent, justifying the increase as necessary for defense against Peru. It was also a way to improve his chances of completing his term. All these programs resulted in deficit spending and by 1956 Ecuador's creditworthiness had sharply declined despite the banana boom.

THE ELECTIONS OF 1956

Velasco Ibarra was constitutionally ineligible to run for another term and he reluctantly accepted that restriction. He decided to throw his support to his former minister of government, Camilo Ponce. Ponce formed a temporary coalition party, Alianza Popular (Popular Alliance or AP), consisting of his own party, Movimiento Social Cristiano (Social Christian Movement or MSC), ARNE, and the traditional Conservative Party. Some Liberals once again combined forces with the Socialists and formed the Frente Democrático Nacional (Democratic National Front or FDN) and nominated Raúl Clemente Huerta, a leftist Guayaquil professor. The mainstream Liberals nominated José Chiriboga Villagómez, while the CFP dutifully supported Guevara Moreno.

Velasco Ibarra threw his support to Ponce because he was the least objectionable of the candidates to the *caudillo*. In reality, Velasco Ibarra campaigned against the other three, especially Huerta and the FDN, which he considered an insult to his legacy. The Catholic establishment strongly supported Ponce, and this, along with Velasco Ibarra's tirades against the others, proved to be decisive. Ponce defeated Huerta by a razor-thin margin of just 3,000 votes.

PONCE AND THE RETURN OF CONSERVATIVE GOVERNMENT

Camilo Ponce was from a long-standing Conservative highland family; many of his ancestors had long been involved in Ecuadorian politics. His first challenge came from Velasco Ibarra on the evening of his inauguration. Velasco delayed his arrival at the ceremony for 90 minutes as crowds gathered chanting, "Velasco sí, ¡Ponce no!" Evidently, he was hoping for a groundswell of last-minute support so that he could initiate an *autogolpe*. When Velasco Ibarra ascertained that he did not have the support of the armed forces, he proceeded to transfer the presidential sash to Ponce, a man he now detested. Thus Ponce faced immense problems including limited popular support, a complete lack of respect by the Liberals, and a nation brought to the brink of bankruptcy by Velasco Ibarra's deficit spending.[8]

Ponce proved to be an effective, if somewhat colorless, leader, but that was what was needed in the aftermath of the third Velasquismo. He mollified the Liberals and the Socialists by including them in his government, thereby limiting political attacks on his government to the Velaquistas and the Great Absentee. This resulted in a calming of the political waters. Ponce did continue to spend freely, acquiring a national airline, building a steel mill, and expanding existing industries. A large project was undertaken to make Guayaquil a deepwater port and to eliminate the need for lighters to load ships. Ecuador supported the improvement of portions of the Pan American Highway and the completion of a rail link from Ibarra to San Lorenzo. New public buildings, including the Social Security Building, were erected in Quito. The Ponce government and the city prepared to host the 11th Inter-American Conference in 1960 by constructing a new conference center and the Hotel Intercontinental. To finance many of these projects, Ponce secured loans from the World Bank and the Import Export Bank. Unfortunately for Ponce and Ecuador, the banana boom was waning. Conservatives were disappointed with Ponce because of his continuance of deficit spending and his failure to reestablish Catholic influence in public education. Ponce's other achievement was to fully complete his term. Unfortunately this example would not be heeded and Ecuador soon devolved into its characteristic political turmoil.

THE ELECTIONS OF 1960

Ecuador's flirtation with democracy came to a dramatic end with the ugly and violent 1960 presidential campaign among four candidates. Antonio Parra Velasco, rector of the University of Guayaquil and a radical socialist, headed a newly created party, Movimiento de la Segunda Independencia (Movement of the Second Independence or MSI). Gonzalo Cordero Crespo, a former minister of social welfare, was the Conservative Party choice, while former president Galo Plaza led the moderate liberal coalition, Frente Democrático Nacional (National Democratic Front or FDN). Velasco Ibarra returned to make his fourth bid for the presidency and, as usual, proclaimed himself to be independent of any political party. One of his supporters was Cañarte who, despite the closing of his papers during the third Velasquismo, decided to back the aging *caudillo*.

There was trouble from the start. On March 19 Velasco Ibarra's speech at the Bolívar monument in downtown Quito was interrupted by gunfire, killing seven bystanders and wounding scores of others. Police dispersed the crowd with tear gas. Velasco Ibarra blamed Ponce and Plaza even though there were no Velasquistas among the dead or wounded. Velasquistas went on a rampage, attacking Plaza's Quito residence and vandalizing anti-Velasco papers and radio stations. Conservatives smeared Velasco Ibarra's personal life, denouncing his divorce, questioning the legality of his second marriage, and accusing him of being a Freemason. In return Velasquistas denounced Plaza as a stooge of the United Fruit Company and an agent of the United States government. Velasco Ibarra won his greatest electoral victory with 323,585 votes to Plaza's 175,076, Cordero's 172,690, and Parra's 46,173. The campaign was so bitter and personal that Ponce refused to attend the inauguration of his successor. He resigned shortly before the ceremony and sent the vice president to transfer power to Velasco Ibarra, a man he once supported and served but whom he now held in contempt.

THE FOURTH VELASQUISMO

Velasco Ibarra showed incredible energy for his age as he donned the presidential sash for the fourth time on September 1, 1960. The first months of his presidency saw a whirlwind of initiatives and spending. The Institute of Electrification was founded to create a national plan to bring electricity to most of the country. He established the Banco Ecuatoriano de la Vivienda (Ecuadorian Housing Bank) to provide low-cost housing for the poor. The government set up health dispensaries for the poor in Quito and Guayaquil and dispatched mobile health units to rural areas. Almacenes de Subsistencias (Stores of Basic Foodstuffs) provided groceries at reduced prices to the impoverished.

Sixty-five schools were built in 10 months and ground broken for 86 more. The president personally approved hundreds of community projects and allocated money to get them under way. Every Thursday morning he invited the public to present personal petitions and he passed out small gifts to the needy for several hours.

Velasco Ibarra renewed the territorial dispute with Peru on September 29, 1960, when he directed Ecuador's ambassador to the United Nations to declare the 1942 Río Protocol null and void before the General Assembly. This was a sharp departure from Ecuador's policy, started during the Plaza administration, to seek a revision to the protocol to gain access to the Amazon but to accept the major provisions. Ecuador cited declarations from the First Pan American Congress of 1889, the Seventh Inter-American Conference of 1939, and the charter of the Organization of American States, which stated that territorial cessions resulting from war or the threat of war were invalid. Of course Peru denounced the announcement. The guarantors of the agreement, the United States, Argentina, Brazil, and Chile, announced that the protocol was valid and urged the two nations to continue to negotiate the details of the final demarcation of the border in the Cordillera del Cóndor area. Ecuador did not have the military resources to force Peru to consider territorial concessions but the declaration stirred nationalism and brought the controversy to the fore for the next four decades. It also signaled the beginning of increased tension with the United States.

Another event indicating the deterioration of relations between the United States and Ecuador was the indefinite postponement of the 11th Inter-American Conference scheduled in Quito in 1961. The United States did not want Ecuador to present its nullity argument because Peru had announced it would boycott the conference if the validity of the Río Protocol was placed on the agenda. In addition, the United States was fearful that the regime of Fidel Castro would have an excellent forum to spout revolutionary propaganda. The postponement of the conference diminished Ecuador's international prestige and proved a deep disappointment to the city of Quito.

Velasco Ibarra was one of the few leaders in the hemisphere to question the intention of President John F. Kennedy's Alliance of Progress, which promised an increase in U.S. aid to assist in development. The United States also believed that Ecuador was overly supportive of Castro's Cuba and sent Special Ambassador Adlai Stevenson to talk to Velasco Ibarra. The talk did not go well and the Ecuadorian president bluntly stated that Ecuador would not bow to pressure and would continue its relationship with Cuba.

Ecuador also explored establishing ties with the Soviet Union in hopes of countering the influence of the United States, gaining support for its position on the Río Protocol, and obtaining additional economic assistance.

Talks were started with the Soviet ambassador to Mexico for the exchange of commercial missions. Carlos Julio Arosemena Monroy, Ecuador's vice president, went to Moscow in June 1961 and a Soviet delegation came to Quito in August to discuss the establishment of full diplomatic relations. At the same time, Ecuador expressed sympathy for Cuba and denounced U.S. policy toward the Castro government. On the other hand, Ecuador expressed alarm at the growing Soviet influence in Cuba and was dismayed when Castro announced that he was indeed a Marxist-Leninist.

THE FALL OF THE FOURTH VELASQUISMO

While Velasco Ibarra pleased some of the masses and stirred Ecuadorian patriotism, he could not sustain the popularity that he had enjoyed during his absences and the recent campaign. His movement suffered from a number of inherent weaknesses that would contribute to its doom. The Velasquista movement lacked homogeneity and contained too many contentious factions including Communists, Liberals, Conservatives, and fascists. These groups had little in common except that they hoped to control Velasco Ibarra. Ambitious subordinates wanted to be the new face of the movement as they anticipated the 67-year-old *caudillo's* retirement, including Carlos Julio Arosemena Monroy, the vice president, who would soon openly split with the president. Velasco Ibarra had survived by handing out patronage to his followers but there were no more government jobs left. He had fired civil servants and replaced them with Velasquistas, but those displaced were angry and vengeful. Despite his personal honesty, his government was known to be corrupt. The economy, already in trouble when he assumed the presidency, was in free fall by August of 1961. Inflation was high, revenues plummeted, and Ecuador's reserves dropped. The government responded by raising existing taxes and implementing new ones on essentials including meat, wheat, rice, and electricity. Velasco's pro-Cuba policy, coupled with his desire to establish relations with the Soviet Union, resulted in problems within Ecuador. Cardinal de la Torre, long a critic of the government and the military, became even more vocal. The army was upset about disparaging remarks made by the minister of defense, and resented forced retirements and demotions that had been mandated for officers who were not sycophants of the president. "In eleven months the administration had alienated practically every source of political support."[9]

The volatile political atmosphere was especially evident in the Ecuadorian Congress. The most bizarre incident occurred on October 16, 1961, when Vice President Arosemena, who was also the president of the congress, responded to heckling from the audience by ordering the balconies cleared. Shots rang out and Arosemena dove behind the lectern, pulled out a revolver, and returned fire. He soon exited through a side door. Luckily no one was hurt in the melee, possibly due to the level of alcohol consumed by the shooters, especially Arosemena, whose fondness for fine Scotch in large quantities was well known.

Strikes called by the Confederación de Trabajadores Ecuatorianos (Confederation of Ecuadorian Workers, CTE) soon paralyzed the nation. The government responded with repression and the arrest of three members of congress. Students joined the labor unions and violence occurred in Guayaquil when the police fired on demonstrators, killing 11. Arosemena used the arrest of congressmen and the actions of the police to declare, "In this moment in which the Constitution is broken, he who represents the Constitution of the Country is the President of the National Congress in the name of the National Congress."[10] Velasco Ibarra responded to this challenge by declaring that Arosemena was no longer the vice president. Velasco then surrounded the legislative palace with tanks. Arosemena was placed under arrest and taken to jail where he declared, while being booked, "Carlos Julio Arosemena, 42 years of age, Vice President of the Republic and tomorrow Constitutional President."[11] On November 7 air force units rebelled and were soon joined by the navy. Velasco Ibarra rushed to rally support from the army but found little or none. The following day he sought political asylum in the Mexican Embassy and was soon whisked out of Ecuador into yet another exile. Congress declared Arosemena the constitutional president with the military's support.

Arosemena's adroit rise to power also proved to be ephemeral as his presidency was short-lived. While he calmed the immediate crisis by appointing a representative cabinet, he soon found himself in deep political trouble. His open sympathy for the Cuban Revolution and his decision to have Ecuador vote against the expulsion of Cuba from the OAS in January 1962 raised eyebrows in Washington. Another problem was the inclusion of alleged communists in his administration. There were also reports that a communist insurgency was brewing and the government was doing nothing to oppose it. The president's personal behavior while intoxicated caused embarrassing incidents at both public and private events. There was also the possibility that Velasco Ibarra would return and run for president in 1964. All these factors contributed to cries by the press, conservatives, and other opposition groups for his removal from office. In the meantime elements of the Ecuadorian military met to clandestinely plan a coup. The final straw for the Ecuadorian military came on July 10, 1963, when the obviously inebriated president made disparaging remarks about the United States at a state dinner attended by the U.S. ambassador. On July 11 a mechanized regiment surrounded the Presidential Palace in the center of Quito and demanded Arosemena's resignation. After a brief standoff the president was relieved of his revolver, taken to the airport, and flown to exile in Panama. The military announced that the president would not be replaced by a civilian or even a military man. Instead a military junta was formed with the intention of governing the country for an extended period.

MILITARY RULE, 1963–66

The military junta of 1963 used the famous July Revolution of 1925 as its model and explained that its intervention was not only to end the chaos created by Velasco Ibarra and Arosemena but "to promote a new socioeconomic structure that would permit the state to comply with its function of serving the common interest of its citizens, thus laying the foundation for true democracy."[12] However, prior to initiating reforms, the junta spent nearly 12 months clearing Arosemena's supporters from the government and subduing leftist radicals. Structural reforms began in mid-1964 were heavily influenced by the Alliance for Progress and the infusion of $84.5 million in U.S. aid. A new tax system was at the forefront of the reforms. The junta eliminated 1,216 different local and regional taxes that had been collected to fund autonomous public institutions. In other words, the junta attempted to end pork-barrel spending or earmarked allocations that had been used for decades to gain the support of local or regional elite groups. Moreover, tax collection was centralized through the Central Bank of Ecuador, thus removing accounting for funds from the autonomous institutions and also diminishing the opportunity for fraud and corruption. While this was a noble endeavor, the institutions and their supporters launched vehement protests. The junta responded by imposing martial law and press censorship.[13]

The junta announced the Agrarian Reform Law in July 1964 with the intent to break up the large landed estates in the highlands and redistribute some of the land to agricultural laborers. While some inefficient estates were dismembered, many sierra landowners retained title to the most productive acres. Many of the landowners were glad to relinquish marginal lands and with it responsibility for the indigenous people who had worked there for decades. In addition, the law abolished the *huasipungo* labor system that had long been an embarrassment to progressive elements in Ecuador. *Huasipungo* was a form of tenancy that existed for centuries in the Andean region; it relegated indigenous agricultural labors to a type of medieval serfdom. Despite these advantages, the elite strongly opposed the regime's implementation of this modest land reform program.

Business interests from both the coast and the sierra also opposed the regime because of a downward spiral in the economy in 1964 and 1965 when the growth rate dropped from an annual rate of 8 percent to 3 percent. As government revenues diminished, the junta imposed high import duties. The

Chambers of Commerce in Guayaquil and Quito orchestrated a general strike that other business organizations, students, and labor unions joined. Faced with growing public unrest and frustrated that most elements of Ecuadorian society rejected its reforms, the military yielded power to a civilian, Clemente Yerovi Indaburo, who served as interim president from March to November 1966. The military had made modest social reforms, most notably overhauling the tax system and ending *huasipungo*. To its credit, the junta spent more on education and public works than on arms. However, it failed to rally public support and lacked the political apparatus to organize such support. In the end the military feared a loss of prestige stemming from a realization that "Ecuador is a difficult country to govern."

THE FIFTH AND FINAL VELASQUISTA, 1968–72

The collapse of the military junta led to the formation, in October 1966, of a constituent assembly to restore Ecuador to constitutional rule. In addition to drafting yet another constitution, the assembly selected Otto Arosemena Gómez to replace Yerovi Indaburo as president until the next elections in 1968. As the 1968 election season neared, the front runner appeared to be Assad Bucaram, the radical populist leader of the CFP. Under Bucaram's leadership, the CFP had been expanding its influence from its traditional coastal base into the highlands, where it was starting to win adherents. However, the surprising return of the aging Dr. Velasco Ibarra left no hope for Bucaram, who decided to wait until 1972. The National Personification returned in March from his long exile in Argentina and immediately demonstrated that, even at age 75 he had lost little of his ability to mesmerize the masses. Some political observers, on the other hand, felt that the old *caudillo* had little appeal to the modern and mature Ecuadorian voter. The Conservative party put forth another former president, Camilo Ponce, who had once been a Velasquista and not untypically had also been an anti-Velasquista. Once again the Liberals turned to Andrés F. Córdova, who was one year older than Velasco Ibarra. While Velasco demonstrated that he could mount a vigorous campaign, his appeal was not nearly as strong as it had been in 1960. It was sufficient, however, to win the presidency for the fifth time: Velasco Ibarra defeated his nearest rival by more than 20,000 votes.

Velasco Ibarra faced three major obstacles as he once again attempted to govern Ecuador. First was the stunning fact that his electoral margin of victory was razor-thin and he had no coattails, which meant that his National Velasquista Front did not dominate congress. Second, the economy was in the doldrums and his deficit spending on numerous public works would soon make it worse. As always, there were great expectations that he would actually fulfill his many campaign promises and that the income from recent petroleum discoveries in the Oriente would enable this to be accomplished. Finally, there was the problem that Velasco Ibarra was Velasco Ibarra; as time would prove, the fiery populist had not yet learned to be an elder statesman.

Velasco Ibarra used Ecuador's potential for oil production to increase spending and to borrow heavily. He wanted to control all spending but the proliferation of 1,300 autonomous public institutions prevented this, as they were directly funded. The president faced the same problem that had plagued the military junta: the public institutions had been established to provide local political leaders with a slice of the budget without interference from the central government. In addition, they were used as a sort of check and balance on patronage of the president and his cronies. Velasco Ibarra was frustrated with the restriction and issued emergency decrees, claiming that they were necessary under his emergency powers as the executive. The Supreme Court disagreed and overturned the decrees by ruling them unconstitutional.

On June 22, 1970, with the encouragement of the military, Velasco Ibarra staged an *autogolpe* and assumed dictatorial powers. He dismissed Congress and the Supreme Court but the *caudillo* promised to remain in power only until the end of his term in 1972. He moved rapidly to implement his economic plan by devaluing the sucre by 28 percent, establishing a national sales tax, and abolishing nearly half of the public institutions. He also closed the universities and sent Assad Bucaram and other opposition leaders into exile. For a time Ecuador's economy improved.

As the 1972 elections drew near, Bucaram was allowed to return to Ecuador and polls indicated that he would be a certain winner in the presidential race. At the same time Ecuador's petroleum boom gushed and the country suddenly was enjoying prosperity and a surge in revenues. These developments should have been good news for Velasco Ibarra, who was nearing the end of his term. However, the military and business interests feared that Assad Bucaram would win the election and then proceed to mismanage the nation's newfound wealth. On February 15, 1972, the army, navy, and air force, led by General Guillermo Rodríguez Lara, seized power. The era of Velasco Ibarra had come to its sad and inevitable end as he fled to Buenos Aires. He would return to his homeland in early 1979 to bury Corina, his beloved wife. He remained in Quito until his death on March 30, 1979, at the age of 86. The military would again establish a junta to run the country and again the men in uniform would learn what Velasco Ibarra had long understood—"Ecuador is a very difficult country to govern."

NOTES

1. Steve Striffler, *In the Shadows of State and Capital: The United Fruit Company, Popular Struggle, and Agrarian Restructuring In Ecuador, 1900–1995* (Durham, NC: Duke University Press, 2002), 29.

2. David Schodt, *Ecuador: An Andean Enigma* (Boulder, CO: Westview Press, 1987), 55–66.

3. India is the world's leading producer of bananas, but most of its yield is for domestic consumption.

4. George Blanksten, *Ecuador: Constitutions and Caudillos* (New York: Russell and Russell, 1964), 81.

5. Ibid., 77.

6. Schodt, *Ecuador: An Andean Enigma*, 76–80.

7. Robert M. Norris, "José María Velasco Ibarra: A Charismatic Figure in Ecuadorean Politics, 1934–1961," PhD dissertation, University of New Mexico, 1969, 306.

8. John D. Martz, *Ecuador: Conflicting Political Culture and the Quest for Progress* (Boston: Allyn and Bacon, 1972), 72.

9. Norris, "José María Velasco Ibarra," 308.

10. Ibid., 419.

11. Ibid., 421.

12. Schodt, *Ecuador: An Andean Enigma*, 83.

13. Ibid., 83–84.

8

The Oil Boom, Military Reformers, and a Second Democratic Parenthesis, 1972–96

In 1967 the Texaco Gulf Consortium discovered vast deposits of oil in Sucumbíos Province in remote northeastern Ecuador. The discovery, followed by the exploitation of the fields, resulted in a third economic boom. Like the previous booms (cacao 1890–1914 and bananas 1948–60), this economic upsurge brought dramatic changes. This export product was located in the Oriente instead of on the coast, the traditional center of Ecuador's export-driven economy. An oil rush resulted in the creation of the boom town of Nueva Loja. The 312-mile Trans Ecuadorian Pipeline, completed in 1972, linked the fields to the Pacific port of Balbao and soon transported 360,000 barrels of Ecuadorian crude daily. The construction of the pipeline, service roads, oil rigs, and worker's facilities altered the previously pristine environment and, in some cases, wreaked ecological havoc. Quito became the center of the oil boom, grew dramatically, and soon rivaled Guayaquil in commercial activity. Public expenditures increased at 12 percent per year and rose to 33 percent of GDP; oil accounted for 50 percent of all government revenue. Ecuador's economic output in the 1970s was impressive, for it increased from $4.3 billion to $10.1 billion, a growth rate of 233 percent. Ecuadorians soon benefited from this newfound prosperity as the government initiated development projects and provided subsidies for essential products such as cooking fuel. The upper and middle classes enjoyed a reduction in taxes.[1]

THE MILITARY REFORM GOVERNMENT

The military government, headed by Army General Guillermo Rodríguez Lara, announced that it would be a long-term reform-minded regime that would spur development. It was a propitious opportunity to make structural changes as oil revenues provided the government with financial independence and thus diminished the power of the oligarchy. "Those who directed Ecuador saw oil as an opportunity to modernize, a means to escape both underdevelopment and poverty, and a way to build a dynamic, developed and industrialized society."[2] The military men were also committed to modernizing their own institution and allocated 45 percent of all revenues to the armed forces. The various services created their own industries. For example the navy built FLOPEC, a fleet of oil transport ships, while the air force established TAME, a domestic airline. Of course, all the services purchased modern weapons systems.

The Rodríguez Lara government took firm control of the economy and soon consolidated its hold on power. It launched an anticorruption campaign and tried former president Otto Arosemena for corruption. Velasco and Bucaram supporters were likewise indicted or harassed. However laudable, these measures failed to generate widespread popular support for Rodríguez Lara or his government.

The public did welcome a flurry of infrastructure improvements that included highway, sanitation, electrification, potable water, and medical services projects. In addition to military enterprises, the state launched and assumed ownership of industries in petroleum, transportation, communications, and public utilities. The government created thousands of other public sector jobs and provided enhanced job opportunities to the middle class. The government hoped that its import substitution plan would stimulate manufacturing, increase domestic employment, and above all else, prevent social unrest. Later high tariffs protected the fledgling industries, and the Committee for Economic Planning and Coordination announced a five-year plan.

The regime moved quickly to take control of the petroleum industry by establishing the Ecuadorian State Petroleum Corporation, CEPE, later renamed Petroecuador. Ecuador proudly joined the Organization of Petroleum Exporting Nations, OPEC, in 1973. Gustavo Jarrín Ampudia, the minister of resources, was soon elected president of OPEC, a tremendous national honor for Ecuador, which accounted for barely 1 percent of OPEC's oil production. The regime hoped to increase its share of national oil earnings to fund

Street vendors and their colorful wares can be found in every
Ecuadorian town. (Courtesy of the author)

development. To accomplish this the government put pressure on the Texaco-
Gulf consortium for a larger slice of the pie by proposing that CEPE become
the majority stockholder. The oil giants balked and cut back production, which
resulted in the loss of hundreds of millions of dollars during the nine-month
period from October 1974 to July 1975. In the end the government realized it
had overplayed its hand and cut taxes on the oil firm's exports.

While the state-directed economy produced some improvements, market
forces soon derailed the five-year plan. Inflation rose steadily and reached

22 percent in 1974, erasing the gains of the middle class. When the export sector faltered in response to the regime's oil policy, imports increased. The government increased tariffs in an attempt to bring down inflation and improve the balance of trade, but succeeded only in causing a sharp downturn in imports, also a source of taxes. The business community in Guayaquil was particularly hard-hit and began to clamor for relief. Another problem was the use of projected petroleum revenues as collateral to secure loans to fund many of the infrastructure projects. Ecuador's oil reserves turned out to be not even remotely as large as those of Venezuela or Saudi Arabia, despite what some analysts had predicted. Rodríguez Lara's government had overspent, overborrowed, overpromised, and been overly generous with subsidies and public sector job creation. When the bubble burst in 1975, the public blamed the military as an institution for failing to fulfill its social contract any differently than civilian politicians had in the past. Within the military establishment doubts grew about Rodríguez Lara's leadership. More importantly, officers began to question whether their institution should continue to govern and how much damage would be done to its reputation if they persisted in doing so.

On September 1, 1975, General Raúl González Alvear led a bloody but unsuccessful coup to force Rodríguez Lara from power. Thirty troops were killed in the encounter, which deeply fractured the military. Rodríguez Lara was unable to restore unity within the armed forces and was eased out of power on January 11, 1976, in a bloodless coup orchestrated by the commanders of the army, navy, and air force. A Supreme Council designated the commander of the Ecuadorian navy, Vice Admiral Alfredo Poveda Burbano, as president. Poveda Burbano governed with two other council members, army general Guillermo Durán and air force general Luis Leoro Franco. The generals decided to transition Ecuador to a civilian government in an attempt to reclaim esteem for their now discredited institution. They moved cautiously as commissions were formed to draft two proposed constitutions and new election laws. The process took three years and nine months.

A new constitution was drafted and the 1945 constitution was dusted off and revised. The two charters were presented to the electorate on January 15, 1978. Forty-four percent of Ecuadorians preferred the new constitution. However, 23 percent of voters voided their ballots to show their disapproval of both documents, or perhaps their support for a continuance of the military regime. Thirty-one percent of the population voted for the revised 1945 constitution. Despite the rejection by a majority of the electorate, the new constitution proved to be a workable and progressive document. It recognized the role of the state in economic development, created a unicameral legislature, limited the president to a four-year term with no immediate reelection, and provided for universal suffrage, including illiterates.

THE SECOND DEMOCRATIC
PARENTHESIS, 1979–96

Whether intended or not, the military regime's decision to return Ecuador to civilian constitutional government ushered in a 17-year period of political stability and democratic government. Open elections drew record participation and international observers characterized them as fair and free. In addition, there were peaceful transfers of power from one side of the political spectrum to the other on three occasions. Moreover, the one serious attempt to remove a president by force failed. It seemed that Ecuador, at last, had reached political maturity.

THE 1978 AND 1979 ELECTIONS

One reason for the military's prolonged hold on power after removing Rodríguez Lara in 1976 was the fear that the populist rabble-rouser Assad Bucaram of the Concentration of Popular Forces (CFP) would be elected president, but the Supreme Council declared him ineligible on a technicality. Bucaram then selected Jaime Roldós as his stand-in. Anxious to win an election, Roldós chose Osvaldo Hurtado, the leader of the Christian Democratic Party, as his running mate. Despite CFP's attempt to broaden its support by adding Hurtado to the ticket, most observers expected Rodrigo Borja of the moderate socialist Izquierda Democrática (Democratic Left-ID) party to prevail. Another major contender was Sixto Durán Ballén of the National Constitutional Front, a right-leaning coalition. The first round was held on July 16, 1978, and Roldós was the surprise winner with 27 percent of the vote. Almost as shocking was Sixto Durán's second-place finish with 24 percent. Under the new constitution Roldós and Durán had to compete in a second round. The election was not scheduled until April 1979 and the intervening nine-month campaign was filled with tension. The government hoped that the extensive interval would provide time for Durán to organize an effective campaign and win. It was not to be, for on April 29, 1979, the Roldós- Hurtado ticket won in a monumental landslide with 68.5 percent of the vote. The size of the victory convinced the military to move forward with democratization but with certain conditions. There was to be no investigation of possible human rights abuses during military rule and certain state corporations would remain under military control.

A PRESIDENCY CUT SHORT: THE
TRAGEDY OF JAIME ROLDÓS

At the August 10, 1979, inauguration of Roldós, Admiral Poveda Burbano lauded the accomplishments of seven years of military government, including a 540 percent expansion in the budget and a 500 percent increase in per capita income. He also listed many infrastructure improvement projects and the development of new industries. While it was true that the military technocrats had improved Ecuador's economic output and in some instances had raised the standard of living for many Ecuadorians, they had failed to solve the problems of regionalism and personalism or to resolve the power struggles between the presidency and the congress that historically plagued the country.[3]

Roldós was soon challenged by his former mentor, Assad Bucaram, who became president of congress. Roldós adroitly built a new power base independent of Bucaram's CFP and won several congressional victories. He also initiated some significant social reforms including a reduction of the work week from 44 hours to 40, a doubling of the minimum wage, and establishment of retirement for women after 25 years of work. As commander in chief he presided during a brief but bloody encounter with Peru over the disputed border. On May 24, 1981, President Roldós, his wife, the minister of defense, and a number of military men died in an airplane crash in Loja Province in the south. Intense speculation surrounded the crash, leading to rumors that the president had been murdered by either his political opponents, the U.S. Central Intelligence Agency, the Ecuadorian military, or the government of Peru. However, an investigation by the Ecuadorian air force concluded pilot fatigue caused the tragedy. The incident might have fueled a crisis and a possible *golpe,* but this was avoided by a rare phenomenon in Ecuador: strict adherence to the constitution! Vice President Osvaldo Hurtado was immediately sworn in as Ecuador's new president with no objections from the military, the congress, or the people.

THE HURTADO PRESIDENCY

Hurtado faced the daunting task of replacing the popular Roldós just as the oil boom ended. The national debt had soared to $7 billion, fed by massive borrowing during the three previous governments. Moreover, Ecuador's oil reserves dwindled under the pressure of increased domestic consumption and production problems. Additional fields proved elusive. The situation worsened in 1983 with the arrival of El Niño, an unusually warm Pacific current that caused severe flooding in coastal areas. The floods damaged or destroyed roads, bridges, levees, shrimp farms, tuna processing plants, and banana plantations, causing $640 million in damage and a $300 million loss in exports. By 1983 the economy had a negative growth rate of 3.3 percent and inflation climbed to 52.5 percent, the highest in Ecuador's history.[4]

Hurtado was able to deal with the constantly shifting party alignments in Congress and was further helped when Assad Bucaram died in November 1981. He also moved to the center and realized he had to deal with Ecuador's faltering economy. He orchestrated the passage of Law 101, an amendment to the 1978 Hydrocarbons Act that allowed CEPE to sign contracts with private companies for petroleum exploration and production. This legislation attracted much-needed foreign investment and increased petroleum output by 12 percent. Nevertheless, Hurtado faced growing opposition from the business sector and organized labor. In 1983, falling oil prices and natural disasters caused the economy to come to a standstill. Private banks stopped lending money to Ecuador and Hurtado turned to the International Monetary Fund to renegotiate Ecuador's external debt. Hurtado initiated austerity measures, cutting back on public spending and investments and devaluing the sucre by 21 percent. As expected, the business sector reacted by closing down commerce while labor unions organized strikes. Hurtado survived the crisis when leaders of the Frente Unitario de Trabajadores (United Worker's Front or FUT), Ecuador's largest labor organization, realized that strikes might result in a military takeover. The FUT reached an agreement with the government to suspend labor unrest. Businessmen also reached an accommodation with the government as it assumed some of the burden of the private sector's dollar debts. In addition, the business sector believed they could elect their own man in the 1984 election and also wanted to avoid military intervention.[5]

Hurtado obtained some modest social advances, including a new labor code for rural workers, worker representation on corporate boards, and improved literacy, but his greatest accomplishment was completing Roldós's term and overseeing a smooth transition to a second democratically elected government. Although an accidental president, he demonstrated calm leadership in the aftermath of the tragic death of Roldós and guided Ecuador during a very difficult time.

THE 1984 ELECTIONS

The Ecuadorian right unified for the 1984 election by forming the Frente de Reconstrucción (National Reconstruction Front) with León Febres Cordero as its standard bearer. The Democratic Left once again backed Rodrigo Borja. Other major candidates included Angel Durante of CFP and Jaime Hurtado of Movimiento Democrático Popular (Popular Democratic Movement, MPD). Borja and Cordero ran neck and neck in the first round, with the former garnering 28.7 percent and the latter 27.2 percent of the votes. In the second round Febres Cordero shifted his strategy from one of right-wing ideologue to populist advocate promising "pan, techo, y empleo" (bread, housing, and jobs).[6] He also quietly reassured his supporters in the business community that he would support a free market economy. Febres Cordero won an overwhelming victory in his native Guayaquil and Guayas Province, took four other nearby provinces, and defeated Borja by obtaining 51.5 percent of the vote. The election was historic as it was the first victory for conservatives since 1956, the first time illiterates could vote in a presidential election, and the first transfer of power to an opposition candidate under the new constitution.

FEBRES CORDERO: A NEOLIBERAL AGENDA

León Febres Cordero was from an elite Ecuadorian family that had long been involved in Ecuadorian politics. He was educated in the United States, first at the prestigious Charlotte Hill Military School in Maryland, and later at Stevens Institute of Technology in New Jersey, where he earned an engineering degree. Upon returning to Ecuador in 1953, he commenced a career in business and soon rose to prominence as an executive for the Noboa Group, Ecuador's largest banana exporter. He later served as president of the Association of Latin American Industries and the Guayas Chamber of Industry. He entered politics in the 1960s and was shot three times while campaigning for congress in 1970. Elected to congress in 1979, he became the leading right-wing critic of Roldós and Hurtado. Febres Cordero did not mind being called by his first name, León, which means lion. He tried to project a macho image by wearing Texas cowboy boots and carrying a pistol.

He immediately implemented free-market principles to recast the Ecuadorian economy. These included ending price controls, floating exchange rates, sharply reducing tariffs, and courting foreign investors. Febres Cordero limited direct social spending to public housing projects, a program that he had promised during the campaign. Like U.S. president Ronald Reagan, Febres Cordero believed that the average citizen's life would be improved by freeing market forces that would allow prosperity to trickle down. While Febres Cordero's approach was not unique, he was the first democratically elected Latin American president to implement neoliberal economic programs. In many ways Ecuador needed this approach at a time when its international debt was at an all-time high, oil output was leveling off, and the bureaucracy was bloated and inefficient.

Febres Cordero faced many obstacles to implementing his free-market agenda. The already anemic economy declined further under the shock of these new measures and living standards and per capita GDP declined in the last months of 1984. As usual Febres Cordero faced a hostile Congress because his coalition controlled only 16 seats out of 71. He also lacked an electoral mandate, as his election in the second round was not so much a confirmation of the public's agreement with his proposals as it was a rejection of his left-of-center predecessors. Nevertheless, the president pushed ahead, issuing decrees to float the sucre, reducing tariffs and most import quotas, eliminating the majority of price controls, and raising interest rates. He formulated low-risk contract legislation to entice foreign oil companies to again invest in Ecuadorian crude. Agreements followed with Occidental, Exxon, and five other oil firms. Because of his willingness to embrace neoliberal policies, Febres Cordero could restructure Ecuador's foreign debt in 1985, to lengthen the payment period and to suspend principal payments for three years. This was followed by $319 million in new loans from the United States and an invitation to participate in U.S. Treasury Secretary James A. Baker's plan to aid debt-ridden developing countries. These policies resulted in modest improvements in the economy in 1985, although other problems emerged the following year.

The FUT had tolerated Febres Cordero's experiments but began to criticize the government when it failed to generate an economic miracle. A more serious challenge came from Air Force General Frank Vargas, who held the president captive for nearly 12 hours during an official visit to the Taura Air Base in March 1986. The revolt soon petered out when Vargas failed to obtain the support of the other service chiefs.

Febres Cordero faced other problems, including a dramatic drop in the price of oil from $27 to $8 per barrel. This drastic reduction cost Ecuador $700 million in revenue and necessitated a temporary suspension of debt payments. To make matters worse, an earthquake ruptured the Trans Ecuadorian Pipeline in March 1987, disrupting the nation's main source of revenue for five months. Ecuador's dependency on oil was evident; oil accounted for two-thirds of export earnings, 60 percent of government income, and 16 percent of Ecuador's GDP. By the end of Febres Cordero's term, the sucre had lost 75 percent of its value, unemployment and underemployment were on the rise, and the foreign debt exceeded $10 billion. While Febres Cordero had not solved Ecuador's economic or social woes, he did improve public housing, made some infrastructure improvements on the coast, and implemented a national program of free infant health care. He also claimed that Ecuador would have been in even worse shape if it had continued on the state-directed path advocated by the left. Perhaps his most notable achievement was to complete his full term in a country that is known as very difficult to govern.

THE 1988 ELECTIONS

Febres Cordero's low approval ratings, coupled with a bleak economic outlook, boosted the hopes of the Ecuadorian left to win the presidency. The seasoned Rodrigo Borja, the perennial candidate of ID, led in the first round held on January 31 with 20.8 percent of the vote. The surprise second-place finisher, with 15.6 percent, was Abdalá Bucaram, nephew of the late Assad Bucaram, and founder of the Partido Rolodista Ecuatoriano (Ecuadorian Roldista Party) formed by splitting with the CFP. The Conservative, Sixto Durán, ran a distant third with 12.7 percent. The mercurial former Air Force General Frank Vargas, running as a socialist, took 10.6 percent and Jamil Mahuad of Democracia Popular (Popular Democracy, DP) had 10.3 percent. An oddity of this election was that all but Vargas would eventually be presidents of Ecuador. The poor showing by Durán was an indicator that the electorate had had enough of neoliberal economic policy. In the May 8 runoff Borja defeated Bucaram 47 percent to 40 percent to win the presidency on his third try.

BORJA'S MODERATE SHIFT TO THE LEFT

Borja assumed the presidency on August 10, 1988, with the intention of radically altering the policies of Febres Cordero. He called for state intervention to curb the excesses of the private sector and to even the distribution of wealth. As a former professor of constitutional law at Quito's Central University, he made respect for law a key point in forming his administration. His government vigorously investigated human rights abuses of the previous administration and Abdalá Bucaram fled the country during an investigation into his financial dealings. Borja buttered up the military by pardoning air force infantry troops who had held Febres Cordero hostage. He also quelled Ecuador's nascent insurgent group, Fuerzas Armadas Populares Eloy Alfaro (Eloy Alfaro Popular Armed Forces FAP-EA), also known as Alfaro Vive ¡Carajo! (Alfaro Lives Damn It!), by negotiating an amnesty agreement in exchange for the group's disarming.

Ecuador's internal and external debt and the fluctuating price of oil limited Borja's ability to enact his socialist agenda. In a spectacular about-face, Borja initiated a number of austerity measures in order to secure more loans and prevent Ecuador from defaulting on its debt payments. In August 1989 he secured $135 million from the IMF and an additional $136 million in February 1991.[7] These cash infusions kept Ecuador going, but at a cost. For example, Borja could not increase public spending, nor meet the demands of organized labor for increased wages nor satisfy the demands of indigenous groups for land reform. In 1989 he reduced inflation to 25 percent from its previous high of 88 percent. He also enticed some international oil companies to return to Ecuador. In 1991 he had a brief respite from economic crisis created by a spike in oil prices brought on by the First Gulf War. In June 1990 Borja became the first Ecuadorian president to face the rising militancy of the indigenous population during the first nationwide *levantamiento* (uprising) organized by the Confederation of Indigenous Nationalities of Ecuador (CONAIE). Borja's most significant social achievement was a successful literacy campaign. Despite four general strikes by FUT, major indigenous uprisings, constant shifts in his center left coalition, and impeachment threats, Borja completed his term and oversaw fair and free elections in 1992.

THE 1992 ELECTIONS: DURÁN'S COMEBACK

Sixto Durán Ballén, a self-styled Conservative, announced his retirement from politics after his disappointing finish in the first round of the 1988 elections, his second bid for the presidency. He had a change of heart and entered the 1992 race as the candidate of the right-of-center Partido Unidad Republicana (United Republican Party, PUR). Abdalá Bucaram was the wild card in the race, once again representing the PRE, and many felt the military would intervene if he advanced to the second round. Jaime Nebot Saadi, a Guayaquil businessman, was the third major candidate; he represented former president Hurtado's PSC. Most of Ecuador applauded when the flamboyant Bucaram finished third with 21.5 percent of the vote to Durán's 32.9 percent and Nebot's 25.1 percent, with lesser candidates splitting the remaining votes. In the second round, held on July 5, Durán, the veteran politician, defeated the newcomer Nebot 57.8 percent to 42.2 percent.

SIXTO DURÁN BALLÉN: ANOTHER FOUR-YEAR SURVIVOR

Durán was the second president of Ecuador to have been born in the United States (Galo Plaza was the first). He was 70 years old when he donned the presidential sash and had a long record of achievement as minister of public works, mayor of Quito, and president of the Ecuadorian Home Mortgage Bank. He was also a successful architect and a professor of art theory at the Catholic University in Quito.

Durán spent much of his presidency negotiating loans from the IMF and then battling Congress to meet the conditions demanded by the bankers. For example, Ecuador secured $180 million from the IMF in March 1994 by agreeing to increase the value-added tax from 10 to 18 percent. Congress blocked the proposal, forcing the president to implement other austerity measures, including increasing utility rates by 50 percent and reducing gasoline subsidies, which resulted in a 115 percent price increase. These measures were met with the usual round of strikes and protests. Another problem was the shortfall in budget projections that were based on oil being sold at a minimum of $17 per barrel, but the price was seldom over $10. A corruption scandal involving the vice president, Alberto Dahik, accused of misappropriating millions of dollars from the treasury, proved a major embarrassment. He soon sought asylum in Costa Rica and was removed from office for abandoning his post. Durán appointed a new vice president with the approval of Congress, one of his few domestic political victories. Durán's pet public works project was making potable water available to rural villages and he managed to oversee a number of other successful projects.

CONFLICTS WITH PERU

Ecuador and Peru continued to quarrel over the provisions of the 1942 Río Protocol in the remote Cordillera del Cóndor region, and hostilities began anew on January 28, 1981. In a week of fighting Peruvian commandos and air force planes attacked three Ecuadorian outposts and forced them to be abandoned. After the 1981 incident, Ecuador made a concerted effort to upgrade its armed forces in preparation for future conflicts. Ecuador obtained Kifir fighter aircraft from Israel and purchased state-of-the-art shoulder-fired surface-to-air missiles. In January 1995 Peru attempted to dislodge Ecuadorian troops from fortified positions in the disputed zone. The Ecuadorian military's modernization program paid off as surface-to-air missiles and Ecuadorian fighter jets shot down three Peruvian war planes and five helicopters and Ecuador held its positions. Peru suffered 300 casualties while Ecuadorian losses were fewer than 50. This was the first time in the 155 years of the dispute that Ecuador had bested Peru in a military conflict. The United States, Argentina, Brazil, and Chile, the guarantors of the protocol, arranged a ceasefire. The Durán government enjoyed a brief period of national unity and the prestige of the Ecuadorian military reached an all-time high with the public. This was the last major military confrontation between Ecuador and Peru and both became more earnest in diplomatic negotiations to find a permanent settlement to the dispute.

POSITIVE ASPECTS OF THE MILITARY REFORMERS AND THE SECOND DEMOCRATIC PARENTHESIS

The two military reform governments of the 1970s have often been criticized for wasteful spending, authoritarian tactics, and failing to transform the country into a developed state. While some of these criticism are well founded, they also overshadow the accomplishments of the military reformers. At the very least the military men provided Ecuador with a respite from the convoluted antics of civilian politicians and enacted agrarian reform legislation. They also started the process of modernization and development that provided Ecuadorians with more schools, hospitals, electricity, potable water, and roads than ever before. Finally, the military oversaw a transition to democracy that was orderly and, for the most part, peaceful.

To many observers it appeared that presidents Roldós, Hurtado, Febres Cordero, Borja, and Durán only managed to muddle through their terms. While these five presidents failed to lift Ecuador out of the economic doldrums following the oil boom, they did make some significant changes. Popular voting participation greatly increased, thereby institutionalizing democracy. The

1978 constitution gave the right to vote to illiterates starting with the 1982 elections. Voter participation steadily increased. International observers, including former U.S. president Jimmy Carter, pronounced the Ecuadorian elections to be among the most open, violence-free, and accurately tabulated in the entire world. In fact, Ecuador's computer programs would have served the United States well in 2000. Another positive indicator was the emergence, for the first time on a large scale, of the indigenous people in Ecuador's political process. Each president had a unique social program that served the marginalized segments of Ecuadorian society. Life expectancy increased and more Ecuadorians could read and write than ever before. There were many improvements to Ecuador's urban centers. For example, Quito was transformed from a sleepy, sedate, colonial town into a bustling modern metropolis. The 1995 Victory on the Cenapa, as Ecuadorians refer to the clash with Peru, lifted Ecuadorian spirits and provided the country with a face-saving event that would ultimately result in a permanent settlement in 1998. Unfortunately, the moderate policies of these five presidents were not enough to permanently resolve the issues of regionalism, personalism, and dictatorial tendencies that have long plagued the Ecuadorian political landscape.

NOTES

1. Allen Gerlach, *Indians, Oil, and Politics: A Recent History of Ecuador* (Wilmington, DE: Scholarly Resources, 2003), 36.

2. Ibid., 37.

3. Dennis M. Hanratty, ed., *Ecuador: A Country Study* (Washington, DC: Library of Congress Federal Research Division, 1991), 46.

4. Ibid., 48.

5. David Schodt, *Ecuador: An Andean Enigma* (Boulder, CO: Westview Press, 1987), 144–53.

6. Ibid., 159.

7. Gerlach, *Indians, Oil, and Politics*, 45.

9

Populism, Political Instability, and the Citizen's Revolution

As illustrated in the previous chapter, Ecuador enjoyed a relative period of political stability from 1979 to 1996 that surpassed the Democratic Parenthesis of 1948–60. It seemed that Ecuador had discovered its own version of checks and balances as presidents alternated from the political left and right. Sixteen years of well-managed open elections and the peaceful transfer of power from one end of the political spectrum to the other were unprecedented in the volatile political history of Ecuador. This respite from military coups and *autogolpes* helped Ecuador shed its image as the quintessential banana republic. Unfortunately, this trend toward political maturity was undone by the presidential election of 1996.

THE BUCARAM DEBACLE

In 1996 the Ecuadorian right had hopes of retaining the presidency when Jaime Nebot of the Social Christian Party (PSC) led a crowded field of nine candidates in the opinion polls. Nebot, a Guayaquil lawyer of Lebanese descent, had served as governor of Guayas Province and promised to continue the neoliberal program of Sixto Durán, including further reduction in trade barriers and the privatization of more state-owned enterprises. Nebot had strong support from both the business sector and former president Febres Cordero.

Nebot's nemesis, and a strong contender for the presidency, was Abdalá Bucaram, also of Lebanese background and the founder of the Ecuadorian Roldista Party. The 44-year-old Bucaram had a colorful political record as mayor of Guayaquil and later as a member of Congress. He had made two previous runs for the presidency in 1988 and 1992. Bucaram's uncle, Assad Bucaram, had helped organize the Concentration of Popular Forces in the 1950s and was a perennial candidate for the presidency until his death. Abdalá's sister was the wife of President Roldós and died with him in the tragic plane crash. When Assad Bucaram died, his CFP split into rival factions with Abdalá heading one, the Ecuadorian Roldista Party, which he named in memory of his brother-in-law. Like his uncle, Abdalá was a spellbinding campaigner who appealed to Ecuador's poor. His erratic behavior, in and out of office, had earned him the nickname *El Loco,* or the crazy one. It was a sobriquet that Bucaram relished and used to great effect in the 1996 campaign.

Under Ecuador's 1978 constitution, a candidate had to earn more than 50 percent of the vote to be elected president. The nine-man field made it nearly impossible for any candidate to be elected during the first round, necessitating a second round between the top two finishers. Two other candidates had polled well. The left-of-center Nuevo País (New Country) coalition supported Freddy Elhers, a popular television commentator without domestic political baggage. Rodrigo Paz, a prominent businessman and former mayor of Quito, headed the ticket of the conservative Popular Democracy Party.

The first round votes were cast in May 1996 and, as the polls predicted, Nebot led the pack but with a disappointing 27.4 percent of the vote. Bucaram finished second with 25.5 percent.

In the second round Bucaram used his political acumen to best Nebot. He had wooed Rosalía Arteaga, a conservative politician from a prominent upper-class Cuenca family, to be his running mate. Arteaga provided respectability to the flamboyant Bucaram among some of Ecuador's conservative voters. She also appealed to women as she campaigned to be Ecuador's first female vice president. Additionally, she provided the perfect prop for Bucaram's anti-oligarchy rhetoric, which became a major theme of the campaign. At rallies, Bucaram would lift up a compliant Arteaga's skirt to show her shapely legs. The stunt showed Bucaram as a man of the masses who could humiliate a woman from the upper class with impunity. In fact, Bucaram's net worth of several million U.S. dollars hardly qualified him as a member of Ecuador's poor. Other antics included descending from a helicopter in a Batman costume, spontaneous singing, removal of his shirt, and impromptu games of *indor,* small sided soccer contests that demonstrated his athletic prowess. Bucaram also made promises of social improvement and vowed to build more than 700,000 houses for low income families.

On July 7, Abdalá Bucaram was elected president of Ecuador, winning 54.3 percent of the votes to Nebot's 45.7 percent.[1] On August 10 he assumed the presidential sash and became the first Lebanese-Ecuadorian president of the republic. He would soon learn that Velasco Ibarra's analysis was true: Ecuador is a very difficult country to govern.

Bucaram faced a dilemma as he entered the presidency. He had promised increased social spending and the poor were a large portion of his constituency. However, Ecuador was mired in a recession because of the drop in oil prices from $18.04 a barrel to $15.58. Inflation soared to 37 percent while tax revenues plummeted by nearly 20 percent. Ecuador's foreign debt reached $14.58 billion.[2] Ecuador did not have the funds to carry out Bucaram's promises and its low credit rating prohibited obtaining favorable loans.

Bucaram decided that in the short term he needed to adopt a conservative economic policy that included balancing the budget, fixing the sucre to the U.S. dollar, and seeking investments from abroad. He hired Domingo Cavallo, the former Argentine finance minister, to implement a painful austerity program similar to one that had worked in Argentina. The plan called for cutting the budget, selling off state-owned enterprises, ending subsidies, and cutting jobs in Ecuador's bloated government bureaucracy. Bucaram realized that increased prices would cause a negative reaction among his supporters but he hoped that his personal appeals for sacrifice in the short run, coupled with promises of long-term improvements in living conditions, would assuage his supporters. In order to raise revenue, Bucaram enacted numerous tax increases including a 103 percent increase on light tobacco, 48 percent on dark tobacco, 63 percent on alcohol, and 10 percent on the already high automobile tax. The reduction in price supports caused electricity rates to increase by 115 percent, public transportation 25 percent and gasoline 20 percent, hardly the relief that Ecuador's masses had been expecting from the charismatic Bucaram.[3]

While Bucaram had inherited a terrible economic situation that he made worse, other wounds were self-inflicted. Nepotism has always been part of Ecuadorian politics, but Abdalá raised it to new levels. Not only did he appoint scores of friends and relatives to key government posts, but also they exceeded the normal levels of corruption. The Bucaram government rapidly became a kleptocracy. For example, the president's 19-year-old son, Jacoabo, stole millions of dollars while holding a position in the customs house in Guayaquil. Bribes had long been part of doing business in Ecuador, but Bucaram's cronies increased the rates threefold. An investigation by the top echelons of the military confirmed that corruption was endemic and the generals urged the president to curb it. Bucaram cavalierly dismissed the problem of corruption when he commented that everyone steals.

Bucaram's blundering extended to foreign policy. In 1995 Ecuador had achieved its first military success in its long territorial dispute with Peru in the Cordillera del Condor region, a source of pride to most Ecuadorians with the exception of the indigenous movement. Bucaram, on the other hand, called the conflict "stupid" and was skeptical of the armed forces' requests for increased funding to prepare for future confrontations.[4] Apparently he saw an opportunity to be remembered as a statesman and, during a state visit to Peru in January 1997, he called for mutual forgiveness between the two adversaries. His conciliatory speech to the Peruvian Congress was well received in Lima but had the opposite effect in Ecuador. The president was portrayed as pandering to the Peruvians and his approval ratings sank to all-time lows. Few understood why Bucaram took this course. Other populists, especially Velasco Ibarra, used the territorial dispute to rally popular support during times of domestic unrest. The issue was also popular with one of Bucaram's main constituencies, the urban poor, a group with which he was rapidly losing favor.

When Bucaram returned to Quito the Ecuadorian high command apprised him that opposition to his government was growing and included all economic and social sectors. The generals pointed out that his economic measures, peace with Peru pronouncements, and widespread corruption had put him in peril. Bucaram understood his situation but believed that he could weather the storm. He felt that Ecuador would not depose a democratically elected president and that other presidents of Ecuador and in other Latin American countries had also implemented unpopular austerity measures and survived politically. He was determined to wait it out and would change course only slightly if protests and strikes erupted.

On February 5, 1997, the United Workers Front (FUT) initiated a general strike that other labor unions and the business groups quickly joined. The major indigenous organization CONAIE, Coordinated Social Movements, and the Women's Political Movement also participated. Protesters closed banks, factories, and the public transportation system throughout the country. Roadblocks were established by CONAIE on the Pan American Highway, shutting down the main north–south artery that connected the highland provinces from Tulcán to Loja. Even Bucaram's critics were amazed at the extent of the strike and the public anger that it represented. Bucaram addressed the nation on television and radio and called on the armed forces to break the state of siege and to maintain order. However, the armed forces, under General Paco Mancayo, withdrew their support in hopes that Bucaram would resign and quietly leave the country. When Bucaram refused to resign, the country faced a constitutional crisis.

Under Ecuador's 1978 constitution a president could be impeached by a two-thirds vote of the congress on charges of treason, bribery, or actions that

affected the national honor. Bucaram still had supporters in Congress; therefore a two-thirds impeachment vote seemed unlikely. In addition, a lengthy
trial would take time, further disrupting an already volatile situation. Article 100, however, provided that a president could be removed by a simple
majority of congress for the cause of physical or mental incapacity. While
Bucaram's behavior was erratic, he did not meet the clinical definition of mental incapacity and he was in fine physical condition. Nevertheless, Congress
had enough votes to pass the measure. Choosing his successor proved more
contentious. On February 6 three contenders claimed the presidency: Bucaram,
who had not resigned and denied the legality of the congressional action;
Rosalía Arteaga, the vice president, who claimed succession under the terms
of the constitution; and Fabián Alarcón, the president of congress, whom the
Congress named to replace Bucaram. The situation created increasing embarrassment for Ecuador in international circles and the military reluctantly decided to end the crisis without taking direct control of the government.

The military decided to back the decision of Congress that Bucaram was
mentally incompetent to continue as president and to usher him into a golden
exile in Panama. Arteaga would be allowed to assume the presidency briefly,
thus fulfilling the constitutional requirement before resigning in favor of
Alarcón, who would oversee new elections. On February 9, Arteaga became
the first female president of Ecuador. Although she wanted to hold executive
power for longer, Congress and the military forced her out on February 11,
naming Alarcón as interim president.

THE ALARCÓN INTERREGNUM

A lawyer, Fabián Alarcón was from a politically active Quito family. His
father, Ruperto Alarcón, had once been president of the Chamber of Deputies. Fabián had served on the Quito City Council and had earlier made two
unsuccessful bids to become the mayor. Elected to congress in 1991, he later
became president of that body. His political base was the small Frente Radical
Alfarista (Radical Alfarista Front, FRA), a left-of-center party. Alarcón realized that a major political problem was his legitimacy. It was an issue that
the ambitious and politically frustrated Rosalía Arteaga intended to use to regain the presidency. Alarcón wisely endorsed Arteaga's call for a plebiscite
to endorse or recant the congressional decision to install him as president.
Realizing that she had been outmaneuvered, Arteaga now called for a general election for president, vice president, and congress, and a constitutional
convention to write a new constitution. In May the voters spoke and 65 percent
of them approved of the decision to remove Bucaram and replace him with
Alarcón. The voters also passed the proposition to write a new constitution,
which a convention finished on June 5, 1998. The new constitution expanded

the number of deputies in Congress to 123 and placed modest restrictions on congressional power over the executive. New presidential elections were set for May 31, 1998.

With his legitimacy established, Alarcón proposed to revive the economy by cutting expenditures, imposing new taxes, seeking private investment, and selling state-owned enterprises. While these proposals assuaged Ecuador's creditors, Alarcón pursued a more realistic agenda to calm the stormy waters of the Bucaram presidency. For example, he lowered taxes by 30 percent and the Ministry of Agriculture and Livestock established the Popular Fund to subsidize essential food items including milk, rice, bread, and cooking oil. These measures resulted in the budget deficit increasing by $470 million. Despite these efforts, Alarcón also faced public protests and strikes, but they lacked the fervor that had undone his predecessor.

The new government also exposed the corruption of Bucaram and his cronies and attempted to prosecute the former president. Bucaram was accused of taking 20 million sucres from the national treasury when he fled to Panama. Documents implicated his brother, Santiago, in fraudulent purchases of computers and backpacks for the public schools. The Supreme Court ordered Bucaram's arrest, froze his bank accounts, and prohibited the sale of his real property. All of this played well to the public but had little effect on the exiled president and his friends.

Alarcón also had moderate success in resolving the long-standing territorial dispute with Peru. His diplomats entered talks with Peru in Brasilia and hammered out preliminary drafts that would result in a final accord by the next administration.

Alarcón's brief presidency had brought a measure of political calm to Ecuador and prepared the way for the 1998 elections, a remarkable feat considering the events that brought him to power. The political spectacle of three presidents in one day had damaged Ecuador's international reputation but, to its credit, the nation did not resort to dictatorship or a military junta to sort things out as in the past. Instead, Alarcón and the military sought constitutional means to continue on the democratic path.

THE 1998 ELECTIONS

The May 1998 elections marked an opportunity for Ecuador to demonstrate that the problems with *El Loco* had been a temporary departure from political stability. The candidate field was historic and offered promise. For the first time in history two women, Rosalía Arteaga of the Movement for an Independent and Authentic Republic (MIRA), and María Eugenia Lima of the Popular Democratic Movement (MDR), sought election to Ecuador's highest office. Freddy Elhers, a popular television personality, headed the New Country coalition and ran on the theme of combating corruption for a new Ecuador. In addition to the fresh faces, there was the familiar former president, Rodrigo Borja of the traditional Democratic Left party. Alvaro Noboa, scion to the Noboa banana enterprises, headed the Roldista ticket with the slogan "Forward Ecuador! Forward!" The leading candidate from the Popular Democracy party was the popular but reserved mayor of Quito, Jamil Mahuad, a Lebanese Ecuadorian. He told the electorate, "I know what to do and how to do it."[5] Noticeably absent was a candidate from the Social Christian Party, Ecuador's strongest conservative political party. Mahuad easily won the first round with 36.66 percent of the vote while Noboa finished second with 29.75 percent.

The heated second round of campaigning was surprisingly close. Mahuad gained the support of the parties on both the right and left, as his former opponents, Borja and Elhers, threw their support to him. Jaime Nebot, the leader of PSC, also endorsed Mahuad. Noboa, on the other hand, offered an end to corruption and told the people to elect him because "I'm too rich to steal."[6] In the end Mahuad won by just 110,000 votes out of the nearly 5 million ballots cast. A bitter Noboa claimed fraud but international observers confirmed that the election had been fair and free.

MAHUAD'S DISAPPOINTING PRESIDENCY

At first Jamil Mahuad appeared to be a breath of fresh air in the stultifying atmosphere of Ecuadorian politics. His record as a competent and progressive mayor, his reputation for personal honesty, and an impressive academic background, including a master's degree in public policy from Harvard, was the basis of this optimism. However, Mahuad faced enormous political and economic challenges. Like most Ecuadorian presidents, his Popular Democracy party did not have a majority, or even a plurality, in congress, holding only 20 percent of the seats. The support he had from Borja and Nebot during the campaign soon evaporated. In addition, the economy went into recession as the price of oil dropped, causing Mahuad to seek additional loans that required him to implement unpopular austerity measures. A banking crisis revealed corruption and the president was soon linked to the scandal. Mahuad's poor leadership skills, coupled with a bland speaking style, contributed to his woes and led to an uprising by Ecuador's indigenous population. Early in his presidency, Mahuad saw an opportunity to resolve Ecuador's long-standing territorial dispute with Peru, but this successful negotiation, instead of winning praise, backfired and resulted in the military participating in his overthrow.

On October 26, 1998, Ecuador and Peru signed peace papers in Brasilia, ending a dispute that originated in 1830, when Ecuador established its independence from Gran Colombia. Resolving the dispute at this time made perfect sense to most observers. Ecuador had vindicated its national honor with military victories in the 1995 war with Peru and continued confrontation would be costly for both. If hostilities broke out again it was uncertain if Ecuador could repeat its 1995 military success. Moreover, the peace proposal brokered by the United States, Brazil, Argentina, and Chile was reasonable, realistic, and the best possible deal for Ecuador. Finally, most Ecuadorians were weary of the conflict and had hopes that a peace dividend would enable a measure of domestic prosperity.

The peace agreement led to Mahuad formulating a new role for the Ecuadorian armed forces. The new missions included combating narcotic trafficking, subduing Colombian guerrillas who used Ecuador as a sanctuary, and focusing on internal security. The armed forces were less than enthusiastic about these missions. In addition, Mahuad cut defense appropriations and reduced conscription by 40 percent. The generals and field grade officers resented these dramatic changes. While Mahuad had made the correct decision in brokering peace with Peru, his sudden shift in defense priorities had created doubt about his leadership among the armed forces, the best organized and most powerful institution in Ecuador.

On the domestic scene Mahuad implemented tax increases and reduced subsidies that he felt were needed to make Ecuador creditworthy in order to secure additional loans. Thus, in the first six months of his administration, electricity costs increased by 410 percent, gasoline by 174 percent, and public transportation by 40 percent. Strikes and other public demonstrations occurred, but Mahuad weathered these initial storms.

The next crisis involved the failure of three of Ecuador's largest banks, Filanbanco, Banco de Progreso, and Banco de Préstamos. Exuberant expansion and risky loans that the bankers had made under the assumption that the government would bail them out if the borrowers defaulted brought on the crisis, in part because many believed that these three banks were too big to fail. The lack of government oversight contributed to the banking crisis. Mahuad took action to shore up the banks with the creation of the Deposit Guarantee Agency (AGD), an Ecuadorian version of the U.S. Federal Deposit Insurance Corporation (FDIC). Although a wise idea, the 1 percent tax on deposits was too high and depositors' confidence had already been shattered. Ecuadorians started to buy dollars and hoard them in safe deposit boxes or other secure places, including the reliable mattress. Ecuadorians quipped that the country had a new bank—The Mattress Bank. Mahuad declared a banking holiday to counter the run on the banks, but this was met with stiff resistance, as were attempts to bail out the banks with an infusion of government cash. When journalists discovered that bailout funds ended up in the pockets of bank directors who fled the country, demonstrations intensified and

Mahuad's approval rating dipped to 22 percent. In March 1999 a nationwide strike supported by taxi and bus drivers closed down the transportation system and Mahuad declared a state of emergency. The strikes and protests were temporarily suspended but flared up again in July. Once again Mahuad declared a state of emergency and ordered the armed forces to deal with civil strife. The strikes resulted in three deaths and scores of injuries. The violence resulted in a reassessment and Mahuad backed down on some price increases. The International Monetary Fund turned down Ecuador's request for a $1.5 billion loan and the military warned the beleaguered president that he was in trouble with the public. In August Mahuad's popularity rating stood at a paltry 16 percent but he still hoped to continue as president and complete his constitutional term.

More bad news came in October when sources revealed that Mahuad had received $3.5 million in campaign contributions from Fernando Aspiazu, one of the bankers arrested in the corruption scandal. All perceptions of his honesty vanished and the embattled president was now viewed as just another corrupt politician. Nevertheless, Mahuad hoped to rally support with two initiatives: a deal to lease a portion of the Ecuadorian Air Force Base at Manta on the coast to the United States, and a plan to make the U.S. dollar the national currency.

In 1998 the United States was in the final stages of phasing out military operations in Panama in compliance with the Panama Canal treaties. For years the United States had used Howard Air Force Base in Panama as the center of antidrug monitoring operations. The Eloy Alfaro Air Base at Manta was an attractive alternative to Howard. Ecuador entered into a 10-year lease of a section of the Manta base and received $70 million in improvements to the base, U.S. support for much-needed international loans, a yearly rent income, and help for the local economy. The primary disadvantage was a possible reaction by the Revolutionary Armed Forces of Colombia (FARC), the Colombian insurgents who were heavily involved in narcotic trafficking. Mahuad felt that Ecuador was not immune to FARC and would have to deal with this problem with or without the lease of the Manta facility. Another problem that he discounted was a rise in nationalist fervor opposing the introduction of foreign troops on Ecuadorian soil. The plan pleased the Ecuadorian air force and did improve the economy of Manta and the surrounding area. Later, the plan would be used against the beleaguered president but was not a significant factor in his downfall.

A more controversial action was Mahuad's plan, announced in January 9, 2000, to replace the sucre, Ecuador's national currency, with the U.S. dollar. The recession was deepening as Ecuador entered the 21st century. Inflation had reached 67 percent in 1999 and the sucre plunged 17 percent in the first week of 2000. Poverty was increasing and unemployment had gone from bad to worse. Ecuadorian workers left for the United States or Europe, seeking a better life abroad. Ecuador's economic performance was the worst in South America, the poverty rate was 62.5 percent, per capita income stood at $1,150 per person, and the debt burden had reached $13.5 billion while the GDP was only $14.5 billion. Mahuad promised that his dollar scheme would stabilize the monetary system, curb inflation, lower interest rates, and spur investment. Critics pointed out that Ecuador would give up economic sovereignty and that monetary policy would not solve the underlying economic problems. An additional concern was that the use of the green dollar would create confusion for indigenous groups who were used to sucre denominations in a variety of colors.

THE INDIGENOUS UPRISING

Business groups, the middle and upper classes, and international lenders endorsed Mahuad's dollar plan and he gained modestly in opinion polls to 22 percent. A few days after his announcement, CONAIE's Parliament of the People met in Quito and sternly denounced the plan. By now CONAIE had given up on Mahuad and intended to force his resignation with a nationwide protest slated for January 15. The indigenous coalition also wanted to replace the old political system with a new order that would address their needs. Their plan was to paralyze the country by blocking roads and access to public buildings, as they hoped that 40,000 indigenous would converge on Quito to demonstrate the power of CONAIE.

Mahuad declared a state of emergency and ordered 30,000 troops and police to mobilize to maintain law and order. The armed forces decided to protect public property but refused orders to arrest protesters or to subject them to military tribunals. The protest started peacefully as scheduled and soldiers did nothing to break up the protest.

On January 17, workers at Petroecuador, Ecuador's state-owned oil company, went out on strike and joined the indigenous in calling for Mahuad's resignation. Their action added momentum to the uprising as oil production plummeted from 373,000 barrels as day to 260,000. Two days later student groups and unions joined the protest. A critical juncture was reached on January 20 when Indians surrounded the Congress and Supreme Court buildings. In the process they encircled the soldiers and police who were guarding the buildings as well as trapping civil servants and elected officials in the buildings. The military joint command decided not to clear the Indians or attempt to rescue the people confined in the buildings. Events soon took a dramatic twist when three busloads of junior officers from the Military Polytechnic School were allowed to pass through both the Indian and troop lines. Their arrival broke the government lines and Indian protesters occupied both the

Congress and Supreme Court buildings. The famous Cenepa Brigade, which had been guarding the buildings, joined the Indians. Army Colonel Lucio Gutiérrez, who had been plotting to topple Mahuad, became the leader of the rebel military forces. Inside the Congress, Vargas, Gutiérrez, and Carlos Solórzano, a former Supreme Court president, announced the formation of a Junta of National Salvation and issued a manifesto that promised to end corruption and introduce radical changes to Ecuador's political, economic, and social systems.

General Carlos Mendoza, head of the joint command, now realized the gravity of the situation. His main concern was the breakdown in the unity of the military as an institution. Determined to prevent a fracture within the military, he decided that Mahuad could not remain as president. Mendoza informed the president that he must resign. When Mahuad stubbornly refused, Mendoza withdrew the president's personal security force. Mahuad addressed the nation on television and announced that he would not leave the presidency. However, within a matter of hours he took refuge in the Chilean Embassy and soon departed the country, still claiming that he was the legitimate president of Ecuador. Mendoza took charge of executive functions and negotiated with the rebel junta.

While Mahuad's departure led to a certain euphoria, the junta soon faced pressure that it was not the legitimate government of Ecuador. The Organization of American States, the United States, numerous European countries, Chile, and the United Nations all warned the junta that it could not hold power indefinitely. General Mendoza realized that the junta could not survive such pressure, so he offered to replace Gutiérrez on the junta. Vargas realized that the junta could not survive without the support of the military and agreed. A few hours later Mendoza abruptly resigned from the junta and announced his retirement from the Armed Forces. He also announced that the military would support Vice President Gustavo Noboa as the constitutional president of Ecuador. Naboa was sworn in on January 22 and the Indian uprising soon petered out. Vargas and CONAIE had succeeded in forcing Mahuad out, but the uprising fell far short of its other goal of radical change to Ecuador's social structure.

NOBOA AT THE HELM

Gustavo Noboa was from a prominent Guayaquil family; his great-grandfather, Diego Noboa, had served briefly as president in 1851. Before he was elected vice president, he had devoted most of his life to academic pursuits, eventually serving as the rector of the University of Guayaquil, where he also headed the law school. As vice president, Noboa took charge of coastal highway reconstruction in the aftermath of floods caused by the El Niño effect and achieved a reputation of competence and honesty. Ironically, Noboa had better political instincts than Mahuad and he also had better luck.

His first act as president was to unfreeze bank accounts, a very popular move that calmed the wave of protests despite the fact that the AGD did not have enough funds to cover all accounts. He pushed forward with implementation of the dollar plan. On March 1, 2000, Ecuador became the second Latin American country to adopt the U.S. dollar as its currency (Panama was the first). He set the exchange rate at 25,000 sucres to one dollar and Ecuadorians had a month to complete the conversion. At first there were problems. Prices rose and illiterates who had been used to each denomination of sucre being a different color were confused. In addition, the government had not issued fractional currency or coins. Suddenly the minimum price for anything in Ecuador was one U.S. dollar! These problems were resolved in time when the government minted Ecuadorian coins that were the same value as U.S. coins and the population became used to all paper money being the same color. In the long run the dollar plan was a moderate success. Inflation declined and the government could no longer attempt to solve its debt problems by merely running the money presses longer. The upper and middle classes found credit easier to obtain. The indigenous peoples were disappointed that their demand for a referendum on the dollar plan had been thwarted. However, the fervor of previous protests diminished and Noboa benefited from Mahuad's taking the heat for proposing dollarization. Noboa's dollar initiative also paid dividends when the United States pledged support for IMF loans. César Gaviria, the secretary general of the Organization of American States, came to Ecuador and offered assistance in an anticorruption campaign and also aid in negotiations with disparate interest groups in Ecuador. Ecuador soon secured $2 billion in new loans to ease the impact of the recession. Oil prices soared from $8.50 a barrel to $24, bloating government coffers. Improved pipeline capacity boosted Ecuador's output from 330,000 barrels per day to 390,000. Noboa's pragmatism and his gradualist approach to problems inspired confidence.

The indigenous movement that had brought on Mahuad's downfall took a more moderate course during Noboa's tenure. For example, Salvador Quishpe, the radical leader of ECUARUNARI, lost his reelection bid as the group's president. The Indians abandoned their demands for a complete restructuring of society and turned to more moderate proposals. The Indigenous Chamber of Commerce was formed, a step toward capitalism rather than radical socialism.

Noboa skillfully managed the problem of what to do with the military men who had participated in the *golpe* that ended Mahuad's presidency. Amnesty was granted to the coup participants, including Colonel Gutiérrez, and the plotters were quietly eased out of the ranks. Noboa seemed to instinctively understand that, in Ecuador, a president cannot endure if he persists with vastly unpopular programs such as freezing bank accounts. He also realized that the military must be accommodated. He was fortunate that Mahuad had absorbed the wrath of the military for the treaty with Peru and the discontent of the indigenous organizations for his dollarization plan. The restoration of calm and the steady improvement of the economy were the hallmarks of Noboa's brief presidency. By October 2002 Ecuador was ready to hold elections to select his successor.

COLONEL GUTIÉRREZ GETS HIS CHANCE

Despite the difficulty of governing Ecuador, there was no dearth of candidates for the 2002 elections. Thirteen men initially entered the race, including former presidents Rodrigo Borja and Osvaldo Hurtado. Alvaro Noboa, the banana baron, made another bid, this time under the banner of his newly created Institutional Renewal Party of National Action (PIRAN). Antonio Vargas, former president of CONAIE and a leader of the coup that ousted Mahuad, decided to run as well. Vargas had lost credibility with Patachutik, CONAIE's political party, and formed the Amauta Jatari Movement (MAJ). His fellow coup conspirator, Colonel Lucio Gutiérrez, was the candidate of another new party, the January 21 Patriotic Society Movement (M21). Throughout the campaign Noboa led in the polls with former president Borja a close second. Political polling in Latin America is not as exact as in the United States and Europe and observers were stunned when, on October 24, Gutiérrez won the first round with 943,123 votes or 20.3 percent of the total votes cast. Alvaro Noboa finished second with 17.4 percent, despite having spent $2.3 million on his campaign to Gutiérrez's paltry $393,374.

The 2002 election was a major disappointment to the Democratic Left, the Social Christian Party, and the Ecuadorian Roldista Party, Ecuador's traditional political parties, as it was the third consecutive election in which they failed to elect a president. Gutiérrez and Noboa each sought the favor of the traditional parties but the indigenous vote became increasingly important. Noboa attempted to win the indigenous vote, as well as the votes of other impoverished groups, by promising to spur foreign investment. He claimed that he could accomplish this because he was a rich capitalist who could negotiate with other rich capitalists. Gutiérrez took a more populist stance by promising to curb corruption and to increase spending for health and improved education. In the end, Gutiérrez won an overwhelming victory, garnering 2.7 million votes or 54.4 percent to Noboa's 2.3 million or 45.6 percent.[7]

GUTIÉRREZ CONFRONTS REALITY

Gutiérrez became Ecuador's sixth president in as many years and, like his five predecessors, faced a host of economic and political problems. Despite a fairly robust economy, a $300 million budget deficit, and a $2.5 billion annual debt payment, the president faced a fragmented Congress in which his party held few seats. As a former colonel, he was viewed with suspicion by the generals, who felt that he had attempted to fracture the unity of the military establishment. He had strong support in the indigenous sector but he himself was a mestizo.

Quickly, he met with U.S. President George W. Bush and pledged Ecuadorian support in fighting drug trafficking and international terrorism. He kept his campaign promise that the United States would retain its presence at the Manta air base. Because of Ecuador's precarious debt problem, he negotiated with the IMF to secure a $205 million loan. The IMF loan came with conditions and Gutiérrez dutifully complied with them. The most controversial was the agreement to earmark one-third of the $6.7 billion budget for debt repayment. The new president also announced that Ecuador would retain the dollar program, which he had opposed during his brief membership on the Junta of National Salvation in 2000. To secure the loan the president announced that there would be cuts to Ecuador's bloated civil service and a reduction of state subsidies. These early moves pleased both the United States and international banking institutions but angered Gutiérrez's core constituencies. Pachakutik, the indigenous political party, soon withdrew support and the erstwhile radical Gutiérrez turned to conservative Christian Socialists for help. A more ominous development was the split with his vice president, Dr. Alfredo Palacio, a 64-year-old heart surgeon who saw political opportunity amid Gutiérrez's flip-flop from his campaign rhetoric.

Gutiérrez had promised to end corruption, but he was soon linked to a scandal when a former governor was arrested for drug trafficking. The accused governor claimed that he had funneled $30 million to the Gutiérrez campaign. An additional accusation alleged that Gutiérrez had received a campaign contribution from Mexico's Labor Party, an illegal act under Ecuadorian law. The president denied these claims and fired some of his cabinet.

The next bombshell came from an unexpected quarter. The president's wife, Ximena Bohorquéz, herself a member of Congress, expressed disappointment over her husband's failure to appoint competent and honest officials to his government. In addition, she refused to play the traditional role of first lady and live in the Carondelet Palace. The couple separated, but reconciled in September 2003. Nevertheless, Bohorquéz continued to criticize her husband and publicly condemned his economic policies, providing Ecuador's tabloids with abundant material.

Despite these difficulties, Gutiérrez muddled through another year in office, surviving protests and shifting political fortune. In October 2004, the Social Christian Party, disenchanted with Gutiérrez, implemented impeachment proceedings. Gutiérrez weathered this storm by forming a coalition with his former political rivals, the Roldistas, and Noboa's PIRAN. With their support, he easily defeated the impeachment initiative. The PSC's move to remove Gutiérrez from office angered him, and he sought revenge by having Congress fire 31 Supreme Court justices. He soon appointed temporary justices sympathetic to his views, and called for a referendum to decide on new procedures for selecting Supreme Court justices. It became clear to many in Ecuador that President Gutiérrez was bent on expanding his power and possibly establishing a dictatorship. Demonstrations broke out in January and February 2005 in both Guayaquil and Quito calling for his resignation. Congress attempted to reverse his firing of the justices and, although the final vote for resignation failed, Gutiérrez's coalition looked fragile. Congress became even more assertive when it decisively rejected the president's nominees for attorney general.

The president's support of exiled president Abdalá Bucaram compounded his problems. The temporary Supreme Court dismissed all charges against *El Loco* Bucaram, paving the way for his return to Ecuador. In addition, Bucaram advised Gutiérrez to declare a state of emergency and dissolve Congress. Demonstrations erupted throughout the country, demanding that Gutiérrez step down. The president declared a state of emergency and announced that he was dismissing the temporary justices, although he did not dissolve the Congress. These measures did not mollify the public and the protests continued. The military refused to disband the demonstrations, thus avoiding a bloody confrontation. As demonstrations intensified, the Congress voted 62–0 to oust Gutiérrez on the grounds that he had abandoned his office. On April 20, 2005, angry protesters surrounded the presidential palace. Gutiérrez escaped by helicopter and sought political asylum in the Brazilian embassy. On April 24 he left the country for Brazil, still claiming to be the legitimate president of Ecuador.

Alfredo Palacio, a 66-year-old heart surgeon, became the sixth president of Ecuador in a span of only seven years, reflecting the nation's recent political instability. Once again a new president faced questions of legitimacy. Although he was backed by the armed forces and recognized by the United States, the Organization of American States investigated Palacio's government to determine if Gutiérrez's removal was constitutional. The OAS concluded that Palacio had been elevated to the presidency in accordance with constitutional procedures. Palacio benefited from the public's disgust with Gutiérrez and was able to consolidate his hold on the presidency. Former President Bucaram fled the country in anticipation that the new president might not be so lenient in prosecuting his alleged corruption. Gutiérrez returned to Ecuador and was quickly placed in jail from October 2005 until March 2006, when the Supreme Court ordered his release for lack of evidence.

Palacio dramatically shifted policy when he suddenly expropriated the assets of Occidental Petroleum, declaring that the U.S. firm had violated its contracts. This move was popular with leftist elements and indigenous groups. The following month the president seemed to contradict the expropriation by hosting a summit with Bolivia, Colombia, and Peru to discuss free-trade agreements with the United States. The president also faced protests during his brief presidency but remained in office to complete his predecessor's term.

From August 10, 1996, until January 15, 2007, Ecuador experienced another period of political instability that threatened its nascent democracy, damaged its international reputation, and slowed the growth of its economy. The balance that had been achieved between right and left in the preceding period was not perfect, but at least political chaos had been avoided for the most part. Much of the blame for this political charade can be placed squarely on the shoulders of the three elected presidents, Bucaram, Mahuad, and Gutiérrez. Bucaram's erratic behavior and corrupt nepotism were too much for the public to bear, even by Ecuadorian standards. In addition, *El Loco* turned his back on the urban poor, the constituency that had elected him. He also lost the support of the military, the most important and well-organized institution in the country. Mahuad offered great promise as an honest technocrat and a man of steady personal behavior. However, he too ignored the groups that had elected him, completely misread the growing strength of indigenous activism, and allowed corruption to taint his image. Additionally, he failed to realize that his new defense policy, announced in the aftermath of the peace treaty with Peru, was offensive to the military. Gutiérrez also allowed early accusations of corruption to mar his reputation as a reformer. He enjoyed a strong economy, but squandered this advantage in a petty fight with Congress over the Supreme Court. He also ignored the indigenous movement that had contributed to his electoral victory. As a former colonel he seemed oblivious to the contempt that the generals had of him for his part in the coup that had ousted Mahuad. All three presidents also had vice presidents who were ambitious and eager to become president.

Some hopeful outcomes emerged during this otherwise dismal political period. The Ecuadorian military acted with restraint and served as a skillful arbiter, preventing the country from sinking into violence, civil war, and dictatorship. Politicians made an effort to find a constitutional resolution to each crisis, even though constitutional provisions for removal of a president were very loosely interpreted in all three cases. In the long run both the peace agreement with Peru and the dollarization plan were beneficial to Ecuador. The three accidental presidents, Alarcón, Noboa, and Palacio, succeeded in calming the political turbulence that engulfed the country each time an elected president went into exile. This enabled Ecuador to have new free and fair elections. The 2006 elections resulted in new trends, a new leader. and a new constitution for the republic.

RAFAEL CORREA AND THE CITIZEN'S REVOLUTION

Even by Ecuadorian standards, the 2006 presidential field was crowded, as 17 people vied for the presidential sash. Early political soothsayers pointed to a victory by Alvaro Noboa, the banana billionaire, who once again headed the PIRAN ticket. Cynthia Veteri, the nominee of the PSC, polled well early on. At the start of the campaign, Rafael Correa Delgado, of the newly formed *Alianza País* (Country Alliance) movement, was relatively unknown and given little chance of finishing in the top five. However, his campaign theme of "Proud and Sovereign Homeland" soon resonated with the urban and rural masses, and he finished a surprising second in the first election round with 23 percent of the vote to Noboa's 27 percent.[8] Correa then faced Noboa in the runoff election and proved to be the new face of populism in Ecuador. His campaign tactics were reminiscent of Velasco Ibarra as he went on the stump giving fiery, but somewhat vague, speeches promising to "whip the mafias," his sarcastic reference to the traditional power structure in Ecuador, and to launch a "Citizen's Revolution."[9] He also vowed to never enter a free trade agreement with the United States and to close the portion of the Manta Air Base that the United States leased for counter-narcotics operations. He claimed a close connection to indigenous peoples, but his obtuse use of a few Quechua phrases exposed this claim as less than genuine. Nevertheless, the indigenous leadership favored him until the last week of the campaign. Like Velasco Ibarra, he did not form a political party, calling Alianza País a movement. He likewise denounced the traditional parties as corrupt and accused them of having created a *partidocracia* (partyocracy). His electoral victory of 56 percent to Noboa's 36 was significant. The *Economist* magazine was less sanguine and attributed Correa's victory not to his charismatic appeal, but rather to the fact that "Ecuador's political and social system has been thoroughly discredited."[10]

Rafael Correa Delgado was born on April 6, 1963, in Guayaquil into a middle-class family. Prior to entering politics, his career was in academics. A brilliant student, he earned an economics degree from the Catholic University in Guayaquil in 1987, followed by a master of arts from the Université Catholique de Louvain in Belgium, and a PhD at the University of Illinois at Urbana-Champaign. He returned to Ecuador and accepted a professorship at the University of San Francisco in Quito and also taught graduate courses at FLACSO, the School of Latin American Social Sciences. In 2005 Palacio appointed Correa finance minister, where he soon promoted programs to reduce poverty and to establish economic sovereignty. He abruptly resigned after only four months in office, claiming a lack of presidential support for his initiatives.

In 1987 Correa volunteered to work at a mission administered by the Salesian order in a remote village of Cotopaxi Province in the north central highlands. This experience helped mold his political philosophy, which is described as Christian left and 21st-century socialism.

YET ANOTHER CONSTITUTION

In his inaugural address, delivered on January 15, 2007, Correa presented the five main points of his Citizen's Revolution. These included a call for a constitutional assembly, an end to corruption, increased spending on health and education, an end to neoliberal economic policies, and regional economic integration. It was soon apparent that Correa's top priority was a new constitution. His number one political problem, somewhat of his own making, was that he had no party support in Congress as his AP movement had not fielded any congressional candidates. His plan was to call for a constituent assembly to write a new constitution and to serve as a temporary legislative body. A constitution drafted mainly by delegates from AP would strengthen the powers of the president, permit presidential reelection, and provide legitimacy for his Citizen's Revolution. Over the next nine months the president proved his political skill by defeating his opponents at every turn. His first victory was gaining approval for a plebiscite to determine if the people agreed to the convocation of a constituent assembly. This was followed by a resounding affirmation on April 15, when 80 percent of Ecuadorians voted in favor of his proposal. Then, on September 30, AP won a majority of the seats in the assembly, insuring that Correa's vision would shape the new constitution.

Not surprisingly, Correa obtained most of what he wanted in the constitution of 2008, Ecuador's 20th. Presidential power was enhanced, congressional power reduced, and future presidents would be eligible for immediate reelection once. Moreover, Correa's current term would not be part of the reelection formula, meaning he could stand for election in 2009 and again in 2013. The draft constitution also provided for a ban on foreign military bases, and reestablished government control of key industries, including petroleum, mining, transportation, and communications. The utopian document provided an extensive list of rights for Ecuadorians including *sumak kawasay*, a Quechua phrase that means the good way of living. While many of these "rights" are laudable goals, they lack little basis in reality and certainly cannot be guaranteed by the state. Nevertheless, Correa won another significant victory on September 28, 2008, when nearly two-thirds of the electorate ratified the new constitution. The constitution went into effect on October 20 and new elections were announced for April 2009.[11]

CORREA: A POPULAR POPULIST

On April 26, 2009, Correa defeated six other candidates to win the presidential race in the first round with 52 percent of the vote, an astounding achievement in view of the fact that the four previously elected presidents had failed to complete even half of their terms. In addition, Correa became the first president to win a first-round election since 1979, and the first sitting president to be reelected since García Moreno in 1875. Moreover, under the new constitution, he is eligible for reelection in 2013 and could possibly serve until 2017. If this scenario comes to pass, he would become the longest-serving chief executive in Ecuador's history.

FOREIGN RELATIONS

During his four years in office Correa has pursued an independent foreign policy. He refused to consider renewing the lease of a portion of the Manta Air Base to the United States, and U.S. personnel departed in November 2009. Relations with the United States suffered another setback when Correa declared Ms. Heather M. Hodges, the U.S. Ambassador, persona non grata, which resulted in her expulsion in April 2011. The incident resulted from a confidential report released by the website WikiLeaks, in which Hodges recommended that the United States revoke a visa for Jaime Aquilino Hurtado, a former national police commander under Correa, because of his involvement in corruption. The cable also suggested that Correa knew of Aquilino's activities at the time of the appointment. Ecuador's foreign minister, Ricardo Patiño, tried to downplay the incident, saying it was an action of one person and not a state-to-state problem. The United States did not agree and responded by expelling the Ecuadorian ambassador and suspending discussions with Ecuador on other issues.

Ecuador's relationship with neighboring Colombia was severely tested on March 1, 2008, when the Colombian military bombed and raided a FARC camp in northern Ecuador. An Ecuadorian national, Franklin Aisalla, allegedly a FARC member, was killed in the raid. The raid also netted computer records indicating that FARC had support from Venezuela and that FARC had contributed to Correa's 2006 election campaign. On March 3 Ecuador broke diplomatic relations with Colombia and filed complaints with the Organization of American States. The two nations did not restore full diplomatic relations until November 2010.

Ecuador's relationship with Brazil has also had its ups and downs. In 2007 Ecuador agreed to purchase 24 Super Tacano jets, desperately needed to upgrade the air force's fighter and training planes. The deal was placed in jeopardy when Ecuador expelled Odebrecht, a Brazilian construction firm, in early 2008 for faulty work on the San Francisco hydroelectric dam. In addition, Ecuador put pressure on Petrobras, Brazil's state oil company, to accept new contracts with more favorable terms. Brazil countered by threatening to end all bilateral trade and recalled its ambassador. This was a surprising development because Ecuador was not only in debt to Brazil, it needed additional development loans. The rift ended in January 2010 when the two nations normalized relations after Ecuador repaid Brazil for the loan it had secured to build the San Francisco dam.

On June 24, 2009, Ecuador formally joined the Bolivarian Alliance for the Peoples of the Americas, better known by its original acronym, ALBA. The creation of Venezuela's president Hugo Chavez, ALBA was established as an alternative to other Western Hemisphere cooperative organizations, such as the Organization of American States. The first two members were Venezuela and Cuba, later joined by Bolivia and Nicaragua. A key goal is the establishment of an organization of socialist governments to work toward regional integration and the adoption of a regional currency. Ecuador and Venezuela experimented with a new regional virtual currency, the sucre, when the two nations signed a bilateral trade deal in June 2010. Ecuador's late entry into ALBA demonstrates Correa's growing confidence that he can pursue a radical leftist agenda in foreign affairs. He had previously been coy about joining ALBA, but his domestic political victories strengthened his hand.

THE ABORTIVE SEPTEMBER 2010 COUP

Correa's smooth sailing in Ecuador's normally troubled political waters encountered storms waves on September 20, 2010, when the national police launched widespread demonstrations to protest a reduction in benefits. Correa decided to confront the police by speaking to protesters at a police installation. While delivering the speech, the president was attacked and tear-gassed by protestors until his security detail whisked him into the police hospital at the installation. Correa holed up on the third floor for the next 10 hours, while angry police surrounded the building, making him a virtual captive. Confusion reigned, Quito's airport was closed, and rumors spread that the coup had succeeded. However, the military high command, most of the subordinate commands, as well as the rank and file, decided not to join in the *golpe* and to rescue the president from his predicament. An elite army special operation unit entered the hospital, safely extricated Correa, and brought him to the presidential palace. However, 5 men were killed and 38 people wounded during the operation. The president soon gave a rousing address to his supporters, who filled the central plaza to celebrate his rescue. Rafael Correa was defiant and triumphant as he waved the Ecuadorian flag from the balcony of the Carondelet, but perhaps he, too, was beginning to realize that Ecuador is a very difficult country to govern.

Rafael Correa has provided Ecuador with more than four years of continuity in the presidency and has survived one attempted coup. Given Ecuador's revolving-door presidency from 1996 to 2007, this is a remarkable achievement. In addition, Correa has won nearly every political battle with his opponents, including a new constitution that greatly strengthens the power of the presidency. His vision for improved health, education, and employment opportunities has provided hope for the marginalized Ecuadorians. He also raised expectations that corruption would be curbed. Correa was embarrassed by *El universo,* the venerable Guayaquil newspaper, for its revelation that his brother, Fabrico Correa, had contracts with the government totaling $300 million. In addition, his failure to deliver any significant promises to the indigenous population has resulted in the withdrawal of the support of the leading Indian organizations. Correa has continued the U.S. dollar as Ecuador's currency despite his promise to restore the sucre. He has also proven to be very harsh with his critics, especially the press. Correa used the obscure Article 230 of Ecuador's penal code, which prohibits disrespect of the president, to bring libel suits against Emilio Palacio, an editor for *El universo.* In July 2011, Palacio and three of the newspaper's directors were found guilty of libel for implying that Correa is a dictator. All four were sentenced to three years in jail and El Universo was fined $40 million. Correa's political victories and his silencing of the opposition press have not yet resulted in significant economic and social change. While there have been improvements to the highway system, an increase in schools and health services for the poor, many are concerned that Correa may be just another populist *caudillo* whose main objective is long-lasting personal power.

NOTES

1. Allen Gerlach, *Indians, Oil and Politics: A Recent History of Ecuador* (Wilmington, DE: Scholarly Resources, 2002), 84.

2. Ibid., 85.

3. Ibid., 86.

4. Ibid., 90.

5. Ibid., 116.

6. Ibid., 121.

7. Ibid., 80–81.

8. Kenneth J. Mijeski and Scott H. Beck, *Pachakutik and the Rise and Decline of the Ecuadorian Indigenous Movement* (Athens: Ohio University Press, 2011), 107.

9. "An Enigmatic Leftist Rides into Town," *Economist,* October 14, 2006, p. 39.

10. Ibid.

11. Marc Becker, *Pachakutik! Indigenous Movements and Electoral Politics in Ecuador* (New York: Rowman and Littlefield, 2011), 127–65.

Notable People in
the History of Ecuador

Atahualpa (ca. 1502–33) Sometimes called the first Ecuadorian because of his birth in Tomebamba, present-day Cuenca, he was the last sovereign emperor of the Inca civilization. He came to the throne after winning a civil war against his half brother, Huáscar. He was captured by Francisco Pizarro, the Spanish Conquistador, in November 1532 and held for ransom. After Atahualpa complied with the ransom demand he was executed on the charge that he had ordered the murder of Huáscar. Atahualpa is venerated in Ecuador on statues, on monuments, and in textbooks.

Alfaro Delgado, Eloy (1842–1912) Known as the "Old Warrior," Alfaro was a radical politician and military officer who led the Liberal Revolution in Ecuador in 1895. At various times he ruled Ecuador as supreme chief or interim president. He served two constitutional presidential terms (1897–1901 and 1907–11). Alfaro initiated many infrastructure improvements including the Guayaquil and Quito Railway. He implemented reforms in public education, established public records of vital statistics, secularized cemeteries, and curbed the power of the Catholic Church. However, he used repressive measures against his opposition and orchestrated electoral fraud. He died a violent death at the hands of a mob following an aborted attempt to regain the presidency by force. Alfaro is an iconic figure for present-day Ecuadorian radicals.

Arroyo del Río, Carlos (1894–1969) As president from 1940 to 1944 he presided over Ecuador's brief but disastrous war with Peru in July 1941 and the subsequent Río Protocol by which Ecuador ceded a vast region of the Amazon. He also cooperated with the United States during World War II and agreed to the construction of air and naval facilities at Salinas and in the Galápagos Islands. He was deposed in 1944 and spent much of the rest of his life trying to restore his reputation after the debacles of 1941 and 1942.

Arteaga Serrano de Fernández, Rosalía (1956–) was the first female vice president (1996–98) and briefly the first female president (February 9–11, 1997). When President Abdalá Bucaram was forced from office by Congress on February 6, 1997, Arteaga became embroiled in a dispute with the president of Congress, Fabián Alarcón, over succession to the presidency. Alarcón was sworn in by Congress but Arteaga claimed this was illegitimate and held her own swearing-in ceremony. Several days later Arteaga resigned and resumed her duties as vice president when she realized she had no support from the Congress or the armed forces. Later she served as secretary-general of the Amazon Cooperation Treaty Organization.

Benalcázar, Sebastián de (ca. 1479–1551) was the Spanish conquistador responsible for defeating the Inca armies in present-day Ecuador. He launched his invasion in 1534 but met stiff resistance from by the Inca general Rumiñahui. On December 6, the Spanish captured Quito, only to discover the defenders had burned the city and hauled off all treasure. Benalcázar founded a new city and named it San Francisco de Quito. His colonial home is now a museum in Quito and a statue honors him as the city's founder.

Borja Cevallos, Rodrigo (1935–) was president from 1988 to 1992, and a founder of the Izquierda Democratica, or ID (Democratic Left), in 1970. Borja's party proposed economic programs to help the poor but he took office during a recession and was forced to implement austerity measures. He is credited with working with other left-of-center parties, including the communists, to create less partisan politics, but he was fiercely opposed by the right. His international policies were more successful. He completed his constitutional term, thus extending an extraordinary period of stability in Ecuadorian politics.

Bucaram Elmhalim, Assad (1916–81) was a leader of Concentration of Popular Forces (CFP), a leftist party, a spellbinding populist, and the first major political figure of Lebanese descent in Ecuadorian history. He was twice mayor of Guayaquil in the 1960s and the leading candidate for the presidency before the military intervened and suspended elections in 1972. He paved the way for other Lebanese Ecuadorians who have been elected president or held other high offices.

Bucaram Ortiz, Abdalá (1952–) was president of Ecuador (1996–97), founder of the Roldista Party, and always a controversial figure in Ecuadorian politics. He campaigned in 1996, proudly using the nickname *El Loco* (The Crazy One) and exhibiting bizarre behavior at rallies by singing American rock n' roll classics and even wearing a Batman costume. Nevertheless he won a runoff election with 54.5 percent of the vote largely on the promise of change and his criticism of the oligarchy. He was unable to deliver on his populist agenda and his embarrassing behavior led Parliament to remove him from the presidency for mental incapacity on February 6, 1997. He spent many years in exile in Panama and returned to Ecuador in April 2005.

Calderón Múñoz, Abdón (1804–22) was the hero of the Battle of Pichincha, May 24, 1822, that ended Spanish rule in Ecuador. Although he was seriously wounded, Calderón continued to fight, and died the following day. He became a symbol of Ecuadorian patriotism and one of Ecuador's highest military decorations is named in his honor.

Cañizares, Manuela (unknown–1814?) was a heroine of the Ecuadorian Independence movement. Her house was used by the patriotic junta to write the first proclamation of independence, which was promulgated on August 10, 1809. She was tried for treason and sentenced to death. Apparently the execution was not carried out, as her will, dated 1814, has been discovered.

Condamine, Charles Marie de la (1701–74) was a scientist and the leader of the French Academy of Sciences expedition sent to Ecuador in 1736 to determine the location of the equator line and measure one degree of the arc of the earth's circumference. His team introduced many books and ideas of the Enlightenment to Ecuador.

Crespo Toral, Remigo (1860–1939) was a poet, intellectual, and educator whose literary works were acclaimed throughout South America. He was also rector of the University of Cuenca and a president of Congress who served in many diplomatic posts during his career.

Espejo, Eugenio de Santa Cruz y (1747–95) was a physician and journalist who founded Ecuador's first journal, *Las primicias de la cultura de Quito*, in 1792. He was strongly critical of Spain's colonial policies and advocated autonomy for Ecuador. His writings resulted in his imprisonment and he became an iconic figure of Ecuadorian nationalism.

Flores, Juan José (1800–64) was the first president of Ecuador (1830–34), and again president from 1839 to 1843. Flores was born in Venezuela and served as a general in Bolívar's army. His Venezuelan birth and numerous attempts to return to power made him a controversial figure of the early republican period.

García Moreno, Gabriel (1821–75) was the Conservative president of Ecuador (1861–65 and 1869–75), known for his modernization projects, strong support of the Vatican, and strongman tactics. Moreno oversaw numerous infrastructure improvements including the Quito to Guayaquil wagon road and improved education. He introduced government reforms, fought corruption, and fostered commercial advances. However, his dictatorial tendencies and close ties to the Roman Catholic Church resulted in numerous enemies. He was assassinated on August 6, 1875.

González Suárez, Federico (1844–1917) was a renowned clergyman and historian who served as archbishop of Quito from 1906 to 1917. His eight-volume *General History of Ecuador* was the first scholarly study of Ecuador's colonial period and is considered a classic. He played a critical role in softening conservative clerical opposition to secular reforms during the liberal period.

Guayasamín, Oswaldo (1919–99) is Ecuador's most internationally acclaimed artist, whose murals and works are displayed throughout the Western world. His most famous works include *The Road of Tears*, 1952, which portrays the sufferings of indigenous and Afro- Ecuadorians; and *As Long as I Live, I Shall Remember You*, a tribute to his mother. His unique style, known as monumentalism, reveals the influence of Picasso and Orozco.

Guevara Moreno, Carlos (1911–74) founded the Concentration of Popular Forces, a radical leftist and populist political party, in 1949. He was elected mayor of Guayaquil in 1951 and was a serious contender for president in 1956. Traditional politicians and the military viewed Guevara Moreno's popularity among the urban masses as a threat and he was exiled or imprisoned a number of times.

Gutiérrez, Lucio (1957–) is a former army colonel who participated in the 2000 uprising that led to the removal of President Jamil Mahuad. He later formed the Patriotic Society Party and was elected president in 2002. He served from 2003 to 2005 and was forced from office by opposition in the Congress with the support of the military. He again ran for president in 2009 but finished second with 26.8 percent of the vote.

Harman, Archer (1859–1911) was the American railroad entrepreneur who contracted with Eloy Alfaro in 1895 to construct the Guayaquil and Quito railway. Harman and his brother John (1865–1907) overcame some of the world's most difficult engineering challenges to complete the line in 1908.

Hassaurek, Friedrich (1832–85) served as U.S. minister resident in Quito from 1861 to 1865. He later wrote *Four Years among the Ecuadorians*, a narrative of his experiences in Ecuador that was for years the main source of information and impressions of Ecuador in the United States. While highly critical of

Ecuador's government, it provides a view of daily life in the Ecuadorian highlands in the 1860s and Hassaurek's fascination with the people and landscape.

Hurtado Larrea, Osvaldo (1939–) assumed the presidency in May 1981 after the death of President Jaime Roldós in a plane crash. He is the founder of the Popular Democracy political party and a strong advocate of the Christian democracy. Hurtado wrote *Political Power in Ecuador* and *Ecuador: Portrait of a Nation,* two influential assessments of Ecuadorian politics.

Icaza, Jorge (1906–78) was the author of *Huasipungo* (The Villagers), the most-read novel in Ecuadorian literature. Icaza was a leading social realist of the 1930s and a proponent of human rights for indigenous peoples. He attempted to expose abuses of the Indians and to raise the social conscience of the white and mestizo population to their plight.

Jaramillo, Julio (1935–78) was a beloved singer and songwriter whose songs are know as *pasillos,* a type of Ecuadorian ballad. They tell stories of unrequited love and broken promises and express the sadness and moral dilemmas of the average Ecuadorian. Jaramillo is as iconic to Ecuadorians as Frank Sinatra or Elvis Presley are to their generations in the United States.

Kemmerer, Edwin W. (1875–1945) was a Princeton University economics professor who helped establish the U.S. Federal Reserve banking system and was contracted by the Ecuadorian government in 1926 to review Ecuador's financial system and make recommendations for improvements. Kemmerer, known as the "money doctor," and his team of experts proposed the establishment of the Banco Central and numerous other reforms to stabilize the economy and minimize inflation. Ecuador adopted many of the Kemmerer reforms, of which the Banco Central proved to be the most enduring.

Kingman, Eduardo (1914–98) was an artist and is considered to be Ecuador's master of social realism: his murals, paintings, and prints express the plight of marginalized groups, including Indians and the urban laborer. His exaggerated depiction of hands earned him the sobriquet as the "Painter of Hands." He served as director of the Quito Museum of Colonial Art and was active throughout his life as a social activist.

Legarda, Bernardo de (ca. 1700–1773) was a colonial sculptor whose masterpiece, *The Winged Virgin of Quito,* the centerpiece of the San Francisco church, is an icon of Ecuador's veneration of the Virgin Mary. The work has been widely copied and is displayed in homes, businesses, and schools throughout the country and a monumental recreation stands on the Panacillo hill overlooking Quito.

Macas, Luis (1951–) is a prominent indigenous political leader, one of the founders and past president of CONAIE (Confederation of Indigenous

Nationalities of Ecuador), former member of Congress, and minister of agriculture in 2003. He was a presidential candidate of the Pachakutik movement in 2006. Macas initially gained international support for indigenous causes but his influence has waned in recent years.

Maldonado, Pedro Vicente (1704–48) was a geographer, astronomer, and mathmetician from Ríobamba who assisted the French scientific team in measuring the equator line starting 1736. He became an internationally recognized scientist and was admitted to the French Academy of Sciences shortly before his death. Maldonado drafted one of the first realistic maps of the Audiencia of Quito and is Ecuador's most famous scientist of the Enlightenment.

Mariana de Jesús, Paredes y Flores (1618–45) was the first Ecuadorian to be canonized by the Roman Catholic Church. At age 10 she took vows of poverty, chastity, and obedience and later assumed a life of solitude in her home that consisted of fasting and austerity. Mariana was known to cure the sick and restored at least one person to life. An earthquake struck Quito in 1645, followed by an epidemic; in the midst of the catastrophe Mariana offered her life to God to spare others and died three days later. Legend has it that a lily sprang from her blood and she is also remembered as "The Lily of Quito."

Marques de Selva Alegre, Juan Pío Montúfar (1759–1818) was a leading figure of the early independence movement and president of the Sovereign Junta of Quito formed on August 10, 1809. In October 1809 royal troops ended the rebellion and crown officials ordered the execution of many of the conspirators. Selva Alegre and others of noble birth were exiled to Spain.

Mera, Juan León (1832–94) was a writer from Ambato who is known as the father of Ecuadorian literature. His novel, *Cumandá,* is considered a classic in Latin American literature and has recently been translated into English. Mera championed criollo culture and wrote the lyrics of Ecuador's national anthem.

Montalvo, Juan (1833–89) is generally considered Ecuador's greatest writer; however, his work focused mostly on essays that promoted the liberal agenda in the 19th century. He opposed the conservative dictator, Gabriel García Moreno, in *The Cosmopolitan,* his magazine that served as a house organ for the Liberal party. His famous essay, *The Perpetual Dictatorship,* may have inspired the men who murdered García Moreno. Montalvo later published *Las cantilinarias,* a critical attack on the regime of General Ignacio Veintemilla.

Moncayo, Paco (1940–) was the army general who orchestrated Ecuador's success in the Upper Cenepa Conflict in 1995. As head of the armed forces he also skillfully managed the chaos surrounding the removal of President

Abdalá Bucaram from office by the congress in 1997. He later served as the mayor of Quito from 2000 to 2009.

Olmedo, José Joaquin de (1780–1847) was a poet and political figure who played a pivotal role in Guayaquil's fight for independence from Spain. He established the Free Province of Guayaquil but it was soon united with Bolívar's Gran Colombia. Olmedo was Ecuador's first vice president and served briefly as president in 1845. His poetry is highly patriotic and his most famous work is *The Victory of Junin.*

Orellana, Francisco de (1511–48) was a Spanish conquistador who served as second in command to Gonzalo Pizarro of an expedition in search of El Dorado in 1541. The adventurers crossed the eastern cordillera and descended to the Napo river. Orellana and 57 men continued downstream in search of food with orders to return in 12 days. The current proved too strong to return upstream and Orellana decided to sail on. Eventually he arrived at the headwaters of the Amazon and later became the first European to traverse the entire length of the great river. Orellana's feat was later used by nationalists to proclaim that Ecuador is an Amazonian nation.

Pérez, Jefferson (1974–) became the first Ecuadorian to win an Olympic gold medal when he finished first in the 20-kilometer race walk at the 1996 Atlanta Olympics. Pérez also won three world championships, three Pan American Games championships, and surprised the world by taking a silver at the 2008 Olympics in Beijing at the age of 34. He is the most successful athlete in Ecuadorian sports history and a national hero.

Plaza Lasso, Galo (1906–87) was a progressive president of Ecuador (1948–52) and an internationally respected statesmen. As president, Plaza ushered in a period of political stability and moderate economic and social reforms. He was a strong advocate of democracy and served as Secretary General of the Organization of American States from 1968 to 1975. Plaza also served the United Nations and worked to resolve crises in Lebanon in 1968, the Congo in 1960 and Cyprus in 1964–65.

Proaño Villaba, Leónidas (1910–88) was the bishop of Ríobamba (1954–85), a leading theologian, and a proponent of liberation theology. His controversial ideas and actions resulted in conservative elements labeling him a Marxist, a description that he denied. Proaño organized Christian Assemblies and Christian Based Communities in his diocese to encourage the poor to form cooperatives and to help each other. In 1960 he started Popular Radio Schools to broadcast educational and religious programs to the poor. In 1962 he founded the Center of Studies and Social Action to assist indigenous villages in development. In 1973 he was tried by a Vatican court for insurgent activity but was cleared of all charges. He was arrested and jailed in 1976 for organizing a meeting of religious leaders that the government declared was subversive. Proaño was later nominated for the Nobel Peace Prize.

Ricke, Jodoco (1498–1575) was a Franciscan friar who began building the famous San Francisco Church and monastery in 1537. Ricke and Friar Pedro Gosseal later founded the St. Andrew School, the first arts and crafts school in Spanish America. This institution spawned the unique artistic style known as the Escuela Quiteña (Quito School of Art) and ushered in the golden age of Ecuadorian colonial art.

Rumiñahui (ca. 1490–1535) was the Inca general who fiercely resisted the Spanish Conquistadors as they marched on Quito in 1534. His scorched-earth retreat through the central and northern highlands partially explains the scarcity of Inca ruins in Ecuador. He was later captured and executed in January 1535. He became a symbol of native resistance and, ironically, an icon of Ecuadorian national identity.

Rocafuerte, Vicente (1783–1847) was a prominent leader in the independence movement, an international statesmen, and the first native-born Ecuadorian to be president of the republic (1835–39). Rocafuerte was a committed liberal who advocated religious freedom, universal education, and republicanism. His essays on liberal principles and political systems were widely read in 19th-century Latin America.

Rodríguez Lara, Guillermo (1924) headed the military junta formed after the overthrow of President Velasco Ibarra in 1972. The junta used Ecuador's newly found oil wealth to initiate numerous infrastructure projects including highways, hospitals, schools, industrial complexes, and modernization of the armed forces. Inflation, a rising international debt, and restrictions on political freedom resulted in the regime's unpopularity. He was removed from power by the military in 1976.

Roldós Aguilera, Jaime (1940–82) was the first civilian to be elected president (1978) after a period of military rule. He was also the first president from the populist Concentration of Popular Forces, a political party that was once considered radical leftist. Roldós died in a plane crash in 1982. After his death Abdalá Bucaram named his new party the Ecuadorian Roldista Party in honor of Roldós.

Sáenz, Manuela (1797–1856) was Simón Bolívar's mistress, advisor, and trusted friend. Sáenz accompanied Bolívar on numerous military campaigns and also preserved many of his papers. In 1828 she saved Bolívar's life during an assassination attempt, causing Bolívar to refer to her as the Liberator of the Liberator. Recent scholarship has revealed that she played a greater role in the independence and early republican period of Latin American history than previously thought.

Sucre Alcalá, Antonio José de (1795–1830) was a general in Bolívar's patriot army, the Liberator's most trusted officer and a brilliant field commander. Sucre led the patriots to victory in the Battle of Pichincha on May 24, 1822, ending Spanish rule in Ecuador. He achieved additional victories in 1824 at Junín and Ayacucho in Peru that ended Spanish rule in South America. Sucre was a native of Venezuela but his wife was Ecuadorian. After serving as president of Bolivia, he returned to Quito in 1828 hoping to retire from public service but was again called to military service in 1829 by Gran Colombia to defeat a Peruvian army that had invaded southern Ecuador. He supported Bolívar in his futile attempt to preserve Gran Colombia. Sucre was assassinated on June 4, 1830. He is a national hero and for many years Ecuador's currency was known as the sucre.

Tituaña, Auki (1965–) was the first indigenous mayor of an Ecuadorian town when he was elected in 1996 as the mayor of Cotacachi. He proved to be an able administrator and Cotacachi was awarded the Cities for Peace prize by UNESCO in 2002.

Tobar Donoso, Julio (1894–1981) was Ecuador's foreign minister at the 1942 Río Conference who signed the infamous Río Protocol that ceded a large and long-disputed Amazonian area to Peru. In 1945 he explained his actions and restated Ecuador's claim with the publication of *The Peruvian Invasion and the Río Protocol.*

Vargas, Antonio (19?) is a leading figure of the indigenous political movement in Ecuador and past president of the Confederation of Indigenous Nationalities of Ecuador (CONAIE). He played a key role in the indigenous uprising in 2000 that toppled the government of Jamil Mahuad. He served as Minster of Social Welfare in the Lucio Gutiérrez government and remains active in advocating for indigenous peoples.

Velasco Ibarra, José María (1893–1979) was five times president of Ecuador (1934–35; 1944–47; 1952–56; 1960–61; and 1968–72), however, he was removed from office by military coups on four occasions and only once completed a full term (in the 1950s). He spent many years in political exile and became known as *El Gran Ausente,* the "Great Absentee." Velasco Ibarra dominated Ecuador's political scene for much of the 20th century, declared himself to be the "National Personification," and invented the Ecuadorian version of the populist political campaign that endures to the present day.

Villamil, José de (1788–1866) was born in New Orleans and became a U.S. citizen as a result of the Louisiana Purchase in 1803. He became involved in the independence movement in Ecuador and participated in the liberation campaigns . He settled in Guayaquil, established buisnesses, and obtained dual citizenship. Villamil pushed for annexation of the Galápagos Islands, served as the first governor of the islands, and was the founder of the Ecuadorian navy. He later served as Ecuador's chargé d'affaires to the United States and was involved in politics throughout his life.

Wolf, Teodoro (1841–1924) was a member of a German scientific team that came to Ecuador in 1870 to teach at the Quito Polytechnic School. Wolf, a geologist, wrote *The Geography and Geology of Ecuador,* the first comprehensive and scholarly study of Ecuador's flora, fauna, and terrain. This classic work contains some of the best early photographs of Ecuador and is beautifully illustrated with maps and charts.

Selected Bibliography

Aguilar-Monsalve, Luis Antonio. "The Separation of Church and State: The Ecuadorian Case." *Thought* 59 (June 1984): 205–18.

Andrien, Kenneth J. *The Kingdom of Quito, 1690–1830*. Cambridge, UK: Cambridge University Press, 1995.

Ayala-Mora, Enrique, ed. *Nueva historia del Ecuador*. Vols. 1–15. Quito: Corporación Editora Nacional, 1996.

Background Notes: Ecuador. Washington, DC: U.S. Department of State, 2011.

Becker, Marc. *Pachakutik: Indigenous Movements and Electoral Politics in Ecuador*. Lanham, MD: Rowman and Littlefield, 2011.

Blanksten, George. *Ecuador: Constitutions and Caudillos*. New York: Russell and Russell, 1964.

Borchart de Moreno, Christiana. "Beyond the Obraje: Handicraft Production in Quito toward the End of the Colonial Period." *The Americas* 52, no.1 (1995):1–24 .

Bork, Albert William, and Georg Maier. *Historical Dictionary of Ecuador*. Metuchen, NJ: Scarecrow Press, 1973.

Brainard, Elizabeth Harman, and Katharine Robinson Brainard. *Railroad in the Sky*. Quito: Corporación para el Desarrollo de la Educación Universitaria, 2007.

Brown, Charles H. *Agents of Manifest Destiny: The Lives and Times of the Filibusters.* Chapel Hill: University of North Carolina Press, 1974.

Clark, Kim A. *The Redemptive Work: Railway and Nation in Ecuador, 1895–1930.* Wilmington, DE: Scholarly Resources, 1998.

Clayton, Lawrence. *The Bolivarian Nations of Latin America.* Arlington Heights, IL: Forum Press, 1984.

Conaghan, Catherine M. *Restructuring Domination: Industrialists and the State in Ecuador.* Pittsburgh: University of Pittsburgh Press, 1988.

Corkill, David. "Democratic Politics in Ecuador, 1979–1984." *Bulletin of Latin American Research* 4, no. 2 (1985): 63–74

Corkill, David, and David Cubitt. *Ecuador: Fragile Democracy.* London: Latin American Bureau, 1988.

Crandall, Russell, Guadalupe Paz, and Riordan Roett, eds. *The Andes in Focus: Security, Democracy, and Economic Reform.* Boulder, CO: Lynne Rienner, 2005.

Cueva, Agustín. *The Process of Political Domination in Ecuador.* New Brunswick, NJ: Transaction Books, 1982.

Drake, Paul W. *The Money Doctor of the Andes.* Durham, NC: Duke University Press, 1989.

Gerlach, Allen. *Indians, Oil, and Politics: A Recent History of Ecuador.* Wilmington, DE: Scholarly Resources, 2003.

Goffin, Alvin M. *The Rise of Protestant Evangelism in Ecuador, 1895–1990.* Gainesville: University Press of Florida, 1994.

Hagedorn, Dan. "Lend Lease to Latin America. Part I: Army Aircraft." *Journal of American Aviation Historical Society* 122 (Summer 1989): 121–25.

Handelsman, Michael. *Culture and Customs of Ecuador.* Westport, CT: Greenwood Press, 2000.

Hanratty, Dennis M., ed. *Ecuador: A Country Study.* Washington, DC: Library of Congress Federal Research Division, 1991.

Henderson, Peter V. N. *Gabriel García Moreno and Conservative State Formation in the Andes.* Austin: University of Texas Press, 2008.

Hey, Jeanne A. K. *Theories of Dependent Foreign Policy and the Case of Ecuador in the 1980s.* Athens, OH: Ohio University Center for International Studies, 1995.

Hurtado, Osvaldo. *Political Power in Ecuador.* Albuquerque: University of New Mexico Press, 1980.

Hurtado, Osvaldo. *Portrait of a Nation: Culture and Progress in Ecuador.* New York: Madison Books, 2010.

Kofas, Jon V. "Politics of Conflict and Containment: Ecuador's Labor Movement and U.S. Foreign Policy, 1944–1963." *Journal of Third World Studies* 13, no. 2 (1996):61–118 .

Kreig, William L. *Ecuadorean–Peruvian Rivalry in the Upper Amazon.* 2nd ed. Washington, DC: Department of State External Research Program, 1986.

Linke, Lilo. *Ecuador: Country of Contrasts.* London: Oxford University Press, 1960.

Linke, Lilo. "Ecuador's Politics: President Velasco's Fourth Exit." *The World Today Chatam House Review* 17 (January–December 1962): 57–69.

Maier, Georg. "Presidential Succession in Ecuador, 1860–1968." *Journal of Inter-American Studies and World Affairs* 13 (July–October 1971): 494–97.

Martz, John D. *Ecuador: Conflicting Political Culture and the Quest for Progress.* Boston: Allyn and Bacon, 1974.

Martz, John D. "Ecuador: The Right Takes Command." *Current History* (February 1985): 69–72, 84.

Martz, John D. "The Quest for Popular Democracy in Ecuador." *Current History* (February 1980): 66–77, 84 .

Martz, John D. "The Regional Expression of Populism: Guayaquil and the CFP, 1948–1960." *Journal of Inter-American Studies and World Affairs* 22, no. 3 (1980): 289–314.

McIntyre, Loren. *The Incredible Incas and Their Timeless Land.* Washington, DC: National Geographic Society, 1975.

Meisch, Lynn A. *Andean Entrepreneurs: Otavalo Merchants and Musicians in the Global Arena.* Austin: University of Texas Press, 2002.

Middleton, Alan. "Division and Cohesion in the Working Class: Artisans and Wage Labourers in Ecuador." *Journal of Latin American Studies* 14, no. 2 (1982): 171–94.

Mijeski, Kenneth J., and Scott H. Beck. *Pachakutik and the Rise and Decline of the Ecuadorian Indigenous Movement.* Athens: Ohio University Press, 2011.

Mikesh, Robert C. *Aichi M6A1 Serian, Japan's Submarine Launched Panama Canal Bomber.* Boylston, MA: Monogram Aviation, 1975.

Murray, Pamela S. *For Glory and Bolívar: The Remarkable Life of Manuela Sáenz.* Austin: University of Texas Press, 2008.

Newson, Linda A. *Life and Death in Early Colonial Ecuador.* Norman: University of Oklahoma Press, 1995.

Norris, Robert E. *Guía bibliográfica para el estudio de la historia Ecuatoriana.* Austin, TX: Institute of Latin American Studies, 1978.

Norris, Robert E. "José María Velasco Ibarra: A Charismatic Figure in Ecuadorean Politics, 1934–1961." PhD diss., University of New Mexico, 1969.

O'Connor, Erin. *Gender, Indian, Nation: The Contradictions of Making Ecuador, 1830–1925.* Tucson: University of Arizona Press, 2007.

Pallares, Amalia. *From Peasant Struggles to Indian Resistance: The Ecuadorian Andes in the Late Twentieth Century.* Norman: University of Oklahoma Press, 2002.

Pineo, Ronn F. *Ecuador and the United States: Useful Strangers.* Athens: University of Georgia Press, 2007.

Pineo, Ronn F. *Social and Economic Reform in Ecuador: Life and Work in Guayaquil.* Gainesville: University Press of Florida, 1996.

Price, Joedd. "Images and Influences: The Legacy of the Founding Fathers and the Federal System in Ecuador." *Latin American Research Review* 10 (1975): 121–33.

Pyne, Peter. "The Politics of Instability in Ecuador: The Overthrow of the President, 1961." *Journal of Latin American Studies* 7, no. 2 (1975): 85–105.

Redclift, M. R. "The Influence of the Agency for International Development (AID) on Ecuador's Agrarian Development Policy." *Journal of Latin American Studies* 2, no. 1 (1979):185–201.

Rodriguez, Linda Alexander. *The Search for Public Policy: Regional Politics and Government Finances in Ecuador, 1830–1940.* Berkeley: University of California Press, 1985.

Rosenberg, Emily S. "Dollar Diplomacy under Wilson: An Ecuadorean Case." *Inter-American Economic Affairs* 25 (Autumn 1971): 49–51.

Rosenberg, Emily S. *Spreading the American Dream: American Economic and Cultural Expansion, 1890–1945.* New York: Hill and Wang, 1982.

Schodt, David. *Ecuador: An Andean Enigma.* Boulder, CO: Westview Press, 1987.

Selverston-Scher, Melina. *Ethnopolitics in Ecuador: Indigenous Rights and the Strengthening of Democracy.* Miami: North-South Center Press, 2001.

Southgate, Douglas, and Morris Whitaker. *Economic Progress and the Environment: One Country's Policy Crisis.* New York: Oxford University Press, 1994.

Spindler, Frank MacDonald. *Nineteenth Century Ecuador: A Historical Introduction.* Fairfax, VA: George Mason University Press, 1987.

Striffler, Steve. *In the Shadows of State and Capital: The United Fruit Company, Popular Struggle, and Agrarian Restructuring in Ecuador, 1900–1995.* Durham, NC: Duke University Press, 2002.

Swanson, Jeffrey. *Echoes of the Call: Identity and Ideology among American Missionaries in Ecuador.* New York: Oxford University Press, 1995.

Thoumi, Francisco E. "The Hidden Logic of 'Irrational' Economic Policies in Ecuador." *Journal of Inter-American Studies and World Affairs* (Fall 1990): 43–68 .

Townsend, Camilla. *Tales of Two Cities: Race and Economic Culture in Early Republican North and South America: Guayaquil, Ecuador and Baltimore, Maryland.* Austin: University of Texas Press, 2000.

Van Aken, Mark J. *King of the Night: Juan José Flores and Ecuador, 1824–1864.* Berkeley: University of California Press, 1974.

Weil, Thomas, Jan Knippers Black, Howard I. Blutstein, David S. McMorris, Milldred Gill Mersereau, Frederick P. Munson, and Kathryn E. Parachini. *Area Handbook for Ecuador.* Washington, DC: United States GPO, 1973.

Whitaker, Robert. *The Mapmaker's Wife.* New York: Basic Books, 2004.

Whitten, Norman E., Jr., ed. *Millennial Ecuador: Critical Essays on Cultural Transformations and Social Dynamics.* Iowa City: University of Iowa Press, 2003.

Wiles, Dawn Ann. "Land Transportation within Ecuador, 1822–1954." PhD diss., Louisiana State University, 1971.

Wilson, Jacques M. P. *The Development of Education in Ecuador.* Coral Gables, FL: University of Miami Press, 1970.

Wood, Bryce. *Aggression and History: The Case of Ecuador and Peru.* Ann Arbor: University Microfilms International, 1978.

Zuvekas, Clarence Jr. "Economic Planning in Ecuador: An Evaluation." *Inter-American Economic Affairs* 25, no. 4 (1992): 39–69.

Index

Acción Revolución Nacionalista Ecuatoriana (ARNE; Ecuadorian Nationalist Revolutionary Party), 119, 120

Afro-Ecuadorians, 11

Alarcón, Fabián, 149, 150

Albion Battalion, 39

Alfaristas, 90

Alfaro, Colon, 108

Alfaro Delgado, Eloy, 12, 16, 71, 83–93

Alfaro Vive ¡Carajo! (Alfaro Lives Damn It!), 140

Alianza Democrática Ecuatoriana (Ecuadorian Democratic Alliance), 108

Alianza País (Country Alliance), 161

Alianza Popular (Popular Alliance), 121

Alliance for Progress, 124, 127

Almacenes de Subsistencias (Stores of Basic Foodstuffs), 123

Almargo, Diego de, 26

Alvardo, Pedro de, 25

Ambato, 5, 27

Amigos del País, 36

Añaquito, battle of, 26

Aranha, Oswaldo, 106

Archipiélago de Colon. *See* Galápagos Islands

Argolla (ring), 93, 95

Arosemena Gómez, Otto, 128, 132

Arosemena Monroy, Carlos Julio, 120, 125

Arosemena Tola, Carlos Julio, 112, 117

Arroyo del Río, Carlos, 105–107

Arteaga, Rosalía, 146, 149, 150

Arteta, José de, 62
Ascásubi, Manuel, 47, 48
Ascásubi, Rosa de, 56
Astronomical Observatory, 67, 77
Atahualpa, 23–25
Aucas, 10
Audiencia, 26, 27
Audiencia of Quito, 27, 35, 37, 43
Autonomous public institutions, 127, 129
Avenue of the Volcanoes, 5
Ayora, Isidro, 98, 99

Baker Plan, 139
Banana boom, 116
Banana production, 13
Banco Central, 98, 99, 127
Banco Comercial y Agrícola (Commerical and Agricultural Bank), 93, 95
Banco de Préstamos, 152
Banco de Progresso, 152
Banco Ecuatoriano de la Vivienda (Ecuadorian Housing Bank), 123
Bank of Ecuador (1869), 66
Baquerizo Moreno, Alfredo, 92
Belén Church, 15, 25, 27
Benalcázar, Sebastían de, 24, 25
Black Charter, 64
Board of Trade, 27
Bolívar, Simón, 38–41
Bonifaz, Neptalí, 99, 100
Borja, Rodrigo, 13, 135, 139, 140
Borrero, Antonio, 72, 73
Borrero, Manuel María, 104
Bourbon reforms, 36, 37
Bucaram, Abdalá, 139–41, 146–48
Bucaram, Assad, 128, 129, 135, 136

Caamaño, José María Plácido, 75–77, 84
Cabildo, 27
Cabildo abierto, 37, 38, 42
Cacao, 13, 66
Cacao boom, 83, 84
Cacique (chief), 20
Cajamarca, 24
Calderón, Albdon, 39
Campaign of 20 days, 90
Cañari, 22, 25
Cañizares, Manuela, 37
Carabineros, 107, 108
Carbo, Luis F., 87
Carbo, Pedro, 62, 75
Carchi Province, 4
Carondelet Palace, 5, 63
Carrión, Jerónimo, 50, 61
Casa de la Cultura, 110
Caspircara, 28
Caudillismo, 51
Cavallo, Domingo, 147
Cenepa Brigade, 155
Central University, 69, 76, 78
Chapetónes, 29
Charles IV, 37
Charter of Slavery, 46, 64
Checa y Barba, José Ignacio, 73, 74
Chimborazo, 2, 5
Cholo, 9, 30
Chota Valley, 11
Christian Brothers, 69
Church of Jesus Christ of Latter Day Saints (Mormons), 15
Cimerrones, 11, 27
Citizen's Revolution, 161–65
Cofán, 10, 20
Coffee Institute, 118
Colorados, 10
Compactación Obrera Nacional (National Consolidation of Workers), 99, 100

Compañia de Jesús Church, 29

Concentration of Popular Forces (CFP) 118, 119, 135

Confederacón de Trabajadores Ecuatorianos (Confederation of Ecuadorian Workers), 126

Confederation of Indigenous Nationalities of Ecuador (CONAIE), 13, 140, 148, 154

Conquistadors, 25

Conservative Party, 56

Constitutions: 1830, 42; 1835, 45; 1843, 46; 1845, 47; 1850, 48; 1851, 48, 1861, 50; 1869, 64; 1878, 75; 1883, 76; 1897, 85, 86; 1906, 91; 1928, 98; 1945, 109; 1966, 128; 1978, 134, 1998, 149; 2008, 162

Cordero, Luis, 76, 79, 80, 85

Cordillera del Condor Region, 124, 142, 148

Cordillera Occidental, 2

Cordillera Oriental, 2

Cordova, Gonzalo S., 95, 96

Correa Delgado, Rafael, 161–65

Cotopaxi, 2, 5, 39

Council of the Indies, 27

Criollo(s), 9, 29, 36

Cuaspud, battle of, 58

Cuban Revolution, 126

Cuenca, 5, 19, 22, 27, 39

Cundurango, 66

Cuzco, 25

Dahik, Alberto, 141

Darwin, Charles, 7

De Soto, Hernando, 24

Dollarization, 154, 156, 160

Durán Ballén, Sixto, 135, 139, 141, 142

Earthquake (1868), 63, 63

Ecuadorian State Petroleum Company, 132

Education, 68–70, 76, 110

Educational Reform Act, 56

El Dorado, 23

El Niño current, 2, 136

El Oro Province, 3, 4, 110

Eleventh Inter-American Conference (1961), 122, 124

Elhers, Freddy, 146, 150

Elliot, Elisabeth, 16

Encomendero, 30

Encomienda system, 30

Enríquez Gallo, Alberto, 104

Esmeralda Affair, 79, 80

Esmeraldas City, 23

Esmeraldas Province, 2, 10, 11, 47

Espejo, Francisco Eugenio de Santa Cruz y, 36

Espinosa, Javier, 62, 63

Estrada, Emilio, 92

Evangelical Protestants, 15

Exxon, 139

FARC (Revolutionary Armed Forces of Colombia), 17, 153, 163

Febres Cordero, León 137–39

Ferdinand VII, 37

Filanbanco, 152

Flores, Juan José, 40–42, 46–48, 51, 58

Flores Jijón, Antonio, 57, 76–78

Flores Jijón, Virginia, 56

Four Day War, 99, 100

Freemasons and Freemasonry, 49, 55, 59, 64, 89, 123

French protectorate plan, 50, 57

Frente Unitario de Trabajadores (FUT; United Workers Front), 137, 139, 140, 148

Fuerzas Armadas Populares Eloy Alfaro (Eloy Alfaro Popular Armed Forces), 140

Galápagos Archipelago. *See* Galápagos Islands
Galápagos Islands, 2, 7, 8, 43, 44, 96
Garcia, Lizardo, 90
García Moreno, Gabriel, 15, 46, 47, 49–57, 59–61, 64, 65, 71, 72
Garroteros, 89, 91
Geographical features, 1–8
González Suárez, Federico, 78
Gran Colombia, 36, 38, 40, 41, 51
Great Absentee. *See* Velasco Ibarra
Guarantors of Río Protocol, 106, 124, 142
Guayaquil, 2, 3, 25
Guayaquil and Quito Railway, 87, 88, 91
Guayaquil Meeting, 40
Guayas Province, 2, 3, 48
Guevara Moreno, Carlos, 118, 119
Gutiérrez, Lucio, 155, 156, 158

Hacienda system, 30
Hall, Francis (Francisco), 43
Harman, Archer, 87, 88
Harman, John, 88
Hassaurek, Frederich, 56
HCJB radio, 16, 17
Hodges, Heather, 163
Huachi, battle of, 38
Huaorani, 10, 12, 16
Huáscar, 23, 24
Huasipungo system, 31, 127
Huayna Cápac, 20, 24, 25
Human Development Index, 12
Humbolt, Alexander, 5

Humbolt current, 2
Hurtado, Osvaldo, 135, 136

Ibarra, city of, 4, 27, 63
Import substitution plan, 132
Inca conquest, 21–23
Inca Empire, 21–23
Incas, 21, 22
Ingapirca, 19
Institute of Electrification, 123
International Monetary Fund (IMF), 137, 141, 153, 158
Izquierda Democrática (Democratic Left), 135

Jambelí, battle of, 61
Jesuits, 29, 62
Jijón y Vivanco, Mercedes, 78
Jirón, Sergio Enrique, 108
Jívaros, 10
Jones, Clarence, 16
July Revolution (Julian Revolution), 96
Junta Nacional de Sufragio Libre (National Committee on Free Suffrage), 101

Kemmerer, Edwin, 98, 99
Kemmerer Mission, 98, 99
Kemmerer Reforms, 98, 99
Kingdom of Quito, 27
Kuraka (chief), 22

Labriolle. *See* Velasco Ibarra, José María
La Condamine, Charles Marie Louis, 31
La Condamine expediton, 31, 32
Lago Agrio, 6, 7
Larsen, Reuben, 16
Lazarists, 70

Lend-Lease program, 106
Letica Crisis, 100
Levantimiento Indígena (Indig-
enous Uprising), 13, 140, 154
Ley de Beneficencia (Law of Charity),
91
Ley de Cultos (Law of Religions), 90
Ley Patronato (Patronage Law), 86,
90
Liberal Party, 57, 83, 92
Liberal Revolution of 1895, 16, 76,
80, 83–93
Liberation theology, 16
Life expectancy, 12
Liga Militar (Military League), 96
Literacy, 12
Loja City, 5, 27
Loja Province, 5, 110

Machala, 4, 39
Mahuad, Jamil, 13, 140, 151, 152,
153
Maldonado, Manuel Tomás, 61
Mamakuna, 23
Manabí Province, 2, 50
Mancheno Cajas, Carlos, 112, 113,
118
Manta air base, 153, 158, 163
Manta City, 27
Marañón River, 43
Martínez, Alberto Guerrero, 100
Martínez Mera, Juan de Dios, 100
Masonic Order. *See* Freemasons and
Freemasonry
Mattress Bank, 152
Media via, 79
Mendoza, Carlos, 155
Mestizo(s), 8, 12, 30
Militarismo (militarism), 51
Military Junta (1963–66), 127
Ministry of Economy, 110
Mita (labor tax), 22, 30, 31

Mitad del Mundo, 32, 51
Mitimaes, 22
Modernization, 58, 59, 65–68, 78,
106, 107, 110, 132
Moncayo, Paco, 148
Montalvo, Aberlado, 101
Montalvo, Juan, 62, 71, 74, 77
Montoneros, 76
Montúfar y Larrea, Juan Pio, 36
Montúfar, Carlos, 38
Mosquera Narváez, Aurelio, 104

National Archives, 77
National Development Bank, 111
National Institute for Development
and Production, 118
National Personification. *See*
Velasco Ibarra
National Planning Committee,
121
National Police Force, 77
National Velasquista Front, 128
Nebot Saadi, Jaime, 141, 145
Neoliberal economic policies, 138,
140
New Granada, 42
Noboa, Alvaro, 151, 157
Noboa, Diego, 48
Noboa Group, 138
Noboa, Gustavo, 155, 156
Non-Govermental Organizations
(NGOs), 12
Nueva Loja, 6, 131
Núñez de Vela, Blasco, 26

Obrajes (worshops or sweatshops),
15, 31
Occidental Petroleum, 139, 159
Oil boom, 14
Olmedo, José Joaquín, 38, 42
Orellana, Francisco de, 25, 26

Organization of American States,
     156, 158
Oriente region, 2, 6, 20
Orphanage, 70
Otavalo, 4, 63

Pachacuti Inca Ypanqui, 22
Pachakutik, 13, 158
Páez, Federico, 104
Palacio, Alfredo, 158, 159
Panama disease, 116
Panama hats, 66
Panóptico prison, 70
Papal Concordat, 59, 79, 85
Partido Rolodista Ecuatoriano
     (Ecuadorian Roldista Party), 139
Peace Agreement with Peru (1998),
     151, 152, 160
Peninsulares, 29
Pentacostal groups, 15
Pepa de oro, 83
Personalismo, 51, 79
Peruvian Conflict (1995), 142
Peruvian territorial dispute, 49
Peruvian War (1941), 105–107
Petroecuador, 132, 154
Pichincha, battle of, 39
Pizarro, Francisco, 23, 24
Pizarro, Gonzalo, 25, 26
Plaza Gutiérrez, Leonídas, 83, 89
Plaza Lasso, Galo, 117–19,
     123
Plazistas, 90
Point Four Program, 118
Polytechnic Institute, 69
Ponce Enríquez, Camilo, 108,
     120–22, 128
Pons, Antonio, 104
Popular Fund, 150
Population, 8, 9, 20, 21
Populism, 101, 102, 115, 145, 163
Postage stamps, 67

Poveda Burbano, Alfredo, 134, 135
Proaño, Leonidas, 17
Protestants, 15

Quechua, 9, 23
Quichua, 9
Quiteño Libre, El, 43
Quito, 2, 4, 5

Radical Decalogue, 85
Railroads, 67, 87, 88, 110
Rayo, Faustino Lemos, 72
Reducciónes, 27, 31
Remittances, 14
Repartimiento de mercancías, 31
Republican Party of Ecuador, 76, 79
Repúblicas de indios, 27, 31
Ricke, Jadoco, 28
Riobamba, 5, 27
Río Protocol of 1942, 96, 106, 118,
     124
Robles, Francisco, 49, 60
Roca, Vicente Ramón, 46, 47
Rocafuerte, Vicente, 43–46
Rodríguez Lara, Guillermo, 129,
     132, 134
Roldós, Jaime, 135, 136
Roman Catholic Church, 14–16
Rumiñahui, 25, 26

Sacred Heart of Jesus, 15
Sáenz, Manuela, 39, 40
Salinas, 3
San Antonio de Ibarra, 5
San Francsico Monastery, 28
San Martín, José de, 38, 39
Santa Elena Peninsula, 3, 20
School of Fine Arts, 78
Selva Alegre, Marquis of, 36–38
Seventh-Day Adventists, 15
Shuar, 9, 10

Sigatoka Leaf Spot, 13, 116
Sisters of Charity, 60, 69
Sisters of the Good Shepherd, 70
Sisters of Providence, 70
Sisters of the Sacred Heart, 60, 69
Sovereign Junta of Quito, 37
Stevenson, Adlai, 124
Sucre, Antonio José de, 38, 42
Summer Institute of Linguistics
  (SIL), 16

Tagua nuts, 66
Tamayo, José Luis, 92
Tambos, 22
Tarqui, battle of, 41
Taura Air Base, 139
Taura Battalion, 48
Tauras, 48, 49
Tawantinsuyu, 23
Telegraph, 67
Tenguel plantation, 13, 116
Terrible Year (1859), 47, 48, 54
Texaco Gulf Consortium, 131,
  133
Tobar Donoso, Julio, 106, 107
Tomebamba, 22
Toquilla hats. *See* Panama hats
Trans Ecuadorian Pipeline, 131,
  139
Transformation, 75
Treaty of Virgina, 47
Tribunal of Gurantees, 111
Tribute system, 20
Trienté, Emilo, 50, 57
Trienté letters, 50
Tsachilas, 10
Tulcán, 4, 58
Tupa Inca Yupanqui, 20

Ultramontanism, 55, 59, 62, 71, 81
United Fruit Company (UFCO), 13,
  116
Urbina, José María, 48, 55, 60
U.S. Bases WWII, 106, 107

Valdiva culture, 20
Vargas, Frank, 139
Vatican Concordat. *See* Papal
  Concordat
Vega, Antonio, 91
Veintemilla, Ignacio de, 63–66,
  73–76
Veintemilla, José de, 63
Vela, Juan Benigno, 77, 78
Velasco Ibarra, José María, 100–104,
  108, 109, 112, 113, 115, 119, 120,
  128, 129
Via media (middle path), 78
Viceroyalty of New Granada, 36
Viceroyalty of Peru, 26
Victory on the Cenepa, 143
Villamil, José de, 38
Viola, Santiago, 61

Wagon road, 59, 60, 66
War of the Chihuahuas, 43
War of the Restoration, 75, 76
Wheelwright, Isaac, 45
WikiLeaks, 163
Wolf, Theodore, 8
World War II, 106, 107

Yanaconas, 23
Yerovi Indaburo, Clemente, 128

Zambos, 28, 30, 36
Zaramilla conflict, 106

About the Author

GEORGE LAUDERBAUGH is associate professor of history at Jacksonville State University in Alabama, where he teaches courses on Latin American, diplomatic, military, and U.S. history. A native of western Pennsylvania, Dr. Lauderbaugh first became interested in Ecuador in 1962 when he was a high school exchange student in Quito. After graduating from Davis and Elkins College with a major in history he began a career in the United States Air Force, retiring after 25 years in the rank of Lt. Colonel. He renewed his interest in Ecuador and Latin America during an assignment in Panama. After retirement he entered the University of Alabama and completed a PhD in history in 1997. Dr. Lauderbaugh is the author of *The United States and Ecuador: Conflict and Convergence, 1830–1946*, published in Spanish by the Corporation for the Development of University Education in Quito in 2011. He and his wife, Sue, reside in Jacksonville, Alabama.

Other Titles in the Greenwood Histories of the Modern Nations
Frank W. Thackeray and John E. Findling, Series Editors

The History of Afghanistan
Meredith L. Runion

The History of Argentina
Daniel K. Lewis

The History of Australia
Frank G. Clarke

The History of the Baltic States
Kevin O'Connor

The History of Brazil
Robert M. Levine

The History of Bulgaria
Frederick B. Chary

The History of Cambodia
Justin Corfield

The History of Canada
Scott W. See

The History of Central America
Thomas Pearcy

The History of the Central Asian
Republics
Peter L. Roudik

The History of Chile
John L. Rector

The History of China, Second
Edition
David C. Wright

The History of Congo
Didier Gondola

The History of Cuba
Clifford L. Staten

The History of the Czech Republic
and Slovakia
William M. Mahoney

The History of Egypt
Glenn E. Perry

The History of El Salvador
Christopher M. White

The History of Ethiopia
Saheed Adejumobi

The History of Finland
Jason Lavery

The History of France
W. Scott Haine

The History of Germany
Eleanor L. Turk

The History of Ghana
Roger S. Gocking

The History of Great Britain
Anne Baltz Rodrick

The History of Greece
Elaine Thomopoulos

The History of Haiti
Steve Coupeau

The History of Holland
Mark T. Hooker

The History of Honduras
Thomas M. Leonard

The History of India
John McLeod

The History of Indonesia
Steven Drakeley

The History of Iran
Elton L. Daniel

The History of Iraq
Courtney Hunt

The History of Ireland
Daniel Webster Hollis III

The History of Israel
Arnold Blumberg

The History of Italy
Charles L. Killinger

The History of Japan, Second
Edition
Louis G. Perez

The History of Korea
Djun Kil Kim

The History of Kuwait
Michael S. Casey

The History of Mexico, Second
Edition
Burton Kirkwood

The History of New Zealand
Tom Brooking

The History of Nicaragua
Clifford L. Staten

The History of Nigeria
Toyin Falola

The History of Pakistan
Iftikhar H. Malik

The History of Panama
Robert C. Harding

The History of Peru
Daniel Masterson

The History of the Philippines
Kathleen M. Nadeau

The History of Poland
M. B. Biskupski

The History of Portugal
James M. Anderson

The History of Puerto Rico
Lisa Pierce Flores

The History of Russia, Second
Edition
Charles E. Ziegler

The History of Saudi Arabia
Wayne H. Bowen

The History of Serbia
John K. Cox

The History of Singapore
Jean E. Abshire

The History of South Africa
Roger B. Beck

The History of Spain
Peter Pierson

The History of Sri Lanka
Patrick Peebles

The History of Sweden
Byron J. Nordstrom

The History of Thailand
Patit Paban Mishra

The History of Turkey
Douglas A. Howard

The History of Ukraine
Paul Kubicek

The History of Venezuela
H. Micheal Tarver and Julia C. Frederick

The History of Vietnam
Justin Corfield